HARVARD HISTORICAL STUDIES

Published under the direction of
The Department of History
From the income of
The Henry Warren Torrey Fund

Volume LXXXV

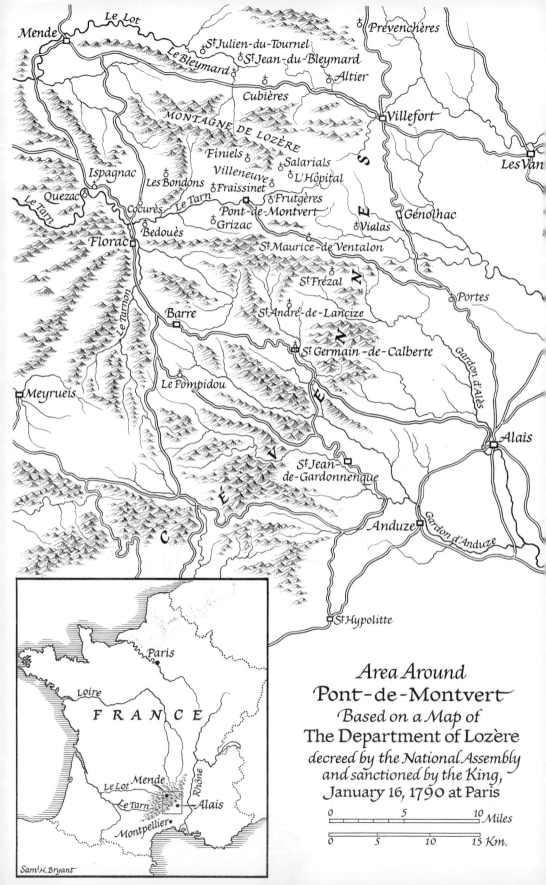

Area Around
Pont-de-Montvert
Based on a Map of
The Department of Lozère
decreed by the National Assembly
and sanctioned by the King,
January 16, 1790 at Paris

PONT–DE–MONTVERT

Social Structure and Politics
in a French Village, 1700–1914

Patrice L.-R. Higonnet

Harvard University Press   Cambridge, Massachusetts   1971

Distributed in Great Britain by Oxford University Press, London

Library of Congress Catalog Card Number 70–133209

SBN 674–68960–7

Printed in the United States of America

Pour mes parents

Pour mes enfants

ACKNOWLEDGMENTS

Since this is my first book, it is only fair that I should thank all those people whose pupil I have been over the years. There are, in the beginning, the Soeurs de Saint-Joseph at Francheville-le-Haut together with Monsieur Beluze, the socialist instituteur of the grammar school, also of Francheville-le-Haut but unlike the sisters, an enemy of Church and State. Less doctrinal but no less useful have been the lessons of the learned men and women under whom I later worked as a graduate student when I first thought of writing this book. Laurence Wylie, Stanley Hoffmann, Paul Bénichou, and David Landes will not, I hope, be too distressed to find in these pages echoes of their books, lectures, and advice. My thanks also to the Social Science Research Council and Harvard University whose generosity enabled me to put these lessons to good use.

But like charity, history begins at home. It is to my mother that I owe my love of history; and to my father, whatever feeling I may have had about what it was like to live in provincial France before the Fall. My most heartfelt thanks go to them here. Gratitude, therefore, is one of the reasons which will make it readily understandable that I should be very pleased that this book was photocomposed, since that is a process of composition which the graphic arts owe to my father's talent.

Then, too, it is a pleasure for me to thank those people who helped me with the actual writing of this book: Benjamin Bardy of the Archives Départementales at Mende who very kindly introduced me to the delights and exasperation of archival work; and my friend Albin Pantel, former mayor of the Pont. I have spent many hours in his office

Acknowledgments

on the edge of the river Tarn, only a few yards away from where the abbé du Chayla was stabbed to death and Esprit Séguier so ruthlessly punished. The recollection of the quiet moments that I have spent with him at the Pont is always a cheering thought.

Lastly, but most importantly, I wish to thank H. Stuart Hughes who encouraged me to write a book of this sort, who directed it when I wrote it as a thesis, and who read and advised on its present form as well. I would fear that I had grossly abused his patience and kindness if I did not know that all of his students have so often been indebted to him for understanding, knowledge, and encouragement.

My thanks go to all of these and to those also whose friendship have helped me to see this through. There are some debts that can not be repaid.

CONTENTS

ILLUSTRATIONS

TABLES

PREFACE

In a short and unfinished story that he wrote in the last years of his life, Pushkin describes the vicissitudes of the life of one Ivan Petrovich Belkin. For years, this officer in a foot regiment had wasted away in the obscure garrison towns whither his career had led him. No wonder, then, that his thoughts should have turned to literary pursuits. To write an epic had been his first intent. This, however, proved more difficult than he had thought, and Ivan Petrovich soon realized that he had aimed too high. Ballads, perhaps, would do. But even here he found it difficult to progress beyond a brief inscription for Rurik's portrait. With regret, "he descended to the level of prose." And yet further, from literature to mere history, from the history of the world to the history of Russia, of the *gubernya,* of the district (which proved impossible, however, since the district had no history). Finally and in despair, Belkin resigned himself to writing the history of his own native village, Gorjukino. With care he assembled his sources: calendars, oral traditions, priestly chronicles, and tales of the mujiks. To no avail. Hardly had he started when he died, and his unfinished manuscript was most ingloriously used to block some windows in the wings of his dilapidated mansion.

From this experience it might be thought that the writing of village histories is somewhat inglorious and not without dangers. Nonetheless it is for many reasons a worthwhile occupation. The story of a village has for us, to begin with, the fascination of rural life. Most of us are city born and bred, but we still often feel that the ways of rural life are not irrelevant to our own thinking and living. Admittedly, ours is an irreversibly industrial society; but it is also one that is only a few

Preface

generations removed from the land. Our frustrations and maladjustments are often the result of an incomplete adaptation to our new environment. In our political organization, in our respect for experience and old age, in our increasingly vain efforts to retain some links between the very different generations of widely scattered families, and even in our wretched suburban lawns, we hark back to an agricultural past which looms over and sometimes even dominates our collective unconscious. But few of us know anything at all about villages or the land. That we should want to fill this gap is not surprising. Rural life is part of our past. If the anthropology of primitive tribes has much to teach us about human nature, how much also can we learn from the study of these cultures from which our own environment directly springs.*

Village studies, then, can tell us something about ourselves, and for that matter about millions of our contemporaries the world over, since most people today do still live in village communities. But we can learn from them also as historians. History is the re-creation and understanding of human situations. It implies both the selection of facts and the integration of concrete events in some theoretical setting. This process can at its simplest be merely sequential, but obviously it can also be infinitely complex. Even a chronicler who arranges his facts in some given order must decide what it is that deserves to be recorded; there is no need to expostulate on the problems faced by those who seek to demonstrate the validity of some abstract idea be it the manifestation of God's will on earth or the workings of dialectical materialism. How historians are to go about their task of combining erudition and intuition depends a good deal on the dimension of their subject—the history of the world cannot be written in quite the same way as that of Gorjukino, which fact can serve as another justification of village histories. A small rural community is a very manageable compass; the problems which it presents enable the historian to think about the applicability and usefulness of abstract concepts, and at the same time to accept or reject *some* facts after he has considered them *all*. These are unusual privileges, and there are few historians of vast topics who would claim today for their work, as Aulard did some

---

* That peasants have much to teach their urban and corrupted brethren is an idea that has been commonly held in France, not only by nineteenth-century romantics like Balzac, George Sand, or Hugo, but by twentieth-century reactionaries as well, and by all those people who thought that "seule la terre ne ment pas." There are eighteenth-century antecedents as well: Rousseau, of course, and Restif de la Bretonne, but also Diderot, who once wrote, "J'aime à causer avec le paysan, j'en apprends toujours quelque chose" (cited in Louis Ducros. *La Société française au xviiie siècle* [Paris, 1894], p. 61).

fifty years ago for his *Political History of the French Revolution,* that it was based on a reading of *all* the available sources. If like Marc Bloch we think of a rural community as a type of microsociety sui generis, its advantages as a field of historical research are clear; it is at once an intellectually meaningful and a technically manageable field of endeavor. At a time when increased specialization appears to be a necessity, village studies provide an unusual opportunity to remain within a specified framework and to consider as well a number of fundamental historical themes, from the relation of concepts and evidence to the interaction of politics and society or the impact of social, intellectual, and technical change.

Finally and most importantly perhaps, village studies are valuable in themselves. We write biographies for what they will tell us about ourselves, about human nature, or to see how other human beings have reacted to those "vast impersonal forces" which mold our own lives. But we also read or write biographies and memoirs because we find them interesting. And so it is with villages: like human beings, they are unique, organic wholes. They appear and disappear, ail and prosper. When we read the memoirs of Saint-Simon, it is sometimes because we want to know more about the world of Louis XIV but sometimes also because curiosity prompts us to do so. We often want to know more about individuals who have left us little beyond the fact that, human beings like ourselves, they lived in worlds very different from our own. In Herzen's words:

> Every life is interesting; if not the personality, then the environment, the country, the life itself is interesting. Man likes to enter into another existence, he likes to touch the subtlest fibers of another's heart, and to listen to its beating.*

The same, it is to be hoped, holds true for Pont-de-Montvert. Independently of what we have to learn from it historically, it is also a world we have lost, a place different from any that we now know. We may want to know more about it for that reason alone. All the more so because the Pont of yesterday is a perfect foil to our own world, since it is at once so close to us and so far away. In contrast to what we find in our own society, life there was very unchanging. It is true that it evolved from century to century, but there never was much change within any single life-span. With very few exceptions, the lives of the people of Pont-de-Montvert followed a set course: peasants would work their land as had been done before them; the poor would remain

---

* Alexander Herzen, *My Past and Thoughts* (London: Chatto and Windus, 1968), I, 347.

Preface

poor, the rich, rich. French peasants are anxious people; they are *inquiets* and always on the lookout for some unusual catastrophe, some stroke of bad luck like disease, bad harvests, or severe winters. But even these can do no more than to affect the inner travails of existences whose broad outlines remain unchanging. Before 1900 the people of Pont-de-Montvert knew where and how they would make a a living, where they would live and die, perhaps even whom they would marry. They could gauge what it was they could expect from whatever effort they expended. For better or worse, we ourselves have none of these things; we are indeed rootless cosmopolites whose cynicism about immutable values and material success often appears to be a mere mechanism of psychic self-defense.

Thus Pont-de-Montvert holds a certain interest for us because it is so different from the world we have, but at the same time it is not an irretrievable world. As Frenchmen, as Protestants, as adherents to the *Grands Principes de 1789,* as loyal believers of nineteenth-century scientism, and even, yes, as Marxists-Leninists, the people of Pont-de-Montvert are often very close to us. We can consider them with an unusual mixture of curiosity and nostalgia, which may well be the best reason for thinking about them at all, about their concerns, their social divisions, and to begin with, about the natural setting in which they live.

PONT–DE–MONTVERT

Durant mes tournées, il m'est arrivé dans les villages de vouloir
quelques fois publiquement faire leur tableau abrégé, leur histoire; il m'est
arrivé même de la commencer: le territoire de la commune est limité . . . la
terre en est argileuse, calcaire, quartzeuse, graniteuse, graveleuse . . . Il est
fou disait on en me montrant.

Le village est situé . . . son église . . . son clocher . . . la maison commune
. . . la halle . . . le lavoir . . . Il est fou! fou, vraiment fou.

L'école, l'instituteur, l'institutrice, le juge de paix, la mairie, le maire . . .
Il est fou! il est fou! Est-ce qu'il peut y avoir l'histoire des villages? Une
tête bien organisée peut elle concevoir qu'il puisse y avoir une histoire de
village?

Amans Alexis Monteil
Histoire des Français de divers états
aux cinq derniers siècles. 1853

The Pont at Pont-de-Montvert.

INTRODUCTION: Pont-de-Montvert in Time and Space

Today Pont-de-Montvert is a small and unimportant, decaying village of the Lozère in south central France. Still, it is not an unpleasant place, particularly in the summertime, which is nowadays when most people see it.[1] It lies in the northern reaches of the Cévennes, a mountain range that stretches, crescent-shaped, from the basin of the Garonne towards the river Rhône.[2] As it name indicates, the village is in a valley near a mountain; a river, whose source is only a few miles away, runs through the town. But when it reaches the Pont, the Tarn is already a large stream which can rise to impressive and even catastrophic heights. In 1890, for example, it rose twenty-six feet over its normal level at the Pont. There are great floods every twenty or thirty years, but none perhaps have been more destructive than those described by Antoine Velay in his notebook,

> On the 17th of August 1697, at two in the morning after it had rained all day, there was such lightning and rain that all the mills of the Pont were carried away together with six or seven houses, without leaving anything behind, and among them that of M. Pons, my brother-in-law, who had married my sister Cassandra, with four grain and fulling mills, and a part of the bridges, all the gardens, and carried away much earth and above all that which was near the river, and left behind neither pasture nor trees.[3]

Three years later, in October of 1700, there was an even greater flood,

> which carried away much earth, and notably the mills of my said brother-in-law which he had had rebuilt, after which my sister died of grief, since she had applied to it much of her constitution.[4]

1

Introduction

Nature is everywhere present in the village and is often very threatening: floods in the summer and fall, snowstorms in winter.[5] And again from Velay's diary, which is a compendium of natural and man-made calamities, there is mention of one Toinette Chaptal who, on February 10, 1725,

> coming from Trêmes, died at the entrance of Villaret, because of the snow and the bad weather, even the mare she was leading died having stayed outside two days and three nights, after Tuesday the 15th she was carried to the Bondons, by order of M. le Curé, as coming from that parish.[6]

People have died in snowstorms as late as the 1950s and the winter blizzards are very fierce. Even today the village is at times completely isolated and until recently many of the hamlets were cut off more or less continuously for weeks on end. In previous decades when medical help was everywhere nonexistent, this prospect was probably not yet terrifying; but today, one of the arguments most often used for leaving the hamlets is that during the winter a serious illness or childbirth can be fatal in an isolated place where it is difficult for help to arrive in time.

Nature here is not only harsh, it is also very erratic. Pont-de-Montvert has a very complicated climatic system. The village lies at the convergence of three geographic zones: it is very high up (between 1000 and 1700 meters) and has in some respects a typically mountainous climate. It is also exposed to Mediterranean and oceanic influences, which explains the abrupt transitions that are frequent there. Cold and wet in winter, the village in summer has a characteristically southern air. Robert Louis Stevenson, who crossed the Mont-Lozère and entered our village astride his donkey Ernestine, was struck by this:

> The whole descent is like a dream to me. I was . . . in a different country from the day before, the stony skeleton of the world was here vigorously displayed to sun and air. The slopes were steep and changeful.[7]

But this area has also been not unjustly described as a "French Siberia," and both judgments are true. The villagers are used to abrupt changes: they have in some ways reified their environment. Like the mountains and fields, the winds have names: Lou Beu, from the south, La Traberso from the ocean, Lau Souredo from the north, and the easterly Ayalas which brings heavy fall rains. But however familiar these winds may be, they are still unpredictable and often savage.

Climate clearly sets definite limits on what one can and cannot do at the Pont, as do also the composition and the lay of the land. The soil of the Pont is granitic, with the exception of a small area near the ham-

Above, a view from the Mont-Lozère; *below*, Pont-de-Montvert looking west.

let of Grizac; and like all the *terres froides* or "cold lands," it is not very productive. Even today, much of it lies fallow one year in two, and only certain types of crops can be grown successfully. Because of these conditions, rye has always been the staple at the Pont since it is very difficult for the villagers to grow wheat (or *blé froment,* as it was called, to distinguish it from just plain *blé* or rye). The soil is light. To make matters worse, it is badly situated, for the area of Pont-de-Montvert is a vast, chaotic jumble of hills and valleys interspersed with granite boulders. There are large farms and *landes* or heaths, on which animals roam at large, but very few fields that are flat and cleared of stones. To some degree, it is possible to counter this environmental determinism, and it is not inconceivable that the gradual switch in the nineteenth century from rye farming to cattle raising was at least in part an effort to stabilize life. Before the development of communications and the advent of scientific or even sensible farming, the yield of the land would fluctuate considerably: the harvest of 1715, for example, was one-fourth greater than that of 1714. If we bear in mind the fact that deductions had to be made for the tithe and for other taxes and that a fixed amount of grain had to be set aside for seed, it can be seen that the amount of net disposable grain could vary widely from one year to the next.[8] Animals, by contrast, could be counted on to graze peaceably rain or shine, but even there Montipontins might have to face other dangers—epidemics or shortages of hay for the winter months.*

The winds, the climate, the altitude, the land are all factors of enormous importance for Pont-de-Montvert. Together they would set the course of village life in a nonindustrial age where there was little or nothing that could be done to combat the vagaries of nature. The inhabitants of the Pont have always been poor, poorer still than their compatriots—even in those days when France as a whole has fallen upon hard times. Because of its setting, the margin of survival for the village before 1800 was always narrow, and a succession of bad harvests could easily precipitate the most striking social upheavals there.

In view of this, it is quite conceivable that the real history of Pont-de-Montvert should be a history of its climate, but such a history cannot be written. Throughout its modern history, the climate of this unusually located village has oscillated between great extremes. In this century average yearly rainfall has risen as high as sixty-three inches and has fallen as low as twenty-nine inches; since climatic changes are

---

* The people of Pont-de-Montvert are known by a variety of names. They are called *Montversois* or *Montipontins,* and sometimes also *Pontois,* although that is usually reserved for those Montversois who live in the town of Pont-de-Montvert itself.

very sudden and even freakish, we cannot reconstruct general or even yearly trends from isolated observations. The fact that there were great floods in 1697, 1700, 1728, or 1890 does not enable us to deduce very much about climatic cycles around those dates or even during these years themselves. Fluctuations are so great that only a long series of readings of rainfall and temperature could provide us with the basic information that would be needed for a climatic history of the village.[9]

The lack of this knowledge does not mean, however, that no history of the village can be written. Indeed, it can be argued that, since nature has always been so rigorous here, we are justified in excluding for the Pont as a possibility what is known to have been a fact elsewhere: the alternation of good and bad climatic periods. At Pont-de-Montvert, environmental determinism has been a constant and depressing factor. It may even be quite possible that a classic social history of this village is more feasible than would be one of the towns in the *garrigues* or moors of the Languedoc, where climate is known to have changed in time.[10] Social transformations at the Pont are more likely to have had purely classical economic or social causes than would be true of similar developments in a region where the climatic margin of change is greater. Montipontins have always been ground down by their environment, whereas others have occasionally been uplifted by theirs. For that reason, it may not matter that we do not know, and cannot know, how the climate of the village in 1700 differed from that before or since. We can simply assume that Pont-de-Montvert has always functioned within clear and narrow limits and it is reasonable to accept and forget these limits in order to concentrate our attention on non-natural historical phenomena.

When then should we begin the history of Pont-de-Montvert? Perhaps, long before the beginning of written records since it has been argued that 3,000 years before Christ, the Lozère or Gévaudan, as it was called before 1789, was already a "geographic and religious unit";[11] and although it would be difficult to substantiate this claim, it is nonetheless a fact that the Lozère was already inhabited long before the Celtic invasions of the eighth century B.C.[12] Men have lived in this part of the world since the end of the neolithic age[13] and excavations of some 300 tumuli have shown that the region was fairly thickly settled in the eighth to fifth centuries before Christ.[14] The syntax of the Lozerian patois also points to pre-Latin and perhaps to pre-Celtic origins, since it has many variants which suggest links to some ancient dialects, to "old and autochthonous sources, which remain unknown today and whose origins are probably very distant."[15] Vestiges of these extinct cultures can be found in the place names of hamlets, rivers, and forests of the Pont.[16] In the name of the river Tarn, for example, the element *ar* is pre-Celtic. Les Balmes nearby has to do with another such root: *balma* or grotto. *Truc, kalm,* and *kros,* which refer, respectively, to a height, rocky plateaus, and a depth, are found in the names Truc de Finiels and possibly Champlong and Le Cros. Celtic names, which are more numerous, testify to the fact that the village was inhabited long before Roman times. One of the most common Gallic roots is *ial* or *ialo* meaning open space, and it bears obvious relevance to the name of one of the hamlets of the Pont, Salarials. As for *Lozère* (and *Mont-Lozère*) it is itself derived either from the Gallic *lausa* "flat stone" or from the pre-Celtic *less* "escarpment" or "steep place." Similarly, the French word *bruyère* and the Montipontin place name Frutgères (which was the original locus of life in the village) are derivatives of *brugères* "heath." There is also in a neighboring commune the place name Rhunes, which, like the name of the river Rhine, finds its origin in the Celtic *renos* "flowing."

Besides these, there are also at the Pont many place names of Latin origin. Grizac, like all names with the ending *ac*, has Roman antecedents. It harks back to Grizacum, from *acum* "camp." There are also the forests of Altefage to the south of the Pont, from Altus Fagus, *altus* "high" and *fagus* "beech." Yet it is interesting to see that the largest number of names of inhabited places in the village, as against names of mountains, rivers or forests, are medieval. Pont-de-Montvert itself is an obviously synthetic name as are those of many hamlets like Villeneuve, le Villaret, or l'Hopital, and Masméjean and le Mazel are also of medieval origin from the Latin *mansus* and the Provençal *mas*.

Something of the medieval history of the village also is known to us thanks to the presence in the region of the Knights of Malta, or Knights of the Hospital of St. John of Jerusalem, as they were called when their order was officially institutionalized by Godfrey of Bouillon, king of Jerusalem. Until the twelfth century the lands of the Pont had been in the sway of the seigneurs du Tournel, whose castle still stands a few miles to the north of the Pont. In 1166, however, on the occasion of the Feast of the Assumption, Odilon du Tournel handed over large tracts of his property to Raymond of Toulouse, master of the order, in whose company he had traveled on a pilgrimage to Le Puy. Subsequently, the donation was rounded out by another gift, this time from Adelbert, bishop of Mende. As was often to be the case, in the next century the heirs of the baron du Tournel had second thoughts and tried to undo the effects of their forbear's catastrophic religiosity. In vain, however, for in 1248 Guigues Meschin de Chateauneuf was obliged to ratify the gift of these lands which once and for all passed into the hands of the order. A further attempt to contest the cession not of the property but of some feudal rights was also nullified by a judgment from the court of the bishop and count of Mende in 1267. Moreover, the Knights continued to acquire rights, titles, and lands at the Pont throughout the thirteenth and fourteenth centuries. In 1238, the Knight-Commander purchased all of Guillaume de Privade's lands in the hamlet of Montgros; and in 1333, the order also acquired from Catherine, widow of Bernard de Cros, the hamlets of Le Cros and of Champlong-de-Lozère, which were places contiguous to the site of Odilon de Tournel's original donation. Before 1166, the locus of all these acquisitions had gone by the name of Gap-Français (from the fact that it was in this place that the suzerainty of the Count of Toulouse yielded to that of the King of France), but in modern times the lands there have always retained the mark of the Knights Hospitallers: hence, as has been pointed out, the existence of the synthetic place name, l'Hopital.

Because of the Order of Jerusalem, therefore, we know many things about the Pont in medieval times. For a similarly fortuitous reason we also know something about another hamlet, Grizac, which in 1362 ascended to sudden fame when Guillaume du Grimoard, who had been born there in 1309 or 1310, became pope under the name of Urban V.[17] By that date, the Grimoards were already reputed one of the most ancient families of the Gévaudan, and they had presumably held sway in the village for two or three centuries. In fact, it is worth noticing that these *notables* already then had connections which extended through the region as a whole, since our future pope had entered the Church at the prompting of his uncle Anglic, the benedictine prior of Chirac. The young Guillaume du Grimoard served in the 1350s as a papal diplomat in Italy and France. As pope, he resided at Avignon. Cracow and Vienna were perhaps the cities which benefited most from his reign, since it was Urban who founded their universities, but Pont-de-Montvert received its share also; and from 1369 to 1579,[18] Grizac was in his honor exempted from the payment of the royal taille.

Yet these institutional and political events do not tell us much about what the village was really like. Indeed, the most direct comment on the circumstances of Montipontine popular life in these years is a stricture drawn from a document dated 1257 according to which the shepherds of the Mont-Lozère were described as much addicted to "adulteria et fornicationes." Some trends do emerge, it is true, but they lack precision. All that we know is that by the twelfth and thirteenth centuries, the pastures of the Mont-Lozère were already important and that transhumance had even then become a part of the agricultural landscape. It is also clear that there existed, scattered among the

7

village hamlets, a number of seigneurial families of which the Grimoard was the most conspicuous. We can likewise assume that these seigneurs were conscious of their rights and even aggressive, since from the thirteenth century onwards they attempted to halt and even to reverse the gifts which had been made to the Church in the twelfth century.[19]

But this is very shadowy. We know nothing for example of the existence of the *frèrèches*. In reaction to the disorder of the fourteenth and fifteenth centuries, the extended family with its communally owned property often replaced the less powerful nuclear family as the focus of social life; and the new system, or *frèrèche,* was typical of the Cévennes from the fourteenth to the first half of the sixteenth century. But we do not know if there were any *frèrèches* at the Pont or not. Nor is there much to be said about what may have been the single most important event in the history of the village: its conversion to Protestantism by 1560. Traditional interpretations of this event have emphasized the fact that the local priests, both at the Pont itself and in neighboring Fraissinet, embraced Protestantism as did for a while also the heirs of Pope Urban V, the Grimoard de Beauvoir du Roure. A more sociological interpretation, however, would not so much dwell on this or on the fact that Theodore de Bèze himself was sent by Calvin to proselytize the region. It would instead emphasize certain aspects of social life in the Cévennes. The economy of the region depended on the multifarious uses of the chestnut tree, and it was linked by numerous trade routes to the cities in the south. Economically, the Cévennes were a "dynamic unity," in the opinion of M. Leroy-Ladurie, who adds that

> the bread tree [by which he means the chestnut tree] supplies food for the numerous peasant-workers, who are weavers or labor in mines, in mills, and it supplies wood as well for the leather trade . . . which will play a decisive role in the development of Protestantism in the Cévennes.[20]

In this perspective, it is the wandering artisans and traders of the Cévennes who carried Calvin's message from the cities to the mountains; and as regards Pont-de-Montvert there is no reason to suppose that this was not the case. But many questions are still unanswered, especially because we really know almost nothing about Montipontine artisan crafts in the sixteenth century. The proximity of sheep pastures and the availability of wool certainly suggest that such crafts should have existed. Yet it is hard to say how meaningful these were, for if we take the eighteenth century as a guide, it will appear that the extension of crafts depended very closely on demographic fluctuations:

artisans, it seems, came into their own not so much when opportunities arose as when an expansion of population drove surplus peasants off the land. And again we do not know very much about the level of population at the Pont before the seventeenth century.

All in all, therefore, the social history of the village in these years remains necessarily episodic. Its political fate is what we know best: in September of 1562, Catholic troops led by a Baron de Goize devastated the region around the Pont, which was again the site of civil war in 1627 and 1628. In that year, we also hear of a battle, "ung combat qui fut rendu le mois de juing dernier, sur la Louzère par le baron du Tournel," from which we can deduce not only the perpetration of more outrages but also the fact that the secretary of the Provincial Estates of 1628 spoke French with something akin to the modern *accent du midi*.[21] Indeed, since one Matthieu Borel received from the Estates of the Gévaudan fifteen livres to recover "from the wounds which he received at Pont-de-Montvert," it is likely that some fighting may have taken place in the village itself. That is all more probable in that du Tournel's opponent, D'Andredieu, who commanded in the region for the Duc de Rohan, had established his general headquarters at the Pont from which he directed the comings and goings, pillaging and arson of no less than 5,000 Protestant troops.

Slowly, however, during the course of the seventeenth century the history of the *people* of Pont-de-Montvert begins to take shape. We have a platt-book for 1631 from which much can be learned.[22] We can see already that even then most of the land of the village belonged to a relatively small group of people, few of whom were nobles and most of whom were simply well-to-do. We also have some information on the demography of the village. Unfortunately, the birth and death records are very incomplete—they exist only for the years 1670–1685 and we do not have figures for total population before 1685—but nonetheless we can see that Pont-de-Montvert in the 1670s was already overpopulated. Indeed, it is perhaps because of this population surplus that artisans had by mid century become a part of the village scene.

In spite of gaps in the evidence it is possible to give for the end of the seventeenth century a coherent description of village life without relying too heavily on inference from other regions and other times. We can see the Pont and its people in our mind's eye, and we can imagine what it would have been like to have arrived there as a traveler in the reign of the Sun King. Of course, it must be said that, to the best of our knowledge, before 1850 no idle traveler had ever gone to the Pont; and this may indeed be a reflection of how hard it was to get there and of how uncomfortable it was to be there after that. But in any case, by

1700 the Pont could be reached from various directions. There was a *chemin* or path which led northward over the Mont-Lozère to Le Bleymard, where Montipontins sometimes went to buy and sell at the fairs that were held there. Our traveler could also have arrived from the diocesan capital of Mende in the northwest by following a larger road which ran parallel to the ancient Roman road that had connected Mimatensis, as Mende was first known, to Alès, Nîmes, and Arles, the important cities of the south and southeast. This was an unusual road in that it did not follow the valley as most modern roads do, but instead ran along the mountainous plateau of the Mont-Lozère, which it reached after a short and abrupt climb near Mende.[23]

In 1700, however, a traveler was far more likely to have arrived from Alès on a road which skirted the Cévennes. These low mountains or hills are more accessible than the Mont-Lozère, and also far more Mediterranean and cheerful. But the quality of the road there depended greatly both on the season of the year, since it was largely unpaved, and on the nature of the times. In 1654, for example, we hear that road building was being resumed after a lapse of many years during which communications for lack of funds had fallen into nearly complete disrepair. Political concerns were also a factor here. After 1670, for fear of rebellion and in order to facilitate the movement of artillery, roads were opened throughout the Protestant Cévennes, and in 1681 the provincial estates of the Gévaudan even agreed to pay for some of the improvement of the road which connected Mende to the Pont. The rest of the cost would be borne by the interested parties, a decision that was not calculated to please, given the basic purpose of this building boom. None of these roads were complicated affairs. They were mere paths, really, and only wide enough to enable two mules to pass by each other without too much trouble.

But however difficult his journey, thanks to the Mediterranean air of the Cévennes, our hypothetical traveler might still have been in good spirits when he arrived at the top of one of the many hills that surround the Pont on all sides. What he would have seen, however, would be very different from what exists today. The town itself would not be much smaller than it now is: with its seventy houses, it was in 1631 only slightly less extensive than it is today. But there would not have been the protestant temple, built during the 1830s, or the Catholic church which dates from the Second Empire, or the town hall and schools which a grateful village owes to the Third Republic. In the seventeenth century, the largest building of the Pont would certainly have been a private home, perhaps that of the André family, a three story affair built of rough and uneven blocks of granite with minuscule windows. We have in fact a description of one of the better village houses for the end of the eighteenth century when housing conditions were still much as they had been a hundred years before:

> At the ground floor, there is a small courtyard, and on the right a small stable. On the right as you enter are two separate rooms, divided by a wooden partition. Between the two rooms is a staircase, also made of wood, with twelve steps, which lead to yet another room; there is also one more room with privies, and on the other side the main room with a chimney. The whole thing is covered with slate and in good condition.[24]

Slate roofs were not unusual by the end of the seventeenth century, and in the bourg or town, as against the hamlets, exactly half of the houses had roofs of this sort. Indeed, the greatest difference between the house of a rich man and that of a poor man was size, not comfort.

The village probably would have looked better from afar than from close up. Many of the houses had a stable on the ground floor; animals were everywhere, and on the whole the town was a dirty, smelly place. It is not inconceivable, therefore, that a traveler might not have wanted to spend the night there, especially since the Pont did not have, as English villages are said to have had, an inn that could provide a focus of communal social life. In 1700 there were three *cabarets* at Pont-de-Montvert where one could buy wine brought up on muleback from the Languedoc, but since the owners of these places were poor men, their establishments cannot have been much to look at.

Of course, if our visitor had seen only the *bourg* or town of Pont-de-Montvert itself, he would hardly have seen the village as a whole. Scattered around this central focus were twenty-two hamlets, which were important social subdivisions.[25] In important ways, the people who lived there led lives which set them apart from the people in the bourg. This was not, as might be thought, because the social structure of the hamlets was different from that of the Pont itself. Many of the smaller communities were still fairly sizable: Finiels and Grizac counted more than a hundred souls each. In each of the larger hamlets, one could find a social hierarchy similar to that of the bourg, and, in the last decades of the seventeenth century, Finiels even had its own notary, Jean Vierne (who died in unfortunate circumstances, since at the age of eighty he was broken on the wheel at Alès). Between bourg and hamlet there was in fact a professional as well as a social similarity. Today, most of the bourg dwellers have a nonagricultural profession, but there was no such distinction in the seventeenth century. Many hamlets then sheltered full time artisans; and in 1700, at the bourg,

11

most Montipontins were still either landless agricultural laborers and tenant farmers, or *mesnagers* and *laboureurs* who tilled their own property.

What did separate the hamlets from the bourg, however, was in the first place, distance. From the Pont to the furthest hamlet, Bellecoste, is a six mile walk, and this distance cannot be ignored in a setting where both roads and climate were so poor. Montipontins who lived in these remote places were even more isolated than their compatriots of the bourg. Often they had their own collective life. Some communal rights, for example, applied to the parish as a whole, but others extended only to the inhabitants of a particular hamlet; common lands were allotted in this same way. Just as the inhabitants of the bourg were entitled to the exclusive use of some common or seigneurial ovens which had been built at their own request in 1678,[26] so the residents of the hamlet of Montgros likewise possessed their own nonbanal mill,[27] and the Grizacois also enjoyed rights in the forests of the Beauvoir du Roure family which they did not share with their neighbors. Even more important were the differences in the incidence of the tithe, which was apportioned not for the parish as a whole but hamlet by hamlet.[28]

Each subcommunity, then, had a particular economic and social personality. Yet, in the end, however important these communal customs may have been (and we shall return to them), it is still clear that Montipontins did have the feeling of being first members of the village, and then of the bourg or the hamlets. This can be seen from their replies when they were required to give their place of birth or residence for some official purpose.

In any case, it should not be thought that the population of the hamlets was very stable. Judging from the names which appear and disappear on tax lists and other papers, the population of the parish as a whole did not change much in that few people came to the Pont as a whole from other villages.[29] The population of the hamlets within the Pont, however, was in great flux. In 1696, for example, at Champlong de Lozère, the capitation lists thirteen taxpayers, twelve of them by name. Five years later, on a similar list (which must be all inclusive, since it mentions one "Marie Mazoyer, widow of André Martin, three children, poor," who paid "0 livre and 0 sou") we now find that there are only nine names, three of which had not been mentioned five years before.[30] The more prosperous people were less mobile—since they owned land that is obviously only to be expected—but the poor of the village constantly moved from one hamlet to the next, although they did not go from one parish to the next.[31]

Another factor which made for a self-contained village was the fact that many activities were carried on throughout the whole parish. Most prominent here were religious ceremonies. Before 1685, Montipontins from all over the village would come on Sunday to the bourg to take part in a Protestant service (there was another temple at Frutgères, but it does not seem to have been much used until the one in the bourg was destroyed by royal order in 1681). After 1685, Catholic priests were installed in two hamlets, Grizac and Frutgères, as well as in the Pont itself, but most Montipontins continued to come to the bourg for mass on Sunday, and it was there also that they came to register births, marriages, and deaths. Indeed, since it was a crime for ex-Protestants to avoid such registrations, the spiritual unity of the parish was in this instance reinforced by actual law. Of course, from the Revocation of the Edict of Nantes until the re-enactment of religious tolerance in 1787, official religious exercises were not a very pleasant part of daily life. Since all Montipontins were convinced Protestants, they cannot have been too proud of themselves when they gathered to worship the "whore of Babylon." But what matters here is that this reluctant hommage implied a communal and general act which brought together all of the villagers, regardless of where they lived. And the village fairs fulfilled a similar, if economic, role. It is true that there were some fairs in the larger hamlets (the one at Bellecoste, for example, took place on July 14) [32] but these were small affairs when compared to the many fairs at the bourg, which took place on August 24, September 5, December 14 and in the first weeks of February. [33] In addition to these, held in virtue of ancient feudal right, there was also at the bourg a weekly market on Wednesday. The inhabitants of Pont-de-Montvert, in virtue of the

> right and faculty which they have, could hold a market on Wednesday of every week where would be sold corn, chestnuts, and animals, without paying any dues, taxes, or duty on the merchandise which enters and leaves the market and have enjoyed this right from time immemorial. [34]

Economics, then, bound the village together; and there were other unifying forces—for example, taxes. From the government administrator or subdelegate who resided nearby at Barre, or from the officials at Mende, orders were received by the "consuls" and other Montipontin notables about the amount of money the village as a whole would have to pay; but the actual apportionment of taxes was done by the village worthies acting in concert at the Pont. Fines and punishments were likewise imposed on the village as a whole rather than on its various parts, and this was no insignificant bond.

13

Introduction

Distance, poor communications, institutions, the primitive conditions of life generally, all of these were important factors that made the village a separate unit, remote from the outside world. This was indeed the fundamental fact of Montipontin life in the seventeenth century, and it is on this note that we could conclude an introduction to the history of Pont-de-Montvert at that time. But, at the same time, it must be interjected that this isolation was never complete. Since the concept of closed village economies has so often been belabored, it may be useful to qualify it here. Pont-de-Montvert, since medieval times, was never totally self-contained. In many important respects, the village was a part of larger units: the area of the northern Cévennes, the Languedoc, France, and even Protestant Europe. Although it can be claimed, and this will indeed be the central theme of our argument, that the effect and impact of the waves which came to it from the outside can best be understood by considering the structure of the Pont-de-Montvert itself, it remains obvious that the history of our village does hinge to a very great degree on what happened elsewhere. Intellectually and religiously, Pont-de-Montvert was obviously dependent on what was taking place in Paris, London, and Geneva; although, again, as shall be seen, the consequences for the Pont of what was taking place in these distant European centers also depended enormously on how Pont-de-Montvert was put together.

The ways in which Pont-de-Montvert was connected to these places are complex and can only be sorted out with some difficulty. To begin with, it is clear that the rich, far more than the poor, had many connections, familial and official, with the outside world. They had more to lose and also more with which to bribe royal officials. They kept a closer watch on what was being decided about them at Barre, Florac, Mende, Alès, or Montpellier, and they were more able to do that because they often had relatives or business friends in these cities.

Commercial ties with the outside were also important, and these did matter for the community as a whole, rich and poor. Unfortunately, the details of these relations will only become clear in the eighteenth century, but for the seventeenth century we can surmise that Pont-de-Montvert probably exported manpower, cattle, and taxes, and imported officials and grain, together with small amounts of metal, salt, books, and paper. Not everybody participated in these dealings, or at least not everyone participated in them in the same way. The poor exported themselves and imported grain; the rich were more likely to export cattle and import whatever meager luxuries the village consumed. But what matters here is that everyone at least had knowledge of what existed elsewhere even if they did not themselves do much about it.

14

This may well be symbolized by the yearly transmigration of the thousands of sheep that came up from the Languedoc every year: certainly only a few people, shepherds and landowners, were directly involved, but the transhumance was a yearly reminder of the magnitude of the village's dealings with other communities.

Yet, ultimately, of course, we must speak in most cases of awareness, of apprehension, rather than of direct participation and involvement. For most Montipontins in the seventeenth century and in most ways, Pont-de-Montvert *was* the essence of all things. Social mobility, or in fact the very concept of social class, was something that was learned within the village, not within France as a whole. Whether one was rich or poor depended largely on where one fitted into village life, and in the end nearly everything that was consumed was village made. Few people traveled to the other large towns of the area, Florac, or Alès, or Montpellier, and there certainly must have been Montipontins who reached adulthood without having ever left the immediate vicinity of the village.

Many of the characteristics which Montipontins shared among themselves, they also shared with other people as well: they were French, loyal subjects of the King, they were Protestants, they were law-abiding citizens. (Criminals were social misfits who were known to be criminals, and had very little to do with the rest of the population.) [35] There are therefore very good reasons to suppose that the overwhelming mass of Montipontins accepted and lived by the general precepts of the Christian and paternalistic life that was typical of French or European society before 1700, and although local Catholics had very harsh things to say about fanaticism and heresy at Pont-de-Montvert, never did they or their officials even suggest that the typical and law-abiding Montversois were morally or culturally different from their Catholic neighbors.

But the point of all this is not to deny that the Pont was ultimately an autonomous unit. It is merely to say that the Pont-de-Montvert, this self-contained unit, very much resembled other similar and self-contained units. Pont-de-Montvert was indeed a part of France, but France itself was a mere conglomeration of discrete units.[36] In the end, therefore, what matters for our purpose is the fact that for most of its inhabitants, and in most respects, Pont-de-Montvert at the end of the seventeenth century was still a world unto itself.

CHAPTER I Social Class on the Eve of the

Camisard Wars (1702–1704)

At the end of the seventeenth century Pont-de-Montvert was in many ways a self-sufficient place. Perhaps because of this, it was also a complicated world, where different individuals with different rights and different responsibilities fulfilled different roles. Indeed, it may perhaps be useful to emphasize this variety, because it does stand in such marked contrast to what Pont-de-Montvert subsequently became and now is, a classless society where social variations, such as they are, are due more to personal worth than inherited status.

This was emphatically not the case in 1700. Of the 1,000 people who lived in the village then, about 700 belonged to what might be called the "lower class."[1] Within this group there were, of course, wide differences: there were those who lived in the hamlets and those who were in the bourg, those who worked the land and those (relatively few— less than one in ten) who were artisans, and here again we should distinguish between the artisans, smiths, and cobblers, who worked for other villagers and those who were in the cloth trade and may have had more to do with the outside world. Yet, since there are many instances of marriages between artisans in the bourg and young girls from the hamlets, as well as of young women of Pont with peasants in Grizac or Villeneuve, it is fair to conclude that socially, the lower class in the seventeenth century was disparate but basically intertwined.

Above them were 200 people, perhaps a few more, who belonged to a distinctly different group. Here the largest element were the landowning peasant families, the *gros paysans,* the *grandes familles,* who are sometimes very revealingly labeled as *les familles* (everyone has a family of sorts, but a real *famille* requires a certain status and wealth).

16

Finally, at the very top were a handful of notables, perhaps fifteen families in all, who were markedly different from the rest.

How well all of these groups got along together must surely have varied from time to time. There are obvious indications, to which we shall return, that they did not see the world through the same eyeglass. But for the three centuries which stand between us and historical darkness, there are no instances of overt and bloody conflict between these three groups, and in a way, it is our overall purpose to show how this could have been. Why indeed have there been, especially since the beginning of the eighteenth century, so few instances of political conflict or even divergence between rich and poor Montipontins?

In part the answer lies in the fact that upper-class Montipontins did fulfill a role that was useful for their lower class compatriots, whom they mercilessly exploited in other ways. In 1676, for example, it became obvious that the inhabitants needed ovens to bake their bread. Quite naturally, the problem was resolved not by the rank and file but by the elite of the village, "les principaux habitants et représentants le plus grand corps du Pont-de-Montvert." [2] The consul Chapelle spoke to the "assembly," which then examined his proposition and made a proposal to the feudal seigneur, the Comte du Roure in this instance (these proposals were then accepted by the count, whose family retained the property of these ovens until 1812). [3] What matters, however, is not the success of the proposals but the fact that the rank and file of the village were never a party to the negotiations. It was the local bourgeois elite that stood as a necessary transmission belt between the very small and the very great, and there are many other similar instances in the history of the village. In 1704, for example, when the region was torn by a running war between the rebel Protestant Camisards and the royal troops, we find that the royal authorities rounded up village notables to act as go-betweens in their negotiations with the rebels. Nothing came of it, but Pierre Pons, the local miller who was sent on this mission for the Pont, was quite pleased with the role he had played. And his role was not unimportant since many locals probably used him as an intermediary with the local commander of the royalist troops who had "honored" Pons with his friendship. [4] Similarly, at a somewhat later date, Antoine Velay must certainly have derived much prestige from the fact that he was so much richer than his neighbors and that they often had to rely on him, as they did in August of 1722. Troops that year had been stationed at Grizac to cordon off the area contaminated by a plague, which had been spreading from Marseille, and it was Velay who had gone to Barre to ask of the local subdelegate that he should lend blankets to the villagers with whom troops had been quartered.[5] In such ways the rich would intercede for the poor; they fulfilled other social functions that were perhaps more ambiguous. The haves would often lend money to the have-nots, who needed it to pay taxes, to buy seeds, or because of some private misfortune.[6]

But in judging how the great and small managed to live together in relative harmony it is perhaps more important to stress those circumstances for which we can garner little evidence, in the strict historical sense of the word. The identity of religious belief, physical proximity, the sense of commonly shared hardships and enmities must all have been important aspects of village life. Certainly, as will be shown, the rich and poor did not see eye to eye on what they should do about the forced conversion of the village to Catholicism; but in spite of this, what remains is that everyone despised and feared the Catholic authorities, the *puissances,* the government officials of Mende and Montpellier who were bearing down on the Pont. Everyone was also faced with the same natural calamities: epidemics, floods, frost. Obviously, some Montipontins were more able to resist these things than others. In 1728–1729, for example, the harvest failed, and in Antoine Velay's words,

> In these years, there was no credit to be found anywhere and the greater part of the people was reduced to beggary and could not find anything. This shortage was general.[7]

Unlike most of his neighbors Velay himself did not go begging. For him this catastrophe only meant that he would have to buy seed for harvest, something which many people may have had to do every year, and whether at this junction Velay's neighbors envied him his independence or thanked him for whatever help he may have given to them, we do not know. But the point is that Antoine Velay was at least *affected* by the same crises which ruined other men. That may not be very much, but it is something. Since the land was ultimately everything for everyone, all social classes shared a number of overriding concerns. It is admittedly difficult to subscribe nowadays to the romantic and corporate concept of organic society. Something of the sort, however, did exist at the Pont around 1700 when the village somehow hung together as a complex and separate unit within which there was relative harmony between the social classes or groups that it comprised.

In spite of this and although there has never been overt social conflict in the village, it is also perfectly obvious that in 1700 there were very wide cleavages within this village society. There were great gaps which separated the three main social groupings from each other, gaps

18

which implied exploitation and resentment, oppression and bitterness. For that reason it is necessary to insist on the fact that the corporateness of the village was most visible in its dealings with the outside. When Montipontins dealt with each other, they did not stand on one plane. Each knew his place, and this place was not the same for all.

The poor and landless were, as has been said, the most numerous. We do not know very much about what they did and thought in normal times, but we do know something of their behavior in moments of crisis and some characteristics of their life-style do emerge. The first of these is that the poorest Montversois lived on a subsistence level. Their actual diet before 1700 is not known, but it must have consisted largely of rye bread and chestnuts, with perhaps some vegetables in the summer months. Meat for them was practically unknown, and there is something quite pathetic in the fact that those Montipontins who tended and raised animals usually did so for others. In many cases, the poor would in fact find themselves so poor that they would have to leave or starve. In moments of great hardships, they begged. This cannot have been thought very degrading, since, after all, professional beggars were not unknown in the Lozère even in normal times. Every parish had them. But for the ordinary run of mortals, beggary was nonetheless a solution of despair, and it is worth noticing that beggars preferred to operate in neighboring parishes rather than in their own.

Naturally, the poor much preferred to emigrate if they could, at least for the harvest season and sometimes for ever. How frequent such emigrations were, we cannot say.[8] The birth and death records for the village at the end of the seventeenth century are very imperfect, since births are nearly always made to outnumber deaths, but the gap is such as to suggest that continuous emigration was already then taking place.[9] Françoise Brès, for example, who was put to death in 1702 at the age of twenty-nine for religious reasons, had spent seven years of her adolescence in this way as a maid at Alès.[10] It was on the way back from there to the Pont, while she was looking for work during the chestnut harvest, that she was seized by the spirit and began to preach against the Catholic Church.

Most of the very poor, like most of the migrants and most of the beggars, were peasants rather than artisans. But the distinction here was not a fundamental one. It would be wrong to suppose that artisans were at this time a distinct group with interests and views widely removed from the agriculturists. The existence of intermarriage between the two occupational groups outweighs the fact that we can discern by 1700 the presence of some characteristically artisan families, where a certain craft was handed down from father to son. One of the first hat

19

makers in the town, for example, was Jean Viala, who was quite well-to-do (since in 1701 he paid a capitation tax of nine livres when most artisans paid less than two livres). In 1747, we now find that both Pierre and Paul Vialla are following this trade. They must surely have been related, perhaps living under the same roof, since their names appear side by side on the tax roll for the *dixième de l'industrie* although there are other Vialas scattered elsewhere on the list; and finally, in 1789, we find yet one more "Viala fils chapellier." [11] It would no doubt be possible to find other such examples; but the overall impression that remains, as has been said, is that artisans were not really in 1700 a separate social entity. Here, it must also be remembered that although artisan crafts had become by the end of the eighteenth century more complex than they had been (hat making, after all, was a complicated trade; carpenters, smiths, and locksmiths also had a skill and began as apprentices) the artisans of 1700 were still usually weavers or spinners. Everyone at the Pont more or less knew how to do that. In the Cévennes, as Chaptal pointed out, every household had a frame for weaving: "all women clean or thread wool, and men weave the cloth." [12] Weaving was not an unusual skill. It was for all a way of earning money in winter time, and for some it was a year-long profession of last resort, something which one did in order to keep body and soul together. There was probably a constant coming and going within the class of the landless, from crafts to agriculture and vice versa. Weavers would work in the fields during the harvest season, and many *valets* would take up weaving during the winter months. [13]

At the end of the seventeenth century what we find therefore at the bottom of the social heap is an occupationally amorphous class, ill-housed, semi-starved, landless, illiterate. The next and intermediate social group was not much better off. Most of the people there, it is true, did own some land, and this gave them a greater margin of survival. But they did not for all that live like *grand seigneurs*. In many cases, the continued existence of their familial independence was conditional on the sacrifice of younger children. It is not infrequently that we find cases like that of the young Bonnicel, one of François Guizot's ancestors, who had by 1701 taken over the farm of his deceased father Guillaume but who had "four brothers and two sisters, most of them serving masters." [14] Many members of the intermediate class were also driven to farm other people's land since their own did not suffice to make ends meet.

Ultimately, what distinguished these middling peasants from the poor was a quantitative rather than a qualitative difference. Unlike the totally destitute, they were not so often obliged to find work in other parishes, nor were they so often or so completely hungry. But like the very poor, peasants of a middling sort were often illiterate; they had little to do with the outside world; they had few contacts with what we might call a market economy. They did own land, but not enough of it to grow a surplus, and it is likely that they too would have to buy rye from the rich. Many of these peasants would be unable to support themselves on the fruits of their property once they had payed the tithe, taxes, and feudal dues. There would be a gap in their finances, which they would have to make up by the sale of some animal or by the remittances of those members of the family who "worked for masters." In short, these middling peasants were also quite miserable, and what separated them from their even more unfortunate neighbors would have been very little indeed if it had not been for the moral and political consequences of the few economic distinctions which did set them apart. For when everything had been said and done, although they may have been poor and even occasionally reduced to beggary, they did own land; and at Pont-de-Montvert, ownership of land was crucial. A starving landowner was not the same as a starving laborer, and he did not think like one. No one could think him a vagabond, an *homme de rien*. Within the community of the Pont, because of his property, he did enjoy some prestige, which was most important if we bear in mind that what was happening outside of Pont-de-Montvert did not concern him very much.

The real cleavage in village society, however, came very close to the top. There one could find a small number of families, some of them rich peasants, most of them bourgeois. These people were quite different from the poor or the middling both in theory and in fact. The rich were literate in all instances and even educated in some—we find among them another Bonnicel, this one *juge et docteur ès droit*. They were able to speak and write French as well as the local dialect or *patois*. They formed a distinct world of their own. Before the Revocation of 1685 we can see their same signatures regularly appearing and reappearing on the occasion of ceremonies, of deaths, and of christenings, which they would attend as witnesses, godfathers, or friends.

Very obvious physical differences set them apart from the rest of the village. Most importantly, they ate better, and on this score we do have some very precise information for the seventeenth century. In these years already, widows or elderly patriarchs would often during their own lifetime pass on to their children their property rights in exchange for a fixed annuity. Since the sums involved were by local standards important and since good accounts make for good friends, these agreements were notarized and are therefore available to us. Naturally, because only the rich or nearly rich would be likely to do this, the information that we get from these *donations* or *donations partage* does not tell us much about life in the lower reaches of the village community, but they are very useful for the understanding of the nature of life at the top, and more particularly, at the top of the peasant hierarchy. We have for 1700 just such a contract. It was signed by Jeanne Pelade, widow of one Alexandre Albaric, whose family property at Villeneuve had counted in 1661 as one of the largest in the village.[15] On April 19, 1700, the widow Albaric signed a paper giving to her son Jean Albaric "each and everyone of her possessions" but to her dying day, her son would have to give to her each year the equivalent of 400 quarts of rye grain, ten pounds of salt pork, four pounds of salt, ten pounds of butter, and ten pounds of cheese, with in addition, every second year, a dress from cloth of local make, one bed sheet, two shirts, one hat every three years, and an initial deposit of twenty livres for her good works.[16] Translated in terms of daily consumption we can see that this unusually rich widow would be able to eat a healthy loaf of bread a day, with once a week an omelet and a bit of salt pork. Not on the whole a sumptuous diet, but the best that could ordinarily be had in the village until the last century. Her days, at least, were not of those "sobre quien tiene jurisdicción la hambre," a fact of no small consequence in the seventeenth century when most Europeans, like the characters of Cervantes, were nearly always in the sway of hunger.

Other very practical matters would set apart this upper group from the two others that we have described. None of the richer people, and no member of their immediate family would have to work in a menial capacity for other masters. Unlike other children who would begin to work and earn something in their early teens at least, the children of the notables would either stay at home or learn some trade or even some profession. Jean Velay, for example, studied law, and his peasant father noted laconically in his diary that this son "has cost his father much money."[17] The rich did not work with their hands, and indeed some of them may not have worked at all. Many of them rented out their property, and one distinction between the notable and intermediate social classes lay in just this fact: those at the top had land to rent out, while those below were forced to lease it.[18]

The village notable differed, then, from their neighbors in the precise, practical circumstances of their lives but they also enjoyed generally a much higher status and greater moral prestige.[19] Many of the notables "lived nobly." This was important in itself, but one must also add that

22

many notables actually *were* nobles or at least aspired to that status. Through the purchase or the possession of seigneurial titles, many bourgeois and even some peasants had achieved an intermediate social rank that set them apart from the rank and file. Admittedly, with the exception of the André family (to which we will return), no one at the Pont either in the seventeenth or the eighteenth century succeeded in passing completely from the bourgeoisie to the aristocracy by purchasing one of these spurious titles. But in spite of this, seigneuries did give prestige to their owners, who became, thanks to them, "almost noble"; and rich bourgeois continued to purchase them to the very end of the ancien régime, although their economic value was by 1700 in many cases already negligible or nonexistent.

It should not be thought, of course, that most of the feudal seigneurs, either in 1700 or in 1789, were bourgeois. At the end of the seventeenth century,[20] most of the valuable titles were still in the hands of the Knights of Malta, or of the great aristocrats of the region, like the Marquis de Grizac, the baron of Barre, the Demoiselle des Portes, the Marquis de la Fare, and the sieur de Valmale.[21] But in the shuffles and purchases that had been going on for decades and even centuries, many bourgeois had managed to find some interstice besides those men who held their claims from "time immemorial." In this way, by the 1690's there had come to be at the Pont nine nonnoble seigneurs, six of whom lived in the village.[22] Little could be squeezed from many of the seigneuries.[23] One of them corresponded to a ruined hamlet, and of two others it was said that

> no one knows that there have been any collections in the fiefs of the Sieur Combes and Mathieu for the last ten years or so.[24]

Yet, although the seigneuries were monetarily unimportant, in some instances even insignificant, they did serve a social purpose by elevating their possessors above the ordinary run of mortals. They also enabled those who owned fiefs to fuse with the real gentry. For one of the characteristic traits of the upper class of the Pont at the end of the seventeenth century was that it included genuine, pseudo, and in-between nobles. The most interesting case here is presented by the Andrés. In 1631, we find already that André André was one of the forty richest men in the village.[25] His family is at this time an honorable one, but there are as yet no titles and no official posts. By 1661, however, the Andrés had already made some progress.[26] There is now a Jean André who is a notary and a "bailiff" for one of the older feudal families. His wife is not a noble, but Claude de Rouvière like himself belongs to a class that is rising and aspiring to a new status. With them in the Pont of 1661, we also find two Marguerite Dandrés, his relatives, one of them married to another bailiff, Pinet, whose family also included notaries and which was to remain an important one in the Pont for a hundred years. The year 1666, however, marks the great social triumph of the André family when another Jean André *fils* married Marie de Beauvoir du Roure, a distant relative of both Pope Urban V and of the baron of Florac.[27] At this point, in the eyes of the villagers the Andrés had in fact become noble, and their house, although relatively modest, was known henceforth as the *château de M. Dandré*.[28] Indeed, the family was now able to withstand André's refusal to convert in 1685. In July of 1686 he was pursued and shot by royal troops; his property, which legally should have been confiscated, was only temporarily taken over by the state; but his sons were forcibly brought up as Catholics, so that one of his grandsons became a musketeer of the King, while another brother, Jacques Scipion, also a Catholic, inherited the title of Seigneur de Montfort.

Ultimately, therefore, although the Andrés did survive socially, they were lost to the village. But they had had the time to pass from the middling bourgeoisie through the upper bourgeoisie to the gentry; and their social saga illustrates the usefulness of a surviving if honorific feudal system. It also points to the amorphous nature of society at the top. The leading class at Pont-de-Montvert in 1680 included many different sorts of people. Some were genuine nobles, others were members of the professions or even rich peasants who had bought seigneuries, and a successful family could within three or four generations climb to the top of the greasy pole of social and seignorial success.

How much change could one find in the social structure of the Pont in the seventeenth century? On the face of it, one could answer "not much." In the 1660s many seigneurs, noble or not, claimed secular possession of their fiefs. One of them, Allier, a peasant from Frutgères, was said to have held his forever; and since his family was declining in these years it is quite likely that this seigneurie had indeed come into his family a long time before. Statistics of a more general sort can also be used to demonstrate that the property structure of the Pont was not changing very much. In 1631, there were at Pont-de-Montvert 213 landowners, which does suggest that nearly every family owned something, but fifty-six people owned 65 percent of the land. Thirty years later, in 1661, the figures were nearly the same: fifty-seven people could then lay claim to 65 percent of the village's landed wealth, and this proportion was largely unchanged in 1701 (at which date, however, it is to be computed from the list for the capitation or head tax rather than from an actual land survey).

A closer look, however, does suggest modifications. Although it is quite true that the general pattern in 1700 was not much altered from what it had been, there was a difference nonetheless in the specific content of the structure, as might have been guessed from the case of the André family. The framework was the same, but individual families were always moving up or down within it. This is readily understandable. For simple biological reasons, the notable class was less stable than one might think from figures alone. Although the rich at Pont-de-Montvert usually married among themselves, they did not always do so. Some marriages brought in people from other villages and other social classes. Like everyone else's, the families of the notables were also often very large, and some of the children could not do as well as others.

Antoine Velay's own brood was a good example of this. Velay himself was the richest man at Grizac and one of the Pont's most notable *gros paysans*. One of seven surviving children, he became the father of twelve more little Velays, six of whom survived. One of them, inspired no doubt by paternal example, had nine children of his own. This made for a lot of Velays, but for a while there was no problem. Antoine Velay, the founding father of the Grizac branch, did quite well and married a wealthy girl from the subregional capital of Florac, where his older brother Jean was a leading citizen, an elder of the Protestant church and a friend of the local Protestant minister. His younger brother Pierre managed equally well. He took over the paternal estate of Racoules, where his grandfather had already been a bailiff or justice of peace, and he married a girl from a neighboring village, Saint-Maurice-de-Ventalon, who brought him with her dowry the seigneury of Marvelhac. Two sisters married bourgeois in the bourg of the Pont. One became the wife of Pierre Desmarets and the other married Pierre Pons, a merchant and miller, and both of these families were to play important political and social roles in the decades to come.[29]

But all of Velay's children did not do as well, and could not do as well, for good management could not continue to provide lands and dowries for so great a number of people. In the absence of birth control, a successful family could rise only if struck by misfortune, by death in childbirth, which enabled the bereaved to remarry and prosper, or by deaths through disease that thinned the ranks of prospective heirs. Such was not Antoine Velay's lot. He and his wife lived to an unusual old age—he was nearly eighty when he died—and his youngest son was born after his daughter had married at the age of twenty-three. His elder children did all right. The oldest daughter married François Deleuze, of Saint-Germain-du-Pradel, who was the seigneur of this place, a kulak like Velay himself, and an elder son married a sister of the local apothecary Roux. But the other children did not do so well, and Velay had to fend for them as best he could. One of his sons he sent as an apprentice to a merchant at Anduze in the South; but Pierre, who was sixteen, did not take to this separation: "he was unable to stay and to his own misfortune came home." [30]

Some families died out; others were too numerous. But in addition to these biological causes, other factors were at work in the village during the last decades of the seventeenth century: movement from the countryside to the bourg, and emigration at the top. In the earlier decades of the century, many of the local notables, as has been seen, belonged to the gentry. This was no longer so true by 1700. A juxtaposition of the cadastres of 1631 and 1661, together with an inspection of birth and death records for the years 1670–1685 clearly show that at the Pont there were fewer aristocrats at the end of the century than there had been at the beginning. Many of them disappeared altogether and sold the lands which they had owned in the village. The Beauvoir du Roures were gone by 1700, and so were the Gabriacs. Before 1685, we have on record a marriage between Pierre Rouvière (or de Rouvière . . .) and Dianne de Nogarède, a relative of Jean de Laurens who was an absentee noble landowner. Later, we will still find Rouvières, but there are no more Nogarèdes.

Yet although this emigration at the top was very conspicuous, it was not a fundamental factor of social change. The departure of the older gentry had no immediate effect because there were new notables who were there to fill the gaps. Although more important than the permanent flux of the poor from hamlet to hamlet, upper-class emigration was not unlike it in nature since it was also barren of consequences. Just as some poor peasants replaced other poor peasants, so did some notables replace other notables in the social system. More crucial, therefore, during the second half of the seventeenth century, was the movement to the bourg of families or branches of families which through luck, hard work, or marriage had risen to prominence in the hamlets.

The impact of this movement is not immediately obvious since the village social structure during these years remained similar to what it had been before. But it derives its importance from the fact that without this flow of new blood, the social pyramid of the Pont would indeed have become very different. In the nineteenth century, this pyramid collapsed when the poor ceased to go from one hamlet to the next and went instead from the hamlets to urban France. And just as the village in 1880 would need replacements for the pool of labor below, so did it need in 1700 replacements for the notable class above. Without the bourgeois migration from hamlet to bourg, the Pont's social structure would in 1700 have fallen to pieces as it did finally after 1880. It was the progression from the hamlets that postponed the fall; it filled the gap left by the gentry and served to perpetuate an inherited but already threatened social pattern.

Many families followed this upward path: the Bonnets, the Andrés, the Jourdans. The case that is best known to us is that of the Servières, who would rise to great eminence in the eighteenth century but had already laid the groundwork for this progression by 1700.[31] The first Servière of whom we know anything was Raymond, who lived in the hamlet of Rieumal during the sixteenth century. Second and third generation Servières did not do much either, but the fourth generation was more lively. Pierre, Jean, and David prospered and created families whose ramifications were to extend so far that in the eighteenth century most notable families of the bourg were in one way or another related to them. The eldest of the three sons, Pierre, remained at Rieumal as its leading kulak. David, the youngest, became a notary in the bourg, but this proved to be a false start, and this branch of the family came to nought. It was the intermediate son, Jean, whose seed did most for the tribe. Jean himself remained on the land and married into another rich peasant family, the Verdeilhans of the Merlet. Antoine and David, his sons (the fifth generation Servières), were both farmers like their forbears, but here one branch of the family did finally move off the land forever. Of Antoine's ten children (the sixth generation Servières), Jean-Antoine did quite well for himself: he married a girl from the neighboring village of Saint-Frézal-de-Ventalon, and in spite of some difficulties during the Camisard wars, he succeeded in later becoming the local bailiff of the Knights of Malta. This gave him an entry into the upper reaches of the village's social pyramid in which his son Jean and all the Servières after him were henceforth securely ensconced. Jean (seventh generation) Servière was also fortunate in that his father died at an opportune moment, enabling his mother to remarry. She did very well for herself and her son and chose as her second husband a Monsieur Desmaret, who was one of the consuls of Pont-de-Montvert. In addition to this stroke of good luck, one of his aunts, Isabeau Servière, had already become in February of 1672 the wife of Bonnet, seigneur de las Cases. All of these things enabled Jean Servière to rise in the world: in 1710, he married Suzanne Talon, whose family was a notch above his own and counted in its midst prosperous millers and notaries. Henceforth, the Servières were well on their way towards the apotheosis that would come to them at the end of the ancien régime and at the beginning of the new one.

Pont-de-Montvert

There are of course many ways of looking at this family saga. One of them would be to insist on how slow this promotion had been. When Jean-Antoine (sixth generation) Servière did finally settle in the bourg, he had behind him one false family start and at least a hundred years of peasant prosperity. But the more important point is that however slow it may have been, the promotion did in the end take place. By 1710, Jean (seventh generation) Servière enjoyed in the village hierarchy the solid possession of a place which a hundred years before had been in the hands of different families, some of them noble. Movement was slow, but it did exist; and because of it Pont-de-Montvert was able to renew and perpetuate itself.

From this it can be seen that although the social structure of the Pont in 1700 appeared to be very steadfast and durable with its three-fold "class" division, it is also clear that this stability was in fact quite deceptive. If at the end of the seventeenth century, the biological attrition and emigration of the older notable families was not crucial, or even visible, it was only because movement from the hamlets to the bourg was making up for emigration from the bourg to the outside. This however was only one half of the diptych, the other half of which was that this substitution ultimately proved incomplete, although this would have been obvious to no one at the beginning of the eighteenth century. Initially, social relationships between the notables and other classes as well as between nobles and the rest of the world remained much as they had been. The new bourgeoisie merely took over where the old gentry had left off. In 1700, it seemed that the newcomers were successfully exercising the important role of intermediary between the villagers and the "powers". Nor did the departure of the gentry bring about any great economic upheaval either. There were no more absentee owners after 1700 than before, and the position of the village as a whole and the role of the poor within it did not greatly change. But it is reasonable to suppose that the disappearance of the local aristocracy affected the morale if not the economic position of the bourgeoisie. Certainly, as we shall see, the bourgeoisie continued in its attempts to penetrate the aristocratic establishment through the purchase of seigneuries, but the situation in the eighteenth century would no longer be the same. At the local level, there was less point in these purchases. In terms of marriage, for example, they could bear no dividends when there were no longer any aristocrats left to marry. Social ascent within the village structure was now less attractive than it had been before; and more important still, the departure of the gentry led to a widening of the moral gap between the village elite and the national and regional establishment.

Social Class on the Eve of the Camisard Wars

This in turn had widespread effects. It is true that the overriding fact of social life at the Pont before 1700 had been its hierarchic divisions of wealth and class. But it is also true that these divisions before 1680 had not been rigid. Many of the Velays, for example, had married beneath themselves. Others had married into families that were related to the Andrés, who were themselves related to great nobles beyond the village; and although it would be misleading to exaggerate the romantic appeal of this great chain of being, it is still undeniable that in the Pont, before the end of the seventeenth century, there were ties which in one way or another linked the very poor to the poor, to the middling, to the rich, to the noble, to the "powers that be." Of course, the bond was very tenuous. It certainly did no more than link contiguous social classes, and it would be silly to claim that because of it the landless laborers thought that they had some claim on the *gros paysans,* or on the local gentry, or on the authorities which really did little more than to oppress and squeeze them. Yet the link was there, and it was important, especially for the bourgeoisie. Through their connection with the gentry above and with the locals below, they had been before 1700 in an intermediary and important position. When this upward tie with the outside was broken in the last decades of the seventeenth and the first decade of the eighteenth century, the immediate social consequences were not important. The bourgeoisie just stepped forward and filled the gap. But there were long-run consequences of this break, and they may perhaps best be brought out by a comparison of the political behavior of the village notables at the beginning and at the end of the eighteenth century.

CHAPTER II Politics in 1700: Pont-de-Montvert

and the Camisard Wars

The political life of most French villages is often muted and hard to reconstruct. Some of them hardly appear to have been touched at all by the great political upheavals of war and revolution. For those that have been marked or even seared, the crisis has often been of recent date. The political turning point for the conservative villages in the west, in the Vendée, came with the French Revolution. In Eastern France, 1870 is a watershed; and in some southern towns the liberation in 1944 marked a new start. The modern political history of Paris itself begins in 1789 and perhaps even with General Boulanger in 1889.

At the Pont, however, the *grands ancêtres,* the founding fathers of modern political tradition, were the Camisards and the great event was the running war which opposed these Protestant rebels to the royal and Catholic troops of Louis XIV. The worst and noblest years of Pont-de-Montvert are 1702–1704, and they are set in the context of the great violence, of the repression and repeated humiliations which followed the imposition of Roman Catholicism on this Protestant community after the end of religious tolerance in 1685. These years are far in the past, but what happened then is still of consequence for the Mont-versois of today.

The Camisard War (or Wars—most of the fighting took place in 1702–1704, but there were revolts until 1710) was very bloody.[1] Pont-de-Montvert was very prominently involved in these conflicts, whose importance for the life of the village cannot be doubted. Yet we do not have much specific or continuous information about the role of the village in these years. Much has to be pieced together since the politics of village life are even more difficult to reconstitute than its social

30

history. Governments, after all, were always interested in village economics (although their reasons for this have not always been to the
liking of the villagers), but before 1789 the powers-that-be were wholly
uninterested in local opinion. Even when trouble arose, officials were
clearly more interested in simply putting it down than they were in
trying to understand it or in taking steps that would prevent its recur-
rence. Later in the eighteenth century, some local functionaries would
occasionally urge the provincial officials to moderation, and it could be
argued that the desire to avoid armed insurrection did imply a certain
concern for local public opinion. That, however, is a tenuous and in any
case infrequent link. Although the elections of the nineteenth century
do provide us with a most useful commentary on the wishes of the
villagers and of the government's reaction to them, there is nothing of
the sort for the years before 1789. As far as Pont-de-Montvert was
concerned, the pattern of the ancien régime was not one of consulta-
tion followed by government action, but of government action followed
by speculation on its possible bloody consequences. Nor was there
much change on this score even in the reign of Louis XVI in the 1770s
and 1780s. Officials in Montpellier or elsewhere may well have been
anxious to know what was thought by important people, but there is no
indication that anyone before 1789 ever bothered to find out what it
was that Montipontins wanted, or whether there were some Montipontins who wanted some things which others would reject.[2]

The background of the Camisard Wars reaches back to 1685. In
that year, Louis XIV decided to revoke the limited tolerance which
his grandfather Henry IV had granted to the French Protestants. At
first, most of them by far abjured Calvinism. What little resistance there
was took the form of emigration to Holland, Prussia, and England.[3]
But there was much resentment and bitterness, even hatred; and a
spark was set to this in 1702 by the murder of a Catholic priest, the
Abbé du Chayla in Pont-de-Montvert itself.

Du Chayla had been sent to the Pont as *archiprêtre des Cévennes* in
charge of missionary work because the Catholic authorities were well
aware that the conversion of the Montipontins, and of the Cévenols
generally, had been purely nominal. Since he was quite determined to
destroy any vestiges of reform and rebellion, it is not surprising that he
was much hated, although it is probably not true that he was, as his
enemies claimed, at once power mad, lascivious, and corrupt. There is
no doubt, however, that Du Chayla was very intransigent in enforcing
coercive laws and in punishing Protestants who were caught while
trying to escape to Switzerland. Feelings were already running very
high in July of 1702 when he arrived at the Pont during one of his cir-

cuits through the Cévennes. The abbé was indifferent to the warnings he received, and he exulted when he heard of the capture on the Mont-Lozère of six young Protestants (three of them women) and of their guide, who was leading them to Geneva. The women, he ordered sent to a convent at Mende. The men were imprisoned in the cellar of his house, the former *chateau de M. Dandré*.

Word of this quickly spread throughout the region. On July 23, sixty to a hundred men from all over the Cévennes assembled in a forest near Grizac. That same night, while the local militia looked the other way, they invaded Pont-de-Montvert, surrounded Du Chayla's house, sang psalms, and shouted "Kill! Kill! We want the prisoners." It is not clear that they did in fact intend to kill the abbé from the beginning. But when a shot was fired on the band by one of his domestics, Du Chayla's fate was settled. Inspired by one of their leaders, or "prophets" as they were called, the rebels set fire to the house. "Never has there been seen a prompter flame," recollected another prophet, Abraham Mazel. Du Chayla tried to escape but he broke his leg and was dragged by the hair to the river Tarn. With a rather macabre humor, Esprit Séguier, who had masterminded the coup, asked Du Chayla if he would abjure Catholicism and follow the band as its Protestant minister. When Du Chayla refused this offer, he was shot twice, stabbed fifty-three times, and thrown into the Tarn.

Retribution was not wanting. Although the rebels or "children of God" managed to kill the curé of Frutgères and some other less important victims, they were quickly surrounded by royal troops. The authorities were determined to be very fierce. Esprit Séguier was tried, convicted, and brought back to the Pont for his execution. His right hand was lopped off, incompletely, and he had to bite off the bits of skin that held it into place. Still unrepentant, he was then burnt at the stake. During his interrogation, he had been asked if he felt remorse for what he had done. Unmoved, he had merely replied, "My soul is a garden full of shade and fountains."

But the ruthless punishment of the "children of God" did not quash the insurrection which now spread throughout the Cévennes. For about one year, the Camisard leaders Roland, Cavalier, and Joanny (who was one of Du Chayla's assassins) led large bands of Protestant rebels, which the royal and Catholic generals Basville and Montrevel were not able to put down. In the summer of 1703, fighting did slacken a little, but only because many of the Camisards went home for the harvest. Their bands were smaller now, but still elusive. At this point, Basville sought and obtained from Versailles the authorization to destroy the whole of the Cévennes: if the rebels themselves could not be sup-

A map of Pont-de-Montvert in its time of troubles (ca. 1704). Gaignères Collection, Cabinet des Estampes, Bibliothèque Nationale, Paris.

pressed directly, they would be suppressed indirectly, through the destruction of their bases of supply. Trees were to be cut down and houses would be wrecked stone by stone. But this was more easily said than done. It took too long to destroy walls and foundations built of massive granite blocks, and winter comes early in the Cévennes. New orders were sent out, and in October of 1703, the royal troops were instructed to burn down 400 villages, including all of the hamlets around Pont-de-Montvert which became a sort of concentration camp for refugees. By December of 1703, the work of destruction was largely completed.[4]

The natural consequence of all this was, of course, to exacerbate Protestant resentment. The bands which had shrunk in the summer of 1703 now became legion. The most famous of the Camisard leaders, Cavalier, was able to put together a small army of 1,800 footsoldiers and 400 horsemen. With them, in December of 1703, he even dared to come down from the highlands towards Montpellier itself. Regular battles took place, and at La Jonquière, in March of 1704, Cavalier surprised a royal troop of 500 elite marines, 300 of whom were killed.

It now seemed obvious that the escalation of governmental and military brutality had only led to an increase in the strength of rebellion. In consequence, Versailles decided to try a new and more moderate tack. Basville was replaced by Villars, who did not yet have the battles of Denain and Malplaquet to his credit but who was already a very prestigious general. The new commander-in-chief ordered that the gallows should be taken down. He traveled throughout the region and urged the Cévenols to submit voluntarily to a force which ultimately they could not resist. Partly because of this, the efforts of the rebels began to wane. There was more fighting in the summer of 1704 (and Pont-de-Montvert itself was attacked on July 19, by 900 rebels, who failed, however, to capture the bourg), but the war was now less intense than it had been. The Cévenol population was weary. The rebel bands were less able than before to count on local support and they gradually fell apart. Cavalier had already surrendered to Villars in May, and in August, another Camisard leader Roland was killed in battle. By September of 1704, the last important rebel band had been destroyed, and in December Villars left the Cévennes and returned to Versailles. The region, it is true, was not yet completely pacified, and for a while, there continued to be an occasional murder with an occasional plot. But even these came to an end in 1710 with the death of Abraham Mazel, the veteran of 1702.[5]

Pont-de-Montvert was deeply affected by these wars. It had been the site of their origin in Du Chayla's death. It had been besieged, and its hamlets were almost wholly destroyed. Yet it would have been difficult to predict in the 1680s that the village would so soon be engulfed in flames, for initially the Revocation of the Edict of Nantes and the end of Protestantism did not seem to have had much effect here. Nearly everyone complied with the orders from Versailles. In a population of over 1,000, only twenty-five people decided to leave the kingdom rather than abjure, and only one person, the bourgeois-noble André, chose to stay and resist the proscription of the new Diocletian.[6] The overwhelming majority of Montipontins offered no resistance of any sort, active or passive. Because so many people at the Pont share patronymics, it is difficult to categorize the handful of émigrés, but none of the people who ought to have resisted or set an example are on the list. There are no Pons, no Servières, no Velays, Jourdans or Albarics, Desmarets or Talons. Those who refused to comply were isolated and poor people, with the possible exception of Lévy, Jacques, and Guillaume Vignes, who may all have been related to Pierre Vignes, a self-sufficient landowner or mesnager from Salarials.[7]

Indeed, the unwillingness of the rich to resist the tyrannical authority of the crown is the most salient trait and the central thread of village politics at the end of the seventeenth century. It is this point which must be described and explained if the political configuration of the Pont at that time is to make sense. For unlike the poor who did eventually resist the *changement de religion*,[8] the rich stayed aloof and distant. They temporized and hedged and waited for better days with admirable fortitude, for they no more than the poor were safe from indignity. Like everyone else, they suffered, but unlike everyone else, they did nothing—which was all the more remarkable because they were the first to be hurt. André was the first to die, and in 1689 Jacques Pons was one of the first to be arrested. He was released soon after, but a nastier fate befell the whole notable class of the village in 1690. The background of this discomfiture was involved. The affair began when the widow of a rich peasant in the hamlet of La Sépedèle, who had been having some trouble in straightening out the finances of her deceased husband, decided to convene all of his twenty-five creditors and debtors. One person who had not been asked wrote to the intendant to denounce this assembly, which he would have liked to attend. These people, he now thought, had met for religious reasons. Everyone was thereupon arrested and one of the culprits was hanged, although local Catholics testified on his behalf.[9]

Soon after this, the whole village fell under continuous oppression. Already in the fall of 1685 there had been some widespread but temporary persecution at the Pont. In his memoirs, Jean Nissole, a merchant of Ganges, recounts that in 1686 he had been imprisoned along with "many prisoners" for having taken part in an illicit "assembly" at the Pont.

> Many of them were tortured. Five of the men were whipped one day, and three more two days later. They wanted them to say who had been present at these assemblies, and above all, who had preached there. But whatever ills they inflicted on them, they were not willing to say anything whatever.[10]

As a consequence of this rebellious act, troops were sent to Pont-de-Montvert, and the villagers were made to disburse "immense sums" for their upkeep.

These soldiers were soon recalled, but they returned once again in the late 1690s on a more or less continuous basis, since it had by now been decided that nonrebellion was not enough. Active participation in Catholic rites would henceforth be required, and this in turn implied active supervision. In 1696, two *compagnies* of dragoons were quartered in the village

> to compel people to go to mass, those who did not do it were fined ten sous or had soldiers quartered on them at will.[11]

The soldiery was momentarily withdrawn in February of 1697,[12] but one year later the troops were back at the Pont [13] and they were to remain there for more than forty years. Word had reached the *puissances* at Montpellier that illegal assemblies had been taking place, and these authorities reacted with great vigor. A force of a thousand men was sent to the village. Many Montipontins were made to confess to a variety of crimes, and this time some of them did accuse their neighbors. Many arrests were made, among them that of two notables Pierre Servière, from l'Hopital, and his brother-in-law, Richard of Saint-Frézal, who were imprisoned for some time.

The arrest of Servière is indeed quite revealing since it shows that the notables of the Pont were not intrinsically hostile to the underground activity of Protestantism at the Pont before 1701. Throughout the 1680s and the 1690s, assemblies were being held there with their knowledge—one Protestant pastor and rebel, Vivens, even stayed at the Pont for some time in 1691 [14]—and it is certain that the notables had not then turned their backs on what was for them the "Olde Religion." But at the same time, as has been said, they would not rebel. When the passive resistance of the population as a whole became after 1701 the overt resistance of a desperate few,[15] the notables moved away, some to the point of siding with the persecutors against their coreligionists, whose excessive zeal had become the source for them

36

of more persecution, fines, and punishment. From then on, they stayed home when other and poorer people became involved, and their aloofness emerges quite clearly with regard to another illegal assembly about which we do have precise information.

On November 13, 1701, thirty to forty people assembled at Montgros, a hamlet on the northern edge of the village. They sang psalms and soon afterwards burst into the house of Jacques Malachane. He did not like this, complained to the authorities, and thereby started an official prosecution. Very revealingly, of the dozen-odd people who were identified by name, nearly all belonged to the "landless proletariat" of the village. Marc Guin, their leader, was a tenant farmer like his accuser, Malachane, but there was a difference between the conditions of the two men. In 1696 Guin had been the richest man at Montgros, where he farmed some land that belonged to Antoine Velay, the author of the Livre de Raison. By 1701, however, Velay must have canceled Guin's lease and given it to Malachane instead, for now we find that Malachane is the richest man at Montgros and that Guin has had to move to the bourg as an innkeeper with a mere subsistence income. The bitterness of the newly impoverished Guin is readily conceivable, and it must have helped him to sympathize with the other participants in the illicit meeting at Montgros because they had always been poor. Suzanne Verdeilhan's father was listed in the tax roll for 1701 as an indigent: *"Pauvre, mendiant."* Jacques and Etienne Boutin of Champlong were not much better off. Etienne paid a tax that was only one-sixth that of Malachane, and the Boutins' sisters were *"chez des Maîtres,"* hired out as domestics. Pierre Martin and Jean Gauch were also very poor: the first was a landless laborer and the other was the only full-time textile artisan of Montgros. Indeed, the only person of substance there was Velay's own daughter, Jeanne, who was marked by smallpox and may have been brought there by her father's former tenant.[16]

In the background of this civil and religious commotion, there clearly lay some private quarrel between the Guins and the Malachanes, particularly as we know from another source that there lived at Champlong, abandoned by his mother, an orphan named Jacques Malachane

aged 10, son of the late Jean Malachane and of Elisabeth Quin . . . The mother is remarried, and has abandoned this boy who has no education and who would become a vagabond.[17]

Yet it is worth noting that this private quarrel had come to overlap with differences in social class. In this particular instance at least, no rich peasants and no bourgeois were involved in sedition.

Pont-de-Montvert

It is very likely that the village notables had very little sympathy for the government officials and police who prosecuted Guin and his fellow psalm singers, but they refused to become involved in active resistance. Since the royal authorities were in the habit of meting out collective punishments on villages where there had been trouble, the rich of course were necessarily involved in the tribulation of Pont-de-Montvert, but in a passive sort of way. They did not lead in the expression of discontent. In fact, they refused to raise their heads even in their hardest hours, and it is not surprising therefore that the first person who resisted and was put to death at the Pont in 1702 was in no way a member of the village establishment. Françoise Brès, quite to the contrary, was in fact very poor. "Pauvre fille, servante de profession," [18] she was accused of having taken part in religious meetings in a neighboring town. She was tried at Alès and condemned to hang, although she was only nineteen years old. She died with great dignity:

> She was executed at Pont-de-Montvert on Wednesday, January 25th, 1702. She walked firmly to the place of her death, refusing with a firm but modest gentleness the missionary who walked with her and was urging her to change her religion. Four drums were rolled from the time she left her jail to her last breath. [19]

Nor did any bourgeois participate in the murder of Du Chayla, whose death had been preached by Françoise Brès. Most members of the band were strangers to the village, but a few were Montipontins and something is known of their social origins. All of them were poor, and curiously enough, most of them were not peasants but artisans. Abraham Mazel, their leader, had family in Grizac although he himself did not live there. [20] His mother, Jeanne Daudé, still had relatives at the Villaret, some of whom were very poor. In 1696, where Velay paid a capitation of ten livres, Suzanne Daudé, a widow with two small children paid only ten sous. Other members of the family were better off. There were two Daudés who were listed as landowning *ménagers,* but their tax of two livres ten sous shows that although they were on the lower rungs of the middle group, they were far from being prosperous. [21] Jean Rampon, a *prédicateur,* was a woolcarder and in all probability the son of Antoine Rampon who had exercised the same occupation. [22] He was arrested at Finialettes with his brother, Antoine, in November of 1702 and spent thirteen years as a galley slave before his release and departure for Switzerland. Pierre Pantel, who was broken on the wheel in 1706, was of similar background. A deserter from the royal army, he was born in Frutgères and must have been related to the only Pantel in the hamlet, Jacques Pantel, a *cabarètier,* who was so poor in 1696 that he paid no capitation at all [23] and died shortly afterwards in 1701 leaving an indigent widow with four small children.[24]

In short, it is very clear that at Pont-de-Montvert only the poor took up arms for the Protestant religion. That so many of them should have been artisans or related to artisans is also worth noting. But this was probably not because these men were more mobile than peasants or more aware of the intellectual or ideological currents that were sweeping the Cévennes at the time. Quite conceivably, the presence of so many artisans in the ranks of the Camisards is simply due to the fact that these people were very poor. An artisan was only a landless laborer who could find no work on the land. The common denominator of rebellion was abject poverty, and the actual occupation of the rebels is in a way irrelevant.

It should not be thought that an explanation of this sort denies the religious or even mystical origin of the conflict. If Protestantism had been a tolerated religion, there would have been no Camisard Wars. This does not, however, invalidate the idea that receptivity to ideological currents was, in the Pont at least, obviously a function of social criteria, and more simply of wealth and poverty. The very poor rebelled; the rich and the nearly rich did not.[25] It would be an exaggeration to claim that class differences at Pont-de-Montvert were so great as to set rich and poor at each other's throats, but the political implications of social cleavage are still very obvious at the beginning of the seventeenth century.

Nonetheless, although the reluctance of notables to become involved was very conspicuous, it has nearly always been overlooked.[26] Because they have been keen on emphasizing the purely spiritual aspects of the Camisard Wars, and perhaps also because French Protestantism has become so closely identified with bourgeois mores, Protestant writers have been generally reluctant to see that the Camisard Wars were in some sense a class conflict, a class movement, and a lower-class movement at that.[27] It is true that the immediate causes of the conflict were undeniably religious. But most Montipontin Camisards were also poor adolescents or young men in their twenties. Very often, they were artisans, that is to say people who found it hard to fit into the system. They were socially marginal, victims perhaps of hard times and overpopulation. They were men who had been sensitized to emotional religious currents by the fact that they had nothing to lose. Of course, had there been no moral indignation, there would also have been no rebellion at the Pont. But there is more to the Camisard revolt than religion alone; there is also a conflict or at least a contrast between social groups.

39

How can this cleavage be explained? Louis Mazoyer has gone a long way towards explaining it, and there is no doubt a great deal to his idea that the rich held off from rebellion because they were more subtle and more able to play the field.[28] The poor, he thinks, were uncritical in their apprehension of the system. For them, Catholicism was the Beast of Babylon, which it was imperative to reject. The rich, however, could see the fissures in the machine; they were able to get away with more infractions because they were often able to bribe officials. Finally, the poor are said to have had a very vivid and immediate apprehension of life and death. They were less able than the rich to see the long instead of the short run; they could not see that it was necessary to bend for the sake of the survival of families. For them it was all or nothing, and all at once.

Unfortunately, it is very difficult for us to pass judgment on the validity of all of these very suggestive explanations. It is true, however, that rich Montipontins, although they were indeed persecuted, were often able to bribe corrupt officials, among them perhaps Du Chayla himself. Also worth noting is that in 1703 during the "burning of Cévennes" a few houses belonging to notables were spared by the royal troops. Without any embarrassment, Jean Velay explains how this was done.

> There were many houses that were not destroyed, like those of the old catholics or of those who had friends close to the powers, among which was the one that we have here at Grizac, for which I had to take many trips to Montpellier and other places.[29]

Pierre Pons had a similar story to tell about his brother Jacques, who had been arrested and was being marched off to Montpellier. Unlike his fellow prisoners who were prosecuted, tried, and convicted, Jacques Pons never went further than Saint-Germain-de-Calberte. "Mr. l'abbé du Chayla, at the request of his friends, kept him from going further."[30] Given what we know about Du Chayla's temperament, such unaccustomed moderation is indeed suspect. More probably, the abbé had been bribed by Pierre Pons, a smooth operator who was not above ingratiating himself with the authorities.

Nonetheless, there is more to the notables' pacifism than their ability to bribe. They had, after all, been sporadically persecuted from the beginning; and although they did sometimes secure favors, they did not always succeed. Even Velay and Pons, to go on with the same men, occasionally ran into serious trouble. In October of 1703, for example, Velay was nearly ruined when he lost most of his animals:

all of the herds were brought together, because the Sieur Viala of Saint-Jean-de-Gardonnenque had promised that we would be payed for them, he had them seized by the soldiers of the Hainaut regiment who came with him and, the bandit, had them removed, without giving anything to anyone and reduced us to beggary.[31]

And five years later, Pierre Pons himself fell victim to the machinations of an agent provocateur, so that in 1708 he left the Pont forever and fled to Geneva. But by then he had already suffered in body and soul. In 1704, he wrote to his brother that he could not hold out much longer:

I am so downtrodden by the quartering of soldiers, that I will not be able to hold on. Besides two beds and two blankets which I had to bring to the barracks, I have staying with me two captains, two lieutenants, and six soldiers. Beyond that, every fifth day I owe two pounds of olive oil and 200 weight of wood . . . my servant can hardly keep us supplied with wood at home . . . I will have to sell my mule for lack of hay, although I brought in more than a 100 weight of it . . . But the soldiers take everything without payment; some of them have been payed at three sous a head. Tomorrow, M. de La Lande and his men will sleep here. In the end, I will have to give everything up. God is my only consolation.[32]

There were clear limits to the prerogatives of the notables, and even their children were threatened. Reeducation of Protestant children for Catholic ends was unusual, but it did exist and it was seriously suggested for the Pont. In 1700, a list was drawn up by the Intendant, Basville, and in his opinion there were six children of the village who were most likely to benefit from such ministrations. Of the six, three were "upper-class": Paul and Louis Talon, who were connected through their mother to the Pons family, and Marie Bonnicel, "aged 12, daughter of Jean Bonnicel, Esq. and of Jeanne de Tinel in the place called Pont-de-Montvert, good family, poor; the mother, badly converted, spoils this child who has some good intentions."[33]

By 1704, then, many of the notables could not have had much to lose. Like everyone else, they had been persecuted, bullied, and exploited. Yet they did nothing, and their reluctance to act in the face of so much suffering is indeed the central problem of village politics in these years. Why did the rich not rally to a cause which the poor took up in spite of the fact that all classes suffered at the hands of the State? The answer is in large part due to the fact that, although the notables may have felt much sympathy for the cause of Protestantism, they had none for the lower-class rebels. Antoine Velay thought that the murder of the abbé du Chayla was an "enormous crime" and he often expressed sympathy for the "unfortunate men," for the poor victims of his rebellious coreligionists. Velay laid stress on the fact that the people who had attacked the abbé were "unknown people," and the kindest thing he had to say for them was that they were "unfortunate rebels".[34] His brother who lived at Florac was no more kindly disposed. He spoke of them sometimes as "these unfortunate men" but more usually as "crowd of rebels," "crowds of vagabonds and faithless men." Jean Velay of Florac had no doubts about the social characteristic of the conflict. It was a frightful thing but some good might yet come of it, he thought, because it would serve

> to teach to posterity how great a crime it is to rebel against one's sovereign. Although the rebellion of these crowds is only from the lowest sort, it does not mean that the highest and wisest do not suffer from this terrible punishment.[35]

Jean Velay even joined the royal troops, and he was part of the force which was sent by the authorities to the Pont in April of 1703.

For the notables of the Pont, and as far as we can see for those of the whole region as well, the Camisards were sincere perhaps, but terribly misguided men. They were a threat directly and indirectly; they stole and they invited official reprisal. But beyond this, their whole style and method was offensive to the notables. The Camisards were labeled by their Catholic opponents as fanatics, and it is true that their methods were somewhat disconcerting. They laid great stress on inspiration and prophecy. Jean Rampon, for example, had received a divine inspiration which enjoined him not to comb his hair.[36] Françoise Brès prefaced and concluded her preachings by screaming and collapsing on the ground. It is also worth noting that the "children of God" were often accused of sexual irregularities. Their bands were accompanied by *prophètesses,* who were said to be more keen in defense of the Protestant religion than in preserving their chastity, a distinction which was probably hard to understand for someone like Antoine Velay, whose life was so completely set in a patriarchal and familial mode. In any case, the mores of the Camisards would probably have shocked even the most broad-minded men. If we are to believe the reporter of the provincial estates, the rebels led

> an abominable life, since the girls sleep freely and shamelessly with the boys that they love, this is notorious. At Esclopier (parish of Saint Etienne) one of them lay between two men, and at Saumanes, two girls were with four boys, claiming that since they had spoken to God, there was no harm in it.[37]

Clearly, these things were not indicative of a style of life suitable to *gens de bien.* Between the rich and the poor, between the notables and the Camisard there existed material differences, certainly, but moral and psychological differences as well. The notables were more calculating, rational, repressed perhaps; and even if they had not had good material reasons for holding aloof, they could hardly have felt much political sympathy for rebels so close to them geographically, but so different from themselves in more important ways.

But this is not a surprising cleavage. Indeed, from what we know about the social structure of Pont-de-Montvert at the end of the seventeenth century, the political cleavage that can be observed in 1702 was certainly in the nature of things. A very great gap separated the rich from the poor, a gap of wealth which had repercussions of all sorts, intellectual, professional, moral, and political. It was only to be expected that the people at the top should have very little sympathy for their impoverished neighbors. Nor can it be said that in "selling out," the notables were moved primarily by material reasons. It is true that they owned seigneuries and had bought an entrance into the feudal system; it is also true that they stood to lose from war and rebellion where others did not. But more important are the moral and psychological differences that separated the notable from the common man. The notables of the village were a part of the village, certainly, but they were also a part of the province and of society as a whole in a way that was not true of the poor. They had relatives who were nobles, they knew government officials, they were bound not only to the village, but to the world beyond it. In short, they were part of a widespread class society, hierarchic and deferential, and their politics were class politics.

For the people of Pont-de-Montvert, the Camisard Wars were therefore a manner of "class war". At the Pont, and probably in the Cévennes as a whole, the lower classes answered the call of the "prophets," but the notables did not. That indeed explains in large measure the failure of the rebels. Devoid of the elite that could have politicized their movements, the Camisards found themselves involved in a dismal, anachronistic, and very savage religious war. Their failure however does not mean that there was no potentially revolutionary force at Pont-de-Montvert. Quite the contrary, the very nature of this movement is a reflection of the social cleavages that were characteristic of Montipontin society at the end of the seventeenth century. Indeed, the greatest paradox in the history of the village during the hundred years that followed the Camisard Wars is that this revolutionary potential was never brought out although some of the divisions that existed in 1700 had become even more acute by the 1780s. The social tensions that have been described did not recede. Indeed, they were heightened, as shall be seen; but in spite of this, Pont-de-Montvert was never to know again what it had seen in 1702, a political division along class lines. Until the end of the nineteenth century, there would still be some Montipontins who were very different and much richer than their neighbors; but for reasons to which we will turn later, the political consequences of this difference would never again be as forceful as they had been during the Camisard Wars.

CHAPTER III   Social Class in the Eighteenth

Century

At the Pont in the 1700s, the politics and the attitudes of the villagers had been closely connected with the class structure of the place as we have described it. There were three social strata in Pont-de-Montvert: the very poor and landless; the middling, small landowners; and the "notables". Surely it cannot have been a simple coincidence that only the very poor revolted, much to the dismay and disapproval of the others, especially of the very rich. But a similar division between the small and the great on a political issue is not to be found for later history of the Pont. In 1789 all Montipontins agreed on what was to be done although that had certainly not been the case eighty years before.

How can this evolution of consensus be explained? Did there take place between the beginning and the end of the eighteenth century some great evolution in the social or economic situation of the village, some diminution of tension between classes that would explain the background of political unanimity at the end of the ancien régime? Indeed, if such changes had taken place, the problem of political allegiance at the Pont would be easily resolvable, but in fact there were no such changes. Quite the contrary, the social structure that had existed before 1700 was in many ways more sharply divided in 1789 than it had been a hundred years before.

The survival of the old system is all the more noteworthy for the fact that so much had been destroyed during the Camisard Wars. What the royal troops had spared, the rebels had demolished.[1] In the bourg itself there had been less physical destruction, but there, also, rich and poor had suffered at the hands of the garrisoned soldiery. Pont-de-Montvert was deeply scarred by this savage conflict and traces of it were to be found for decades in the demographic structure of the village. We are well informed about this particular topic, for in 1738 the *curé* of Frutgères drew up a list of his reticent Protestant parishioners.[2] It is very probably incomplete, since it indicates that there were more ten- to fifteen-year-olds than there were zero- to five-year-olds, which is manifestly wrong. But the population pyramid that can be drawn from it has a reasonable shape for the ages above fifteen and is probably trustworthy. It is most striking in that it shows first how young was the population of the village as a whole. Even if it is assumed that there were no more infants than are indicated by the lists, it still follows that fewer than a quarter of the villagers were over forty. The youthful imbalance is even greater for females, whose life expectancy was shorter, perhaps because of deaths in childbirth. But the population pyramid also reveals the ravages of the Camisard Wars. There is a shortage of men for the age groups that had reached adulthood in 1699–1708, and, demographically even more important, there is also a shortage of births for these same years. Because of the dislocation of village life, perhaps accompanied by an increase in infant mortality, far fewer children were born or survived infancy in 1700–1710 than before or after.

Yet for all that the vitality of Pont-de-Montvert in the eighteenth century cannot be brought into question. Demography again provides the best indication of it. By actual count, the Pont at the end of the seventeenth century was a densely populated place. With its thirteen hundred inhabitants, the village had reached a level that would not be consistently equaled until the second half of the nineteenth century. It could indeed be argued that this vitality was too great, and the despair of the villagers on the eve of the Camisard Wars must have had a great deal to do with the fact that the Pont numbered in 1700 ten percent more people than in 1685.[3] In that sense, it could even be said that the wars of 1702–1710 had beneficial consequences since the level of population from 1710 to 1740 was probably the lowest the village had known for a century. In any case, these three decades proved to be only an interruption of the secular trend of rising population. In the early 1740s there were probably fewer than 1,000 Montipontins; in the early 1750s their number was over 1,000; there were 1200 of them by 1760, and 1350 in 1785 when the curve began to level off. This was a very considerable increase of more than 30 percent in less than forty years, and this rapid population increase can provide the general context for the evolution of agriculture, of artisan crafts, and of course of poverty as well.

Montipontins had never been rich, but now that there were more of them to be fed, some of them at least became even poorer than before. The precise nature of their poverty for the years before 1700 is rather shadowy, but it comes into focus during the last decades of the ancien régime since it is possible to compute the per capita income of Montipontins as a whole for the 1780s by using the capitation or personal head and income tax rolls of the period. At the Pont, in those years, the capitation brought in about 1400 livres, and it is also known that this tax was taken to represent about one percent of real income, if not in France generally, at least in this area.[4] This would give a total personal income of about 140,000 livres, which is keeping the calculations that have been made of late on the value of rural income in France since 1700 by Marczewski, who estimates that the annual value of produce per person living on the land in the 1780s was in the order of 140 francs.[5] If we multiply this figure by 1,300 (the population of Pont-de-Montvert) we would arrive at a total income of about 180,000 livres. This is 40,000 livres more than the figure based on the capitation, but this indeed is as it should be since Pont-de-Montvert certainly stood below the national average of prosperity.

Per capita income in the Pont therefore was about 100 francs a year. To get an idea of what that represents, it is enough to say that in 1790 one franc represented two and one-half pounds of beef, less than one pound of Arabian coffee, and less than two quarts of oil (which was in great demand in the village, where it was used in lieu of butter or lard for cooking).[6] But, of course, coffee, sugar, and the like were unheard of luxuries. Laurent Servière, the richest Montipontin of his day, did own two coffee pots, one of them described as "a great tin coffee pot" valued at two francs and the other, a splendid affair, in silver, worth thirty-six francs. But needless to say this was very unusual. Most Montipontins would have limited their purchases to bare essentials, and even those were for them very costly. A standard item of masculine clothing, for example, was the well-known Auvergnat headgear with a round top and a very wide brim which did double duty as umbrella and parasol. These also were very expensive. The fanciest of them, made out of fine wool with a seven-inch brim, cost seven livres, and the cheapest was three livres, or about one week's wages for an unskilled laborer.[7] Food, of course, accounted for nearly all of the average budget, and even here, there was not much to be had. For a family of four, the two hundred francs or so which a laborer might at best earn during the year, would certainly not go very far. With his wife and children he would live on potatoes, which were less than one sou per pound (there are twenty sous in one livre or franc), on lentils which were twice as expensive as potatoes, and also on chestnuts, which were very cheap. Two hundred pounds of fresh chestnuts could be had for one and one-half francs.

In fact, the consumption of chestnuts is perhaps as good an indication as any of the low subsistence level of village life at the end of the eighteenth century. The importance of chestnuts was consecrated by the complicated customs that regulated their harvest. The problem here had to do with chestnut trees which were on the edge of one man's property but whose branches extended over someone else's. Ordinarily, possession of the land was absolute and entitled its owners to collect everything that was to be found directly above it, even if it were attached to a branch that was connected to a tree that grew in someone else's lot. (Montipontins had such a demanding sense of private property that, unlike many other Lozerians, they did not even recognize the custom called *servitude du tour d'échelle* which entitled one owner to lean his ladder on another person's property in order to repair a dividing wall). But an exception was made for chestnuts, at least in some cases. The owner of the tree always had the right to trespass in order to collect the burrs which had fallen to the ground. As for the nuts, the issue depended on whether the nut was ripe or not. If they were, they belonged to the owner of the tree; if they were not, they belonged to the owner of the soil.[8]

There were many chestnut trees at the Pont, whose location and climate is often suitable for this tree which thrives between altitudes of 400 and 900 meters and which benefits from the alternation of warm days and cold nights, and in 1825 the chataigneraies or chestnut groves of the village covered some fifty acres of the village land.[9] The tree was doubly useful; it provided wood for furniture and fuel; and since it was planted on slopes, it was ideally suited for the fructification of marginal land. The crop was harvested in the fall, usually by young women, like the unfortunate Françoise Brès. The chestnuts could be eaten fresh as soon as they had begun to peel, or they could be roasted and served up in a soup, the *bajano,* mixed with milk, prunes, and wine. Many houses in the Pont also had a *clède* or roasting room. The chestnuts were placed on a lattice above a smoldering and smokey fire which would burn continuously for more than a day. These evening sessions were social occasions as well. The *veillées,* or *castagnados,* as they were called at the Pont, were one more fruit of the bountiful tree.

It is difficult to estimate precisely how important rye, potatoes, and chestnuts each were for the different social groups in the village. In 1790 an observer remarked of the Lozère generally that "when chestnuts are plentiful, they are a *complement* to our subsistence and alleviate the misery of a mediocre harvest."[10] By contrast some forty years later, in 1827, the subprefect of Florac believed that it was "on the chestnut that rested the whole subsistence of the Cévennes." [11] But this testimony is suspicious in view of the fact that one year later the same official ventured the belief that the potato was so important that it would soon supplant rye as the staple crop. What is clear, however, is that the chestnut does not seem to have been essential to the rich or middling peasant class. The wills or *donations partage* of the 1780s and 1790s do not make mention of them. Jean Servière, for example, on May 8, 1787, handed his property over to his son, who agreed to give him each year 320 liters of rye, thirty-six livres in cash, five pounds of salt pork, ten pounds of cheese, five pounds of butter, and seventy-two eggs.[12] Jean Roure *père* of Rieumal struck a somewhat harder bargain with his heir. He held out for Servière's terms plus a suit of clothes every three years, a hat every two years, and a shirt every six months, "the whole thing payable, in case of separation, by advance, in quarters, and without any deductions whatever."[13] But in neither of these instances, or in others like it, do we find mention of cereals other than rye. In 1781 Antoine Chapelle, who appears to have been less well off, did reserve for himself "the right to plant potatoes in a little plot of land where he likes." [14] But even here, chestnuts are not mentioned. Of course, it is possible that even rich peasants traded wheat for something else. Much later in his private accounts for 1909 Albin Molines, who was a prosperous man, mentioned that he had bought forty liters of chestnuts, and no doubt this was true of others at other times as well.[15] Yet, on the whole, diet certainly continued to be one of the factors which separated the rich from the poor. In the eighteenth century, the rich ate bread—the very rich ate white bread— and the poor ate soups of varying but uniformly dubious sorts.* Probably M. Benoit was not far wrong when he wrote in 1830 that in the Cévennes, one could find "families which at home do not taste bread ten times a year; they eat only potatoes and chestnuts." [16]

It can be doubted, however, that M. Benoit was also right in thinking that in spite of their diets, the poor of the Cévennes were nonetheless "robust, vigorous, and enjoying the best of possible health." [17] Quite the contrary, Montipontins may have sometimes been hardy, but most of them often bore the marks of malnutrition. They were, to begin with, very short. The sixty-five Montipontins enrolled in the national guard, in the *Bataillon du district de Florac debout contre les tyrans*, cannot have been too terrifying a sight since only nine of them were over five

* Many observers have commented on this, including Goethe who noted in 1792 that "der Franzos erschrickt vor jeder schwarzen Krume" (*Kampagne in Frankreich,* Collected Works, ed. Cotta [Stuttgart, 1954], X, 327).

feet four. Sixteen of the men were under five feet, and the average height was five feet two.[18] The effects of a poor diet were further aggravated by the almost complete absence of hygienic measures of any sort. Admittedly, the death of the mayor in the neighboring commune of Fraissinet, attributed in an official report to the "dirtiness of the place," was surely an extreme case.[19] But conditions were generally very bad and one could repeat for the Pont what a Napoleonic prefect wrote of all houses in the Lozère, which he describes as "ordinarily unhealthy and uncomfortable. The manure pit, that slimy cesspool which seems to guard its entrance, continually spreads about its putrid effluvia." [20] Another official report of the same period also describes the Cévenols as "not very careful on the question of cleanliness . . . The inhabitants of the mountains do not cut their hair." [21] Scrofula was the most common disease. Some people were covered from head to toe with scrofulous sores. Ophthalmia was another common ailment, and at Pont-de-Montvert, of the thirteen men who were declared unfit for military service in 1799, four were described as having "spots in their eyes" (among the others, one was an idiot and another was an epileptic, one had an arm which was deformed for having been improperly reset after a fracture, and the last suffered from a mysterious ailment described as a *palpitation au creux de l'estomac*.) From a voting list of the same year, we know that there lived in the village a health inspector or *officier de santé* named Joseph Niel, and of course there had been apothecaries at Pont-de-Montvert for at least a century; but it can be doubted that any of these people had any serious knowledge of medicine or surgery.[22] Nor were there even any professional midwives in the village, and at the end of the eighteenth century Montipontins of all social classes were essentially defenseless against the effects of disease, malnutrition, accident, and dirt.

In the last decades of the eighteenth century, the Pont was still a very poor and backward place. Most of its inhabitants were miserable, always hungry and often sick. This is not surprising, for the economy upon which this social structure rested remained inefficient and unproductive. As had been true in the seventeenth century, most of the villagers' efforts, one century later, were still channelled to the growing of rye. It was by far the most important crop and its commercial worth represented one half of the value of total village production. Although the amount grown did not cease to increase in absolute terms during the eighteenth century, it is in the earlier decades that its relative importance was greatest. Grizac in 1728 was described as having "neither trade nor industry: the soil produces rye, a few hops and some hay" and this must have been typical of the whole community, especially since the soil of Grizac is in places calcareous and more suited to the cultivation of wheat and other crops than land at Frutgères, which is nearly exclusively granitic.[23] From time immemorial, a two-crop system prevailed, the *jachère morte,* with the substitution of lentils for potatoes, or oats for rye in the more fertile parts of the parish as its only variation. Techniques were also immutable and very crude. Plowing was done with the traditional plow or *araire* inherited from the Romans. This was by far the most common tool, although there may have been some improvements at the end of the eighteenth century since Laurent Servière, who counted among his books an eight volume edition of the *Cours complet d'agriculture* (valued at twelve francs), had introduced in his own farms, at least, the *charrue* or modern plow. The inventory of his property lists both *araires* and *charrues,* "with their plowshares, old and worn," and this implies some long-continued use.[24]

Naturally this system of agriculture was labor intensive because it was extremely inefficient. The *araires* did not plow very deep, six inches at best. It was necessary to spade the field by hand every other year or so in order to turn the land over to a depth of ten or twelve inches. Nor was there other machinery of any sort. Scythes were not unknown (Servière again owned one), but it is likely that most harvesting was done with a sickle. More labor yet was used—or wasted—in the construction of elaborate terracing and drainage ditches. Drainage was a material necessity for the rich owners of vast pastures. It rains a great deal at the Pont, and it was necessary for landowners to build and rebuild the ditches without which their fields would become bogs unsuitable for grazing. Terracing, by contrast, was more due to psychic necessity than to a rational apportionment of effort. Since land was becoming scarcer in the eighteenth century, hillsides were increasingly adapted for the cultivation of rye, and this involved an enormous and essentially unprofitable expansion of time and labor. Yet, in order to become the *propriétaire* of some plot, however small, the poor would pay the price, any price, provided they could do so in labor alone; and traces of their herculean and ant-like labor are still visible everywhere today.

But in spite of the immense energy expanded, production remained inadequate. There did not seem to be any way of growing better crops and breaking out of the cycle of poor soil, poor crops, poor pastures, inadequate animals, and insufficient manure. At the end of the eighteenth century, Montipontins were perfectly aware of the importance of animal fertilizers, but dung of any sort was a rare and even precious commodity. Not much of it was available except, as shall be seen, for

Farm buildings on the Mont-Lozère.

those people who rented out sheep pastures for the *transhumants.* Yields were often catastrophically low: seldom more than five hecto-liters of rye per hectare (or six bushels per acre) and sometimes one half of that. In a good year, a Montipontin could expect to harvest from four to seven times the amount of seed he had sown; but there were bad years as well when the land would give up only twice as much as had been planted.[25]

Fortunately, rye was not the only pillar of Montipontin economic life. Animals were also important, and here we should distinguish be-tween cattle and sheep as well as between local sheep and the *trans-humants,* whose comings and goings are the most picturesque aspect of husbandry at the Pont. In the early summer, during the first weeks of June, herds of sheep were driven from the parched lowlands of the Languedoc to the greener highland pastures of the Gévaudan and the Auvergne.[26] Shepherds would herd their flocks northwards from the south to towns and villages like Pont-de-Montvert along special paths or *drailles,* sometimes twenty yards wide, of Roman or Celtic origin. There were many advantages to be derived from these *Tierewander-ungen.* In the first place, Montipontins would be paid for the use of their pastures, and in the 1780s the largest local landowners, the Knights of Malta, collected no less than 5,000 livres a year in this way.[27] In addition, the landowners would also benefit from the *nuits de fumature* or night soil. The sheep droppings were valuable fertili-zers, especially for the granitic soil of the Pont, and the precise location of the herd on any given night was a closely argued thing. Landowners would come together and pool their pastures so as to offer for lease areas that would be suitable for very large flocks. Long negotiations would be necessary to iron out the details. Who was it that was entitled to the greater share of night soil? Should it be apportioned according to the size of the plots, to their innate quality, to their accessibility? These were difficult matters to resolve, but the villagers did succeed in working them out. Each year contracts would be drawn up like the one passed on 11 Brumaire, Year II between the shepherd Jean Guérin, *berger du citoyen Cazari, de Vèzenabres district d'Alès* and eleven landowners of the Mont-Lozère by which Guérin agreed to pay 400 livres for the pasture of 1,500 animals and to deliver eighty *nuits de fumature* to the Montipontins as they had agreed to share it.[28]

Some transhumance had probably been taking place since the earliest historic times. The *grande draille* which leads from the south to the Mont-Lozère, by the Palais du Roi, Chateauneuf Randon, and the mountain pass of the Pierre Plantée is also known as the *draye de César* and tradition has elaborated on this. What is certain however is that transhumance was a well organized affair by medieval times. In 1451, it has been estimated that more than 20,000 sheep were herded from the Languedoc to the Gévaudan.[29] By the eighteenth century, this number had increased many fold, although there is little agreement on what it actually was. One writer has estimated that 500,000 sheep were driven annually to the Lozère in the 1720s,[30] and a report on pastures for the various parishes of the Gévaudan estimated that every summer between thirty and sixty thousand animals came to Pont-de-Montvert alone.[31] The impact of transhumance was certainly great and the economy of the region would have been in a bad way without it. As early as 1724 it was described as essential to the region: "without this help, the lands of the Gévaudan would produce almost nothing." [32] It is impossible to follow very closely the evolution of the number of animals involved, but it seems that it grew somewhat during the eighteenth century. In 1775, it was estimated that 60,000 animals pastured on the Mont-Lozère,[33] and as late as 1850, it was thought that there were still 250,000 sheep which grazed in the Gévaudan during the summer.[34]

Transhumance was fundamental in many ways. To the village it brought money and manure, both desirable. Some of the money, it is true, was paid to the Knights of Malta rather than to the villagers; but even then, this cash did not at once leave the village. It was collected for the Knights by local bailiffs, who could be trusted to withhold some small parts of the fees. But all of the manure remained, and so did some of the wool. Nor should it be forgotten that in addition to transhumance the village could draw on its own animal resources. At Grizac alone there were 1,400 sheep in 1724 (for 250 inhabitants), and in the village as a whole, there must have been at that time close to 5000 sheep.[35] This was a most useful addition, for although the animals in question were by modern standards very scraggly beasts, they could be expected to produce as a group some 60,000 pounds of wool, which was the raw material par excellence of most of the village's artisan industries. Transhumance, husbandry, and industry were closely linked at the Pont.

This economic structure, although it was well integrated, was nevertheless inefficient and even wasteful. It could perhaps satisfy the needs of the village in good or even normal times, but demographically speaking, the eighteenth century was highly abnormal. There were now many more mouths to feed, and the agricultural system was not geared to satisfy greater needs. The amount of arable land was largely fixed, and productivity did not increase. How then would the Pont cope with its fundamental problem of a growing population?

Permanent or temporary emigration was one solution, and contemporaries were certainly aware of the fact that many peasants were leaving the Lozère. One eighteenth century text, for example, claims that

> the inhabitants of the Gévaudan are poor and miserable, their misery is well known in all of the Languedoc and in the other neighboring provinces to which they provide a great number of female domestics, farm hands, shepherds and cowherds, and also many beggars. Those who stay at home have to eat chestnuts.[36]

In the neighboring parish of Saint-André-de-Capdèze, the *cahier de doléance* for 1789 echoes the same complaint: people were so poor, they had to leave. Taxes were very high and this had led to

> emigration from this place, since three-quarters of the parish must go the lower Languedoc, to the Vivarais and the Gévaudan in order to earn by the sweat of their brow enough to pay their tithe.[37]

But the contents of documents designed to make the authorities sympathetic and possibly to abate taxes are always somewhat suspect. It is certainly true that during the eighteenth century and well before, hundreds of Cévenols, many of them from the Pont, had indeed sought seasonal work in the south. That had enabled them to live and to pay their taxes and dues at the Pont where many of the migrants owned property. But it is not true that during those same decades most or even many Montipontins left their village forever. We have no specific information on the actual extent of emigration, but the steeply rising curve of village population conclusively proves that only a few Montipontins could have been so tempted by the promises of the newly established textile manufacturers of the Languedoc as to leave their house and home without hope of return.

Most Montversois stayed at home; and they were able to stay there despite an inefficient agriculture and despite the "demographic explosion" of the last decades of the ancien régime thanks to the growth of artisan industries. In all probability there had been at least some artisans in the village from time immemorial. We find them listed in the earliest available tax rolls and records of births and deaths. In 1696 there were already sixteen weavers and carders[38], four of them at Grizac.[39] Their number grew throughout the eighteenth century. In 1737, there were thirty-four persons engaged in the cloth trade,[40] and there were forty in 1789.[41] During the eighteenth century Pont-de-Montvert developed a hat trade which had not existed before at all. There were only two hat makers in 1696; there were seven in 1737, eleven in 1750, and fourteen in 1780. Their number declined on the eve of the revolution—there were only nine of them in 1789—but it had risen again to eleven in 1795 when their handiwork was described as "of very good quality and all in wool." [42] There were therefore at the end of the ancien régime about fifty people in the wool trade where there had been fewer than twenty in 1700, and in addition to these persons who usually worked in the bourg, there were also quite literally hundreds of part-time weavers all over the parish who worked their looms or spindles during the winter months:

> (at the Pont) they manufacture rough cloth which is used to make clothing for the locals: and just about everyone makes enough for his own use and some pieces to sell, none of which have any set length or weight.[43]

Most weavers were of course very poor. In 1789, the thirty-seven landowning *mesnagers* and *laboureurs* of the village had an income that was nearly twice as great as that of the village's seventy-odd artisans. Hat makers, it is true, were markedly more prosperous than weavers, and two of them by local standards were well off. But in spite of this, it is clear that in most instances, artisans were people who had no real material stake in the system. They had taken up their trade because there was no room for them on the land and what they secured from their craft was very meager indeed. It might even be argued that artisans were poorer than those landless laborers who were housed and fed by their masters, the *valets,* who lived on the farm and were paid a standard wage of about 150 livres. Some skilled artisans did earn between three and four hundred livres a year, but from this must be deducted housing and food expenses for their entire household. It is not inconceivable that artisans may have been former *valets* who had become family men and had had to move off the land, from the hamlet to the bourg, one step farther down on the social scale.

It would hardly do, therefore, to claim that Pont-de-Montvert was basking in prosperity at the end of the eighteenth century. The village did not enjoy a very large share of the national well-being that was characteristic of France as a whole in those years. But this may not be the point. Montipontins perhaps did not ask to prosper but merely to survive, and this they did do. In the end, the more important thing is that artisans, however poor they may have been, managed to live on somehow. Inefficient, unproductive, nontechnical, wasteful: the economic system of the Pont in eighteenth century may have been all these things, but it worked. Ultimately, it did absorb the shock of sudden demographic expansion. The artisan crafts provided a solution that was fragile in many ways, but it kept body and soul together for hundreds of people who could find no work on the land. Soon, admittedly, the Montipontine cloth makers would have to face increased competition both from English manufactures and from the factories that would exist in the Languedoc by the end of the ancien régime. But in the middle decades of the eighteenth century, the Pont and the Gévaudan as a whole were still able to market their textiles, perhaps, as was suggested in a mémoire of 1736, because of the consequences of the Protestant emigration. Many Protestant traders had abandoned the region after 1685, but they had now returned as go-betweens; and in 1736, an observer could write that "they have come back here, and are busier at it than ever." [44]

Given the fact, then, that at the end of the eighteenth century the economy of Pont-de-Montvert was not an unbalanced one, it is only to be expected that the three-level class structure of the 1680s should also have remained in the 1780s largely unaltered. Nothing serious had yet happened to rock the village's economic base and Pont-de-Montvert went on as before, particularly since, as shall be seen, its moral and ideological bases had in these same decades also been strengthened. There was, therefore, no reason for it to change, and it did not change. In fact, in many ways the system was reinforced, and the cleavages between social classes were widened. This was in part due to some of the economic and demographic phenomena that have just been outlined. The proportion of village income that flowed into the pockets of the rich remained constant in these years, although the size of the population did not. The forty or fifty richest men of the Pont continued to account for about half of the village's wealth throughout this period. In 1631, the first fifty-six owners accounted for 65 percent of total agricultural income; in 1701 the first fifty-seven tax payers paid over 60 percent of the village's tax; and in 1789, fifty-six people paid 53 percent of the capitation. But the difference between 1700 and 1789 was that there were at least three hundred more villagers. Some of them did create new sources of income, but essentially what happened was that the rich stayed rich and the poor got poorer. The proportion of people living on the edge of total poverty was greater in 1789 than in 1700 even if the village as a whole was somewhat better off (through the sale of cloth, the introduction of potatoes, and some minor improvements in roads and trade).

Even the middling well-to-do peasants were squeezed, although this is less clear and must obviously have affected fewer people. One of the great themes of eighteenth century French rural history is the contraction in the number of farms that were leased and the increase in the average size of leaseholds. Similar developments took place at the Pont after 1700. It is difficult to gauge the precise impact of this change because of the evolution in the meaning of the words that were used by tax collectors to describe tenant farmers. On the face of it, the decline in the number of leaseholds was very great. In 1789 there were fewer than fifteen *rentiers* or tenants at the Pont, although there had been no less than forty of them in 1696. Unfortunately, it is certain that in 1789 the precise meaning of rentier (or tenant) and of *laboureur* and *mesnager* (or landowner) was not what it had been in 1696.[45] At that time, the nomenclature used by tax officials did not clearly distinguish between farmers who were only tenants and farmers who were *also* tenants that is to say, between farmers who owned no land and those who owned some and rented more. In 1696, everyone who rented any land was listed as a tenant; that would not have been true in 1789, when the definition of tenant was narrowed to mean someone who lived principally on someone else's land. Were it not for these terminological changes, we would not have as clear an impression of the decline in the number of leaseholders. Nonetheless, when all has been said and done, the fall from forty-five *rentiers* in 1696 to fifteen in 1789 is a large one, especially if we bear in mind the increase in population between those dates. It is likely that in the eighteenth century the number of tenant farmers at the Pont *did* decline somewhat at least. There are certain eloquent instances of individual cases that can be traced during the century. In 1750, for example, the bourgeois Servière had two farms at Le Cros, one of them tended by Jean Rouvière and the other by J. Martin. In 1789 Servière's son still owned the property but now there was only one *rentier* at Le Cros. The Martins had dropped out altogether, and although the Rouvières survived, they did so in an attenuated way: where, in 1750, as tenants, they had had an income of over 400 livres, by 1789 they had little more than 200 livres as landowning *laboureurs*.[46] Clearly, Servière had consolidated his farm, and perhaps gone over from rye to animal farming since in 1799, when the inventory of his property at Le Cros was drawn up, it included six cows and 117 sheep. It is quite conceivable that the Martins and the Rouvières had been the victims of a form of enclosure movement which, of course, benefitted the rich and drove the poor off the land.

But by 1789 the exploitation of the poor by the rich had assumed a more sophisticated form than this. Indeed, it might be said that it was all but institutionalized in the cooperation of the bourgeoisie with the feudal state system. At the end of the seventeenth century, as has been seen, the local bourgeois notables had already begun to infiltrate the establishment by purchasing honorific if unlucrative seigneuries. This continued during the eighteenth century, and Louis Servière consecrated the rise of his family in just that way when in 1770 he bought the title to the seigneury of Pont-de-Montvert itself.[47] Unlike the Andrés in the previous century, Servière made little use of his new title,[48] but in any case it was not with these prestigious if profitless baubles that lay the kernel of the Montipontine bourgeoisie's relationship to the "system." Monetarily, seigneurial titles were no more valuable in the eighteenth century than they had been in the sevententh; in a way, since most seigneurial dues were paid by peasants to the Knights of Malta, the bourgeoisie was of all social classes the one that was least concerned by that particular aspect of the problem.[49]

But although seigneurial dues were unimportant and the bourgeoisie relatively blameless in this respect, because of the tithe, it remains true that the feudal system was an immense burden for the poor. As was usually the case in France, the tithe at the Pont represented roughly one-eleventh of crops grown, since it was collected

> at the rate of one-eleventh for all the gathered grain and at the same rate for calves, with beyond that one sou for the fleece of every lamb and sheep.[50]

These last provisions for animals, known as the *dîme carnenc,* represented about 500 livres a year in the 1780s, but the tithe on grain was far more important.[51] Each year, it came to more than 200 setiers of grain for Frutgères alone (at twenty to thirty livres a setier, this represented a value of about 5,000 livres a year). Grizac's contribution on this score was pooled with Fraissinet, but it can be estimated that Pont-de-Montvert as a whole handed over yearly a tithe of 300 setiers or 1,500 bushels of grain to the Knights of Malta and to the absentee prior of Fraissinet and Grizac, a layman who lived at Nîmes and doubtless never once saw his priory.

The tithe had many consequences, which can best be gauged if we bear in mind not only the amount of grain collected but also the amount of grain grown at the Pont as well as the amount of grain needed by the villagers to subsist. From the tithe of 300 setiers, we can estimate *grosso modo* that annual production stood at about 3,300 setiers. At the same time, since annual per capita consumption was on the order of two and one-half or three setiers,[52] total consumption of grain at the Pont in the 1780s must have hovered between 3,200 and 4,000 setiers (or 20,000 bushels). Obviously, then, when the population of the Pont rose above a thousand souls, a critical situation ensued because local grain production was no longer sufficient to meet local needs.[53]

Social Class in the Eighteenth Century

The balance of production and consumption was a precarious one. When the amount of grain represented by the tithe was subtracted from production, inevitably there was a shortage of wheat. The producers no longer had enough grain for bread and had to buy it, either from the outside or else from those people who had collected it at the Pont. This situation at once affected the price of grain, the amount of land turned over to the production of grain, and, finally, the status of those few people who did have surplus grain to sell.

The effect on food prices was quite paradoxical, for it is indeed very odd that grain should have been more costly at Pont-de-Montvert, a grain-growing and agricultural community, than it was at the regional capital of Montpellier. But such was the case during the last decades of the eighteenth century and the gap was often sizable. In 1779, wheat at Montpellier sold for twenty-five livres a setier; it must have brought close to thirty livres at the Pont, where rye, which was a third cheaper than wheat, was sold that year for twenty-two livres a setier.[54] In 1785, by the same reckoning, we can estimate that wheat would have cost more than thirty livres at the Pont as against twenty-seven livres at Montpellier. Indeed, how could it have been any other way? Roads were in a very poor state; everything had to be carried on muleback, a costly and inefficient proposition. As soon as Pont-de-Montvert was unable to grow all of its wheat and rye, the price of these commodities rose very quickly.

This in turn serves to explain another aspect of village economics in these years: the deformation of the Montipontine agricultural structure. Since grain was so expensive, everyone tried to grow as much of it as he could, both in order to sell it and so as not to be forced to buy it. In the 1780s the net annual Montipontine production of rye must have been on the order of 3,300 setiers, to which must be added the seed, the result being a gross annual production of about 4,000 setiers of 6,400 hectoliters. In this same decade, the average yield per hectare cannot have been more than ten hectoliters (in 1888, it had only reached that figure).[55] It follows that in any one year, about 640 hectares were turned over to rye (4000 setiers, or 6,400 hectoliters/10 hectoliters = 640). Since land at the Pont would lie fallow one year in two, it can be estimated that, all in all, more than 1,200 hectares of the village's arable surface was used to grow rye. How great a deformation of normal needs this was can be seen if we compare this figure of 1,200 hectares with the fact that in 1888, with a larger population and better techniques, production of rye reached only 5,000 hectoliters on 1000 hectares as against 6,400 hectoliters a hundred years before.[56]

In the 1780s, then, the Pont was producing much more grain than it

61

ever did after 1789 and more, certainly, than it had grown a hundred years before, since in the 1680s the tithe for Frutgères represented 200 setiers of grain only as against 240 in the 1780s.[57] This had yet another consequence, this time of a social rather than of an economic sort: the relative amelioration of the landowners' power and wealth. It was they, and only they, who had a surplus of rye to sell; they could sell it at a high price. In so doing of course, they benefitted from the fact that there was a seller's market for rye: the village as a whole *had* to buy the grain back because it had to eat.

Ordinarily the insufficiency of local production and the need to import rye would not have had particularly important consequences. It is perhaps the order of things that at times in a preindustrial economy a village should have to import foodstuffs. Nor is it surprising to see that it should have endeavored to produce those crops which it needed most. But the situation at the Pont of the eve of the Revolution was different because, thanks to the tithe, a sizable portion of the production was confiscated from its growers who then had to repurchase it in order to subsist. The great benefactors of the system were therefore in part those few individuals who owned enough land to keep their heads above water, who had enough land to grow enough grain to feed themselves, pay their tithe, dues, and taxes, and who still had a surplus which they could sell in a seller's market. But the greatest beneficiaries of all were obviously those people who laid claim to the grain tithe and then resold it to the peasants, who had just been forced to hand it over. And here we must distinguish between the owners of the tithe and feudal dues on the one hand and those people who actually collected the grain from the peasants.

Feudal and religious dues were not collected by the owners directly. The Knights of Malta, the prior of Fraissinet, the baron of Florac had all entrusted their judicial and monetary rights to local bourgeois. Admittedly, these men would all be Protestants; but, as was seen even during the hard days of the Camisard War, they were men who were closer to their purses than to the Good Book and they could certainly be trusted to squeeze the locals for what they were worth. It is no accident therefore that so many Montipontine bourgeois families rose to greatness by riding the coattails of the system. In the seventeenth century already the Andrés had been bailiffs, and the Desmarets and Bonnicels had been judges, empowered to deal out seigneurial justice. But the most spectacular case of enrichment based on an institution was that of the Servières. Jean Servière in 1710 had reached the bottom of the top. He married a demoiselle Talon, whose family was one of the most important in the Pont, and in 1720 he became a seigneur through the acquisition of the seigneury of the *Tour du Viala de Cadoene*. His eldest son, who was known as the seigneur du Viala, was a lawyer and a judge of the *commanderie* of Gap-Français. He did not marry and this enabled the younger son, Louis, to consolidate the family fortunes. On September 22, 1762, this same Louis Servière made the best deal of his life when he took over the farm of all of the order's property and rights in Frutgères and the neighboring communes, for which he agreed to pay the Knights of Malta 10,000 livres a year for the next five years.[58] Since the order owned only one farm in addition to the pastures of the Mont Lozère, most of its income was derived from feudal and religious dues, and it was by collecting these that Servière grew rich during the next twenty years.[59] The amount of the lease was revised from time to time but Servière always ran ahead of the pack. In the first years, the price of wheat increased 30 percent; therefore so did the value of what he collected, but not of what he paid out. The measure of his gain can be seen from the fact that in 1785, the order farmed out these same rights for 21,000 livres where it had collected 10,000 livres in 1760; 7,300 in 1715; and 3,600 in 1687. Naturally, the order was perhaps the greatest beneficiary; but Servière too did all right for himself, as indeed did everyone else in his position during this period of rising prices. In 1750, Louis Servière paid a capitation of twenty livres. In 1789, after the marriage of his son, Laurent, whose wife brought him a dowry of 50,000 francs, Louis Servière's contribution had risen to 150 livres. In forty years, his income had grown more than seven-fold.

This was a spectacular increase, and of course an unusual one. But the process was very usual indeed. In 1701, Antoine Jourdan was a smith, but in the late 1710s he took over the farm of the priory of Fraissinet and received "for his troubles" 150 livres.[60] By the 1750s, the Jourdans were no longer smithies, they were listed on the tax roll as the Sieur Jourdan, a rare distinction which he shared with only six other taxpayers, and in 1789 there was still a Sieur Jourdan, *chirurgien,* who owned a farm which he did not work himself.[61] The Molines of Camargues had followed a similar path. In 1709, Jacques Molines had taken over the farm of the Knights of Malta, and by 1750 the Molines of Camargues were twice as rich as they had been fifty years before. Later in the century, other bourgeois would climb onto this same gravy train, if with less *éclat*. In 1736, the "sieur Pascal" was the bailiff of the Comte du Roure;[62] in 1788 Jean Servière, a cousin of Louis Servière, had likewise taken over the collection of the tithe for the priory of the neighboring parish of Saint-Maurice-de-Ventalon which was worth more than 2,000 livres a year;[63] and a "Sieur Rouvière, *marchand,*" managed to supplement his income from the yearly contract

63

which he received for road repairs from the Estates of the Gévaudan. In one way or another, sometimes spectacularly, sometimes more humbly, the whole Montipontin bourgeois establishment depended on the feudal and religious state complex.

How true that was can be measured in other ways. For the very people who collected the dues were often in charge of dispensing seigneurial justice. They could at will prosecute troublemakers, or, more simply, exploit them yet further, a fusion of roles, of judge and plaintiff, which was aptly described in 1766 as an "infamous judicial comedy." [64] Nor should it be forgotten that the local bourgeoisie also derived a great part of its income from the small loans which it made to the poor. For the poor not only had to buy back the grain they had grown and given up to "the powers" for the tithe, or taxes, or dues, they also had to borrow in order to buy it back. They were sometimes able to repurchase their grain with the money they had earned by selling cloth, wool, or chestnuts,[65] or, as has been said, by working as seasonal laborers in the Languedoc. But more often, their earnings were not enough, and they would then have to turn to the local bourgeois for loans. Rates of interest were very high, and somewhat later, in 1813, loans were being made at the rate of 12 percent per annum, although the net yield of land was not more than 3 percent.[66] Indeed, as late as in 1845 the *conseil général* of the department reported that except in the three or four largest cities, there were no bankers at all, so that the peasants when they were rich borrowed from local landowners, and when poor and incapable of offering a guarantee, from "petty usurers".[67] At the Pont, this state of affairs was obviously of great benefit to those few people who did have money, and especially again to the Servières. When Louis Servière's son Laurent died in 1799, the inventory of his property lists no less than 160 claims on *divers débitants,* or debtors, most of them from Pont-de-Montvert.[68] Some of the loans had been made by Laurent to people like Filhon who had bought confiscated church lands, or *biens nationaux,* or again to fairly prosperous peasants. But most of the claims antedated the Revolution and were owed by poorer people, like Jean Rouvière, Servière's tenant at Le Cros, or Joseph Rampon, an artisan at the Pont.

It is in fact amusing to compare this list with a similar one drawn up by the departmental administration that was in charge of the confiscated property of "Jean Baptiste D'André de Montfort, seigneur de Veluze, le Vialas, Prades, Masméjean, résidant à son chateau de Prades." [69] The D'Andrés, it will be remembered, were descendants of the intransigent Protestant André who had taken to the hills in 1685 and refused to recant. His heirs, brought up as Catholics, had by contrast become true pillars of the State. In 1789, André de Montfort was therefore deeply shocked when local Protestant revolutionaries wrecked his garden walls. He would, he explained, have willingly given more than his

> modest garden, if that sacrifice could have contributed to the welfare and happiness of a people that was formerly gentle, peaceable, and good natured, and which he loves with all his heart. But he can only be indignant about those badly intentioned men who have corrupted and stirred up these poor people to no purpose or usefulness.[70]

Progressively more scandalized, Montfort finally emigrated; his goods (and loans) were fortunately confiscated, and this is why we know of their existence.[71] These loans ranged from three thousand to only six livres, and involved all sorts of peasants and artisans, rich and poor. Similar deeds it can be added had been made and let out at the Pont by Henri de Pelet, captain in the Régiment du Dauphin and "seigneur de la Rouvière," who also emigrated. Of course, it could be supposed that the local bourgeoisie felt a little unhappy about the identity of purpose and method which existed between itself and the "powers," the owners of feudal dues and the Catholic seigneurs of the region. There is, however, no written evidence of that; and we must assume therefore that if the bourgeoisie did suffer, it suffered privately and silently. What remains, nonetheless, is that in the end the local bourgeoisie was benefitting, in some cases quite spectacularly, from a feudal state system which brought to peasants and artisans nothing but exaction, or humiliation, or both.

Thus by 1789 the gap between rich and poor was more extreme than it had been in 1700 when both rich and poor were being actively persecuted by the State. Now the local bourgeoisie was more safely ensconced in the interstices of the system. Other reasons as well made for a greater chasm between haves and have-nots. Most Montipontins in 1789 like most Montipontins in 1700 lived on the land and did not depend for their livelihood on the local bourgeois. But on the eve of the Revolution this had changed greatly for some people at least. Admittedly most landless laborers were still employed by rich peasants (as had been true before) and those farmers who had cattle to sell would drive them to market at Alès or Barre. They did not sell their cows or oxen to unneeded and unwanted middlemen. But, as has been pointed out, the number of artisans grew in the eighteenth century, and *they* probably did need go-betweens. The merchants who fulfilled this function were not actively nefarious. There was no destruction of rural cadres, and as far as we can tell neither was there even a putting-out system. Artisans continued to be self-employed; but in subtle ways the merchants were important nonetheless. There were about fifteen of them on the eve of the Revolution.[72] They would act as intermediaries, buying cloth and hats at the Pont, which they would sell at fairs. From there they brought back merchandise that they would resell perhaps to those same artisans whose cloth they had acquired. It could be argued, therefore, that these local merchants played a useful role and stood between the Pont and the rest of the world as the notables had done for centuries before. Nonetheless there was something anomalous or at least new about their situation. In the past, the bourgeoisie had played a direct, straightforward political and social role. They had been notaries, apothecaries, millers, lawyers. They performed immediate and necessary functions that the peasantry needed but could not duplicate. This was not so true of the new merchants. Of course, they were not idle men, and since they imported to the Pont grain, tools, olive oil, wine, and, in the last decade of the ancien régime, coal from the mines of the Gard they were even necessary to the welfare of the village. But these new bourgeois were now middlemen rather than producers, and this must have affected their status. Some of them were very poor, and the rich peasants of the village must have felt vastly superior to the misery struck muletier or *bastier* whose prosperity hinged on the well-being of some mangy mule. But it is hard to suppose that the weavers or the laborers, the *travailleurs de terre,* could have had much liking for the five or six fairly prosperous merchants with an income of more than a thousand livres. What did they do but live by reselling the handiwork of the poor?

The evolution of village economic life therefore made for more tension between social classes, and this may have been accentuated by yet another social phenomenon: the relatively static nature of social life in the village during the eighteenth century. Although the broad outlines of the social structure had remained unchanged for decades and perhaps centuries, before 1700 there had been a continuous flux that brought families from the hamlets to the bourg and on to the outside world. At the top there had always been some notables, but not the same notables. By 1750, however, the notables of the Pont all belonged to families which had been well-to-do in the 1710s: the Sieur de la Vernède was a relative of Jean Velay; Roux, Jourdan, Velay de Marueilhac, Pagès, and the Servières were also people whose forbears had gotten their foothold in the first decades of the eighteenth century or even before.[73] In 1789, the leading families of the Pont were essentially those that had weathered the turmoil of 1702–1704, the Servières, Pagès, Rouvières, Pinets, Molines, and Jourdans.

Social Class in the Eighteenth Century

Paradoxically, this structural stability implied great change from what had taken place before. In the seventeenth century, the village structure had, it is true, been fixed and steadfastly tripartite. But its content was fluid: within an established system, there had been a considerable turnover, and new families had taken up where old ones had left off. In the eighteenth century, this was no longer so. Now, the structure remained unchanged, but so did the contents. The continuous emigration from the hamlets to the bourg was drying up. On the eve of the Revolution, the line was more clearly drawn than it had been in 1702 between the bourgeois, with their vested interests and *droits acquis,* and the peasants and laborers of the village as a whole. Now the bourgeoisie was not only pressing down more harshly on the other village classes than ever before; it had also become more isolated, both socially and geographically. The links of family and place which still held together the Montipontins of 1700 were weaker in 1789 than before.

Obviously, then, village politics in 1789 ought to have been even more divided than it had been in 1702. At that time, the village had had class politics which corresponded to a class structure; in 1789, the class lines were more sharply drawn and more sharply felt. It follows therefore that Montipontin politics in the French Revolution should have been even more class dominated than before. But that was not the case. In fact, the reverse was true. Of course, the village was very "left wing". In the elections for the Convention the district of Florac chose a Montipontin, and his career in Paris was unimpeachable: he voted with the Montagnards, for the death of the King, and all the rest. But the complexity of the problem is shown by the fact that this ardent Revolutionary was none other than Laurent Servière, the son and only heir of Louis Servière, tax farmer and enemy of the people.

CHAPTER IV Revolutionary Politics

Why was there no class revolution at the Pont in 1789? This is a baffling problem, especially if we bear in mind that social divisions were so pronounced at the end of the century that something *ought* to have happened. The question is also difficult to resolve because it involves matters of method. In our view, the problem of nonrevolution can be resolved within the context of the village alone, but it is only fair to point out that many, perhaps most, historians would not agree. They might point here to the Camisard Wars of 1702–1710 and argue that if the Pont had exploded in those years, it was because it had then been in the path of a widespread religious current. Could not the situation in 1789 have merely been the reverse of what had existed before? Can it not be supposed that if a social revolution did not occur at the Pont in 1789, it is because it did not occur elsewhere as well?

The question of course can never be resolved. Since the region around the Pont did not revolt, we will never know whether the Montversois would have risen up if the villages around them had given them an example to follow. Perhaps they would have. But it is more than sensible to argue that the whole problem of regional involvement is something of a red herring. After all, even in 1702, if Pont-de-Montvert was swept up in an *Inspirationsbewegung,*[1] that was probably because conditions at the Pont resembled those in surrounding and already contaminated communities. What mattered therefore was the *similarity* of conditions between the Pont and its neighbors rather than the existence of a general current. Much the same can be said for 1789. If the Pont did not have a social revolution, that may have been because there was no regional impulse for it to do so; but that in turn may have been because the region, like the Pont itself, was not ripe for it, and this brings us back once again to a description of the village itself.

This reasoning does, it is true, remain an act of faith insofar as conditions in the Cévennes remain unstudied; but the historian is encouraged to accept it because it can be sustained by the evidence that is to be found for the Pont itself. Admittedly, social divisions in the village were extreme in 1789, but other factors explain very cogently why it was that these cleavages did not result in political upheaval. We can find within the context of the Pont itself sufficient and necessary causes for its passivity during the decade of Revolution. We do not need to find explanations from wider context because the history of Pont-de-Montvert in these years makes sense by itself.

Of these "internal" causes, the first and most important is that the poor may have hated other people even more than they hated the rich. The state was their first and greatest enemy. Nor were they absurd in thinking this, since, after all, the "State and Church" did weigh down more heavily on their backs than did anyone else. As has been shown, per capita income was low at the Pont, and the total village income was in the order of 140,000 livres per year. At the same time, religious dues amounted to six or seven thousand livres, and so did taxes. Together these sums alone represent between 10 and 15 percent of total village income, and to that should be added incidental exactions, dues, prosecutions and their legal costs, as well as the fines which were imposed on the villagers from time to time.[2] (See Table 1.) Much if not all of this must have seemed completely indefensible. Religious dues for example must surely have been loathed, not only because the villagers were overwhelmingly Protestant, but also because this money was a net loss for the village, since local clerics received practically none of it.[3]

Table 1.   Taxes paid by Frutgères, and Fraissinet and Grizac

Type of tax	1726		1753	
	Frutgères	Fraissinet and Grizac	Frutgères	Fraissinet and Grizac
Taille	142	200	142	200
Taillon	44	62	44	62
Mortpayes	7	10	7	10
Garnison	53	75	39	55
Ordinaire	731	1030	187	263
Extraordinaire	2666	3756	1476	2080
Capitation	1192	211[a]	993	143[a]
Etapes	—	—	53	73

[a] Grizac only

veuve
Louise Jourdan menagere
pautquinair mediocre

Le berger du lieu

La veissiere

Jean deux ... Jouer
travailleur
pauure

Le berger du lieu
Jean pantet munier pauure

Jouer
mouise pontet travailleur pauure

Lemakel

Jean albaric laboureur ou
Jeanne roux sa belle mere
mediocre
un valet

Jacques roux laboureur pauure

Laboureur
claude gauch travailleur
pauure

Le berger du lieu

11.

Le Seigneur du fief des licorie comme bourgeois

Les biens de pierre vigne, de salanal
confisqués pour cas d'irreligion

Nous soussignés certifions avoir fait l'estat cy devant
... et l'avoir leu en plaine assemblée chés monsieur
le curé ou l'ensemble des habitans à esté convoqué
lequel nous avons fait avec toute l'exactitude
qu'il nous a esté possible ce trantiesme mars mil
sept cens trante six

[signatures]

Total des articles compris
au présent denombrement cy _____

_____ 265.

A tax roll at the Pont, 1736. Inhabitants are listed hamlet by hamlet. Archives
Départementales de la Lozère.

Admittedly the state was not wholly ruthless in its collection of taxes. During the Camisard Wars, tax increases had been a frequent weapon of the authorities in their fight against subversion, but this never occurred in the last decades of the ancien régime. Taxes, it seems, were then collected with an eye not only to what was needed but also to what the locals could bear and they were no longer used as a punitive measure. In fact, judging from the figures on the capitation, taxes did not increase after 1780. They had remained stable for the decades between 1737 and 1760 (we have no complete figures for the years immediately preceding or following these dates); by 1780 they had risen sharply by nearly 20 percent but they remained unchanged after that. The capitation for 1781 was set at 1,237 livres; it fell to 1,180 in 1786 and although it rose again to 1,380 in 1788, it was lowered once again to 1,249 livres for 1789.[4] Since the population of the village had risen by perhaps as much as 25 percent from the 1760s to the 1780s, the increase was not excessive. It must also be said that the authorities sometimes relented and actually gave the village some of its money back. In 1729, for example, during the famine, the bishop did what he could to alleviate suffering:

> Towards the month of July 1729, Mgr. the Bishop of Mende, seeing the general shortage of grain in all of the land and especially in his diocese, solicited the provincial estates for some foreign grain, which was granted to him, a great deal of it was carted to Saint-Jean-de-Gardonnenque and it was distributed to the parishes according to their population. For the parish of Grizac, there were only ten bags of poor grain which was distributed to the poorest.[5]

Similarly in 1753 20,000 livres were distributed to all of the "communities whose harvests had been damaged," but this was a modest sum since the province as a whole paid nearly 800,000 livres in taxes each year.

The state was now more moderate in its fiscal demands, than it had been before, and it was at times positively magnanimous. Nonetheless there is no doubt that taxes were a great burden for the village, and they were deeply resented. To have them diminished was the villagers' overriding political goal. This appears quite clearly from the draft of the *cahier de doléance* which the villagers drafted for the Estates General of 1789.[6] The *cahier* has eleven points; six of them, including the first three, are concerned with this very question of taxation. The first item begins with a description of the Pont: it is situated

> on a very rough and bitter soil, which on all sides offers to those who see it nothing but a sterility that is felt by everyone.

Everyone in the village is poor, and yet taxes are very high: "(they) are so excessive that they exceed one-third of our income." This was too much, thought the Montversois; and indeed it was, since their tax burden was only half as great as they had made it out to be. To solve their problem, they proposed a new fiscal structure much in accord with the latest physiocrat principles. The King, they thought, should accord his special protection to peasants

> by emancipating all the fruits of agriculture from all taxes, tolls, and dues of all kinds and to grant to agriculture all the prerogatives which the nurturing mother of man can and must demand in a well-conceived state.

Other complaints dealt with the salt tax, or *gabelle,* which the villagers wanted suppressed; with the taxes on roads (there should be taxes and roads, rather then just taxes for roads, as was then the case); with the abolition of fiscal exemptions for nobles and *privilégiés;* and with the administrative reorganization of the province of Languedoc, which should be granted "a free and entire constitution" similar to the one that had been granted to the province of Dauphiné. None of the articles of the *cahier* deal with abstract political programs. This is unusual, for even in those cases when the *cahiers* were drawn up by peasants rather than by notables or according to some circulated model, some mention was usually made of *lettres de cachet,* national constitutions, freedom of assembly or of the press. None of these things appear at the Pont, where the whole thrust of local demands was directed against the fiscal exactions of the state.

This motive of course had probably always existed in one form or another. It had been present during the Camisard War: in 1702, the estates of the Gévaudan reported that the "fanatics"

> having interrupted all sorts of commerce by occupying the passes where they have slaughtered many muleteers, even went so far as to forbid the payment of the tithe and of the head tax, and have threatened to kill and burn those who would pay it or collect it; so that nearly all of the communities of the Cévennes, have refused and do refuse to pay the tithe and head tax, for fear of the rebels or in the hope that they will help them.[7]

Yet although the antitax motive is a great constant in the history of this village where Poujade was to have a considerable following, it may have had particular relevance in 1789. Now that Protestantism was tolerated and the garrisons had been withdrawn, fiscal injustice had become the focus of antimonarchism or antistatism. Taxes at this point were perhaps also more often and more keenly felt to represent the

difference between life and death. Since the number of landless un-
employed and artisans had been growing, there were now more
people who were leading increasingly marginal existences, and the
channeling of their hatred away from the bourgeoisie and against the
state was not completely absurd. Money is the blood of the poor, and
it cannot be denied that they had reason to hate. The local bourgeoisie,
it is true, also lived on the backs of the peasants; but their bite was not
so great as the one that had to be delivered to the "powers." Moreover,
the local bourgeoisie, unlike the state, did fulfill at least some useful
functions and others which appeared to be useful (money lending, for
example, to people who could not pay their taxes or buy bread). Then
too, in their own way, the local notables were, for the poor, fellow
sufferers, since they too were Protestants and had taxes to pay. Nor
should we ignore the fact that the ways in which the Servières and their
friends benefitted from the system were relatively obscure, although
the way in which everyone was asked to pay for the upkeep of a distant state that rendered no visible useful service to anyone was obvious
to all.

Memories after 1743 and resentment before that had also fed the
flame of popular antistatism, for it should be remembered that the Pont
had been for four decades a physically subjected land and the headquarters of a royal army of occupation. During the first few years, the
troops in question were drawn from the battalions of the half-wild
Miquelets, the *fusilliers du roy* who were recruited in the mountains of
the Roussillon. After them, at the end of the Camisard Wars, came
regular units, like the Régiment du Bourbonnais, de la Couronne, de
Noailles, and de Croix, whose presence is known to us by the notarized
acts of births, marriages, and deaths. There was, for example, the sad
end and burial of sergeant La Tulype, "no one knew his last or christian
name".[8] There were also socially unfortunate cases like the baptism in
February of 1728 of Joseph Vigne, "the natural and illegitimate son of
Joseph, called Lamotte, a soldier in the company of M. Damtou, of the
Bourbonnais Regiment, as was said and asserted by the bastard's
mother."[9] Interestingly enough, however, although soldiers often
stood in as godfathers in the compulsory Catholic baptisms, there is to
our knowledge no record of any marriage between a local person and
an "occupier," although we have found more than fifty mentions of
individual soldiers in notarial and other archives. Royal troops were
recalled after 1743. They reappeared in 1751 and were still at the Pont
in 1755. Their final departure at that time must have occasioned universal relief.

Resentment against the state and its satraps is one factor that can serve to explain the absence of internal social dissent. Another important cause of this same phenomenon is of a very different sort. It is a truism of revolutionary jargon that in order to have a class struggle, one needs not only classes but class consciousness as well. The potential revolutionary must have an outlook on life that is at least different from that of his bourgeois overlords. If he operates with the same set of mental tools as his master he cannot successfully rebel, even if the material circumstances of his existence are objectively propitious. And the issue here is that from this point of view, the Pont in 1789 was far less ripe for social revolution than it had been a century before. On the eve of the Camisard Wars, the Montipontin lower class (peasants and artisans) had for a quarter of a century been ideologically at loose ends. Like the other Cévenols, they had been largely abandoned by their pastors who had fled abroad or abjured their heresy. Nor had the local notables shown themselves more courageous or inspiring. For this reason, the Camisard movement was in many ways an anarchistic and popular agitation which was opposed to all forms of guidance from above. Not infrequently, the "prophets" of the movements spoke in millenarian terms. The rebels, like Jean Molines of Finialettes claimed to serve "Jesus Christ and his apostles" rather than some particular (bourgeois) institution like the Protestant Church.[10] One prophet, Pierre Clary, even had a world vision in which the Pope and Mohammed presided over humanity reconciled. Indeed, there is much reason to agree with Gagg, who concludes that

> we should not be surprised that some of the inspired looked forward to a new setting where there would be neither Papists nor Calvinists, but where God would be honored by a single christian Church.[11]

Ideologically, the Camisards had been on their own. Protestantism had given them a focus and, ostensibly, a purpose. But at that particular moment it had not given them guidance or inspired them with respect for their betters. That, however was precisely what Protestantism was doing in 1789 and had been doing since the 1720s, when the Montipontine lower classes were once again drawn into the compass of an organized religious movement directed by the local bourgeoisie. Here it is particularly interesting to trace two phenomena, first the attitude of the regular Protestant clergy to the Camisard Wars with its implications of social upheaval, and second, the evolution of the village elite in relation to Protestantism, and their re-espousal of a cause for which they had felt in 1702 a distant interest at best.

To understand the attitude of the Protestant clerics to the Camisards, one need go no further than the opinion of the two leading apostles of the French Protestant revival in the eighteenth century: Antoine Court and his representative in the Cévennes, Corteiz. The latter had himself lived through the Camisard Wars. In 1702, when aged fifteen or sixteen, he had often addressed Protestant crowds, but he had not then been very popular:

> Until 1702, he addressed exhortations to the faithful, and spoke much against the prophets which were covering the land, preaching for war, and ordering that priests should be killed and churches burned. But passions had been unleashed and he was called an unbeliever.[12]

When Corteiz returned from Switzerland in 1716, he began by condemning spontaneous Protestant assemblies in the *Désert*.

> We will not tolerate either fanatics, or pietists, or anabaptists; the word of God is our only rule, and would it please God that you should see with what order and rule we hold to it.[13]

Corteiz himself was only moderately successful, but the movement of Protestant restoration gained much impetus with the arrival in the Languedoc of Antoine Court, who was to be with his son, Court de Gebelin, the architect of the new bourgeois Protestant order. The whole of his public existence was directed to the harnessing of those passions which Corteiz had decried. About the Camisards, he had few doubts. When he returned to France in 1715, he had made up his mind about them: "He divided the inspired into two groups: those who were mad and those who were scoundrels." For him, the Camisard War was the result certainly of Louis XIV's persecutions (and he never ceased to attack those); but the Protestants had their share of the blame: they had succumbed to the most *déplorable fanatisme*.[14] The reformed Religion had had

> ignorant prophets which the people followed with zeal because there were no enlightened pastors, and their absurd predications were received with full confidence and dangerous docility. Thus the vivid light which had shined on the reformed churches of the seventeenth century died out, and in its place came a long darkness.[15]

The origins of the Camisard Wars were not mysterious for Court:

> When the spirit was no longer able to nourish itself from the Testament and truth, it fed on day dreams and chimeras. The War of the Camisards provides an irrefutable proof of that.[16]

It seemed therefore obvious to him that it was in the interest of the government to leave him alone. In 1723, Versailles let it be known that Court would not be harmed if he would agree to leave the country and give up the Languedoc, where a price had been set on his head. Court refused and argued that Versailles

> instead of laboring to have me expelled from the kingdom, (they) should work to keep me back, and should be convinced of the fact that I am giving useful service by molding good subjects.[17]

In his view, the interests of the state and of the Protestant church were identical in that both depended on the "education" of the rank and file.[18] Court's own courage cannot be questioned, and there is no doubt that he argued in this way from conviction rather than opportunism; but his devotion to the powers was little less than fawning. Indeed, he went so far as to put loyalty above his own private welfare. In 1727, a Protestant minister, Alexandre Roussel, had been captured by the constabulary and two hundred men had gathered to free him. Court objected; they should not rescue Roussel just as they should not rescue him if he were captured:

> By my advice, I led them away from this, since I preferred to give some martyrs to the Church than to bring troubles to the region or condemnations to the religion.[19]

Court's attitude is all the more important for the fact that he was very successful in his campaign to reach the faithful who had gone astray since 1685. By 1721, a network of underground churches had been set up throughout the Cévennes:

> The churches of the Lozère, of Pont-de-Montvert, of Castagnols, of Saint-Juilhan, of Florac made great progress and were raised again with the marvelous assistance of God, being favored by the plague which had brought about the withdrawal of the troups from our mountains and from the Cévennes.[20]

Court himself came to preach at the Pont on June 6, 1728 and his mission was a great success.

> The next day, on Sunday, the churches of Genolhac, of Frutgères and of Pont-de-Montvert were convoked, and the church of C.... also came. The assembly was very numerous. We saw there what had perhaps not been seen since 1685: five children being baptized at the head of the assembly. This ceremony was tenderly felt by all those present. How many tears were shed during the sermon! Rain did bother us, not only during the ceremony, but afterwards as well. When the exercise had been completed, and the rain had ceased, some left and others took a small meal on the grass. There one could see a large number of groups of people, sitting on the grass who ate with great simplicity ... And the whole thing was closed with the singing of some holy hymn. That is how assemblies are usually con-

ducted in that part of the country. Before I left, I blessed five marriages.[21]

Prophetism had made great inroads in the Pont, and the martyrs of the Camisard Wars did find heirs. On April 22, 1723, Jacob Bonnicel was hanged at Montpellier for having belonged to a secret Protestant sect. What official Protestantism thought of this sort of thing shows in the tone of Corteiz's description of this affair:

> Poor Bonnicel from Pont-de-Montvert who had been sent to study and become a priest but who later decided to become a merchant, was an attendant in a shop at Montpellier . . . he too was condemned to be hanged.[22]

But this was the last case of unrestrained prophetism in the village. Thanks to Court's preachings and efforts, the natives' energies were harnessed to different ends. Just as Bonnicel's fate was typical of an earlier period, the course of eighteenth-century Montipontin Protestantism was symbolized by one Viala, who was born at the Pont, studied abroad, and became a Protestant minister "after having taken an exam given by Corteiz, Claris, and Brétine."[23]

In itself, the ideological emasculation of the village's working class was an important fact. But it was made more complete yet by the fact that the Protestant bourgeoisie itself also responded to Antoine Court's appeal and rejoined the fold. From 1685 to the Camisard War, as has been seen, the working class had drifted out of the control of the notables who had in these same decades become very opportunistic. In spite of the fact that the loyalty of the upper class was not always rewarded, the rich had remained steadfastly opposed to resistance and collaborated willingly, if joylessly, with their persecutors. But after 1720, a reverse pattern was created. The poor were brought back to the established fold and the rich also came back to it of their own accord. Henceforth religion would provide not only a framework for social thought, but also the grounds for mutual understanding and sympathy between rich and poor. The reintegration of the notables was perhaps unhurried (unfortunately, for lack of documents we cannot follow it in detail for the village) but it appears to have been completed by the 1740s. By then the *assemblées du desert* were tacitly accepted by the royal officials. Some of them were attended by as many as twenty thousand people, and more importantly, by people of all social milieus. Nobles and bourgeois alike were keen to be forgiven their "past cowardice." "The country gentleman," wrote Court, "the lawyer, the doctor, the honorable bourgeois, and the rich merchant come with the same zeal . . . as the farmer or the artisan." [24] In 1744, the bishop of Uzès concurred but with less satisfaction:

> everyone is going to the Protestant assemblies, even those people who before would never have thought of going there: proctors, notaries, merchants, bourgeois, notables, gentry even, and the local seigneurs; even children who are just learning how to walk are being taken there.[25]

The bishop, however, was overly cynical in his appreciation of these people's motives:

> When you ask people of a certain status, who used to disdain the assemblies why it is that they go to them now, they reply that in so doing they do not think that they are disobeying the orders of the king, because the king knows about them and tolerates them.[26]

There was no doubt something of that, but that is not the whole truth. Clearly, by the middle of the eighteenth century, the Protestant notables had undergone some sort of spiritual rebirth. There is no reason to doubt the sincerity of their actions, especially since in Pont-de-Montvert itself we can find proof that the renewal of their faith was not without its dangers. Even passive religious resistance, as will be seen, could bring down the wrath of the authorities.

In any case, the change of heart of the Montipontine bourgeoisie was very thorough, and its participation in Protestant underground activities was as obvious in the 1750s as it had been hesitant in the early 1700s. In 1701, a revival meeting in one of the hamlets had come to the attention of the authorities,[27] and thanks to the documents of the subsequent investigation, it had been possible to ascertain the lower-class origin of all but one of the people involved. A similar meeting took place at the Pont in 1751. It also was investigated, and the contrast between the two meetings is very revealing of the social and ideological evolution that had taken place in the first half of the century. To begin with, the case in 1751 was different from what had happened in 1701. The subdelegate Campredon was now unable to find any native witnesses, although that had not been true before. Campredon himself went from Barre to the Pont. There he found a field which he thought could hold 2,000 people

> set in the center of a wood on a lawn where there is an infinite number of stones suitable for sitting.[28]

He himself did not see anything there except for a few sticks and some horse dung, circumstantial evidence at best. But one soldier of the local garrison, Beaujolais, had seen a few people whom he was able to identify. Naturally it is to be expected that he should have named prominent people first, but what is interesting is that he should have been able to name any notables at all. That would not have been possible in 1701. In 1751, of the eight people seen by Beaujolais, only two were artisans. But both Jacques Felgerolles and David Servière, both hatmakers, were unusually rich artisans since they each paid three livres six sous in capitation or three times as much as the average for an unskilled laborer. Also interesting is the presence of Jacques Pons and his sister, whose behavior is in sharp contrast to that of the Pons who was a royal collaborator in the Camisard Wars. More surprising yet is the fact that three leading families of the Pont and of the neighboring hamlet of Fraissinet were also represented by Madame de Velay, *femme du juge*,[29] Madame Rouvière, whose husband paid a capitation of twelve livres, and Madame Boissier, whose husband was the leading light of Fraissinet and whose tribe would supplant the Servières at the Pont in the first decades of the nineteenth century.

As it happens, in this particular instance, the culprits did not come to any tragic end. Although Saint-Florentin who was in charge of Protestant affairs at Versailles was "annoyed to see by the affair that has taken place at Pont-de-Montvert that Protestants are becoming every day more audacious,"[30] nothing much was done, perhaps in part because of the entreaties of the local Catholic authorities. Bancilhon, the curé of the Pont, pleaded for mercy on the grounds of poverty. "My parish," he wrote of the Pont,

> is full of wretched people and has been so for some years, the crops have failed, and there is at the moment a great mortality among the animals.[31]

And the subdelegate concurred:

> The bad harvests that we have known for the last few years in these mountains have put the inhabitants in a great misery and it is to be feared that they would commit some great mistake if they found themselves unable to pay the fine, should it be too great.[32]

Their advice was more or less heeded since the Pont was only required to pay a fine of 1,000 livres, with 167 livres for procedural expenses. But more serious things did sometimes happen. Louis and Paul Servière's sister Suzanne was forcibly cloistered at the Carmelite Convent in Mende,[33] and the Sieur Pierre Roux, *practicien* and apothecary, was locked up at Alès. His sister was also hounded for awhile, although Campredon was forced to admit that she was no more guilty than "a multitude of others."[34]

It is of course conceivable that the ardor of the Protestant bourgeoisie did to some degree vary with the intensity of persecution: they
may have become more enthusiastic after 1743 when the authorities
relented, and more cautious again in 1751 with the last wave of organized persecution; but there is nothing to prove it as far as Pont-de-
Montvert is concerned. All the evidence points to the fact that the return of the local bourgeoisie to Protestant orthodoxy was as sincere
as that of the working class had been thorough; and from 1740 to our
own day, Pont-de-Montvert has nearly always been united in its loyalty
to the Protestant establishment.[35] The official reappearance of a Protestant pastor in the village after the edict of 1787 is therefore something of a symbol if of a clouded sort since the comings and goings of
Pierre Bonnicel remain somewhat mysterious. What is known, is that
he was born at the Pont in 1751, that he was a collateral ancestor of
François Guizot, and that he was educated at Lausanne. In 1803, after
the Revolutionary upheaval, he returned to the Pont where he stayed
until his death in 1819.[36] But he had been there before the Concordat
since he had begun his career in the *désert* and he may well have been
at the Pont with interruptions from 1787 on. In any case, his appearance on the scene at the end of the eighteenth century marked both the
close of a century of neglect and the official reimposition of an elitist
framework for ideological speculation.[37]

We can therefore explain in part at least why the resentments of the
village working class were channeled into an attack of the state rather
than of the possessing classes. But this does not explain why the
possessing class itself became politically revolutionary. It is perhaps
baffling that the Montipontins should have sent Louis Servière's son
to the Convention, but it is also strange that Louis Servière's son
should have wanted to go there at all. Was he not a prosperous man?
Had not his father done well out of the clerical and feudal state system, and could he not look forward to doing as well? Here again we can
propose various explanations. Most obviously and cynically, Servière
and his friends could hope to do well out of the Revolution, and in fact
they did just that. They may also have thought from the onset that it
would be better to go along with the tide, which might in any case push
some church-owned lands their way. In the same order of morality
would be their desire to have access to jobs which until then had been
the prerogative of nobles.

However, it must be said that for the Pont there is practically no
evidence to support this. True, Louis Servière had, late in his life,
quarreled with the Knights of Malta and had even sued them. He
certainly had his own reasons to dislike these pseudoclerics, but there

is no reason to suppose that he had greedily envisaged in 1789 the gains that his son would make in 1795; nor is there any evidence that Servière or any of the bourgeois notables aspired to some official post. They seem to have been content in their moneymaking enterprises. Indeed, the great stability of Montipontin social structure in the eighteenth century and the lack of bourgeois geographical mobility indicate anything but a restless quest for new and better state jobs.

Socially, the local bourgeois were supine, but much evidence, direct and indirect, suggests that many of them may have had intellectual or ideological reasons to dislike the system by which they had done so well. To begin with, in consequence of their return to Protestantism, many bourgeois (including Servière himself) had had relatives who had been imprisoned by a persecuting state. Independently of these personal considerations, their sympathy for Protestantism generally may also have predisposed them to Revolutionary endeavors. On May 10, 1790, on the occasion of some suppressed royalist plot, the Protestant Jeanbon Saint-André, future member of the Committee of Public Safety and future Bonapartist prefect, is reported to have said "It is the day of vengeance, and we have been waiting for it for more than a hundred years." [38] Of course, this is no proof at all that all Protestants thought this way, or that Servière and his friends thought this way, but it is not an unthinkable idea.

What is certain, however, is that Servière at least did have ideological motives. Fortunately we possess an inventory of the books that he kept in his home at the Pont, and it is indeed revealing.[39] Strikingly, Servière owned practically no books on the physical sciences or on practical matters generally. He did have a *Cours complet d'agriculteur,* as well as selections from Pliny, and some of the forty-two volumes which are not described by name may also have been of a scientific sort. But the thirty-seven titles that we do know are those of books that deal with quite different things. Many of them are works of literature, French, Latin, and English. The works of Racine, La Fontaine, "Boilo," and Colardeau (1732–1776) coexist with those of Homer, Plato, Virgil, Lucian, Tacitus, and those of Cervantes and Pope. More interesting from our point of view are those works which deal with purely historical or philosophical topics: histories of Joan the *pucelle,* of Japan, of ancient Greece, of the war in India [sic], of the inquisition, and of Persia; descriptions of voyages to Guinea and Greece with a *discours sur le gouvernement* as well as the works of Machiavelli, Helvetius, "la matrie," and Marat. No less curious are titles like *Les Fastes de Louis XV, Les Oracles des sibiles,* and *Le Vrai Fransmasson.* (The appraiser of the estate, it must be said, did not think much of that one:

he rated it at fifty centimes. Barthélémy's *Young Anarcharsis* did best: thirty francs, which incidentally was two months' wages for one of the downtrodden men whom Servière would have wished to liberate.)

If libraries are any indication of their owners' tastes, Servière had obviously been won over to the *lumières* of the eighteenth century. And it is all the more tempting to suppose that ideological motivations must have been important for Servière, since there are so few concrete reasons which could otherwise have served to make him a revolutionary.

The poor hated the state, and so did the bourgeoisie. Divided against itself, the Pont was nonetheless united against the clerical and feudal state, and the course of Revolution in the village followed more or less along these lines. The Revolution met with the united approval of the whole community; but since the poor had been taken in tow by the bourgeoisie, it was the bourgeoisie that stole the show. Participations in the events of the day were unequal; and the rewards of rebellion were not shared as equally as they might have been. The rich, whether bourgeois or peasants, did more and got more also.

As in many other parts of France, discontent had both general and specific causes. The winter of 1788 and the spring of 1789 were disastrous. The temperature dropped below freezing on June 13, 14, and 15. Two years later, an ecologically minded observer wrote, "The misfortunes of this department go back to 1789. The rigor of the winter was for the prairies and pastures as bad as that of 1709." [40] Times were very hard, and the Revolution was greeted with some enthusiasm if only as a palliative to these acts of God. Many Lozèrians apparently thought that their taxes would be halved and that they would henceforth pay "neither salt, nor tithe, nor dues." [41] Initially everyone was pleased, and the Revolution in the Lozère met with unanimous approval.

The specific manifestations of this good will are hard to follow insofar as the Pont is concerned. Unfortunately the departmental archives went up in flames in 1887; [42] many records were lost, among them the minutes and correspondence of nearly all of the *comités de surveillance*, so that we do not know of any specifically revolutionary institution at the Pont, although some must certainly have existed. [43] Insofar as we can make out what happened, it seems that at the Pont enthusiasm for the Revolution was sustained. In 1790 and 1791, some opposition to the Revolution began to develop in other parts of the Lozère; on August 22, 1791, the mayor of the neighboring and Catholic commune of Le Bleymard could already write to the Departmental Directorate that the people seem sensitive to the deprivation of masses and it is our opinion that this dissatisfaction is the only thing which might drive it to some insurrection.[44]

But in Protestant Pont-de-Montvert, all was quiet and harmony. On July 14, 1790, the Montipontin national guard celebrated the fall of the Bastille with their neighbors from Villefort. There was a great deal of emotion; everyone swore fidelity *à la Nation, à la loy, et au roi;*[45] and shortly afterwards the two Catholic priests of the Pont accepted the civil constitution of the clergy.[46] All Montipontins, rich and poor, Catholic and Protestant, appeared to be very pleased with the new state of affairs.

A closer look at electoral rolls, however, does suggest some corrections. It would be wrong to say that many, perhaps any, Montversois disapproved of the Revolution; but it is true that many of them do not appear to have cared much either way. There were many villagers who should have voted but who did not do so. They were certainly not deterred by voting requirements. At the Pont as in the rest of France the franchise of 1789 was the widest in the world, not excluding any of the recently independent thirteen colonies. In order to estimate its extent for the village, it can be assumed for the sake of argument that half of the population (1,245 persons) were males, one-half of whom again were adults. That would make about 310 potential voters, and we know that there were in fact 225 "active" or enfranchised citizens at the Pont.[47] This was a most generous extension of political rights, but many Montversois did not avail themselves of this newfound prerogative. Electoral involvement at the Pont was well below the national average. Napoleon's coup of 18 Brumaire, for example, was ratified by 3,000,000 votes in France as a whole. Proportionately, 150 Montipontins should therefore have come to the polls on 6 Nivose, Year VIII. But the canton as a whole was represented by a mere ninety-three voters, and of these only fifty-three were from the Pont itself, a small and disappointing number even if we bear in mind that no one of them saw fit to disapprove of the new order of things.[48] Some progress in participation was made during the empire itself. One hundred and forty-two people approved of the life consulate, and 158 voters gave their consent to the hereditary empire on 13 Messidor, Year XII.[49] But these are figures for the canton as a whole, and they remain considerably below the number of people who had been enfranchised to vote in the village alone as active citizens in 1789–1791. Indeed, it does seem that in 1789–1815 no more than one Montipontin in two ever bothered to manifest his political will. Most surprisingly,

Laurent Servière, the Pont's own favorite son, was sent to the Convention by less than 225 votes for the district of Florac as a whole. Probably it was universal military conscription rather than universal manhood suffrage that had the largest impact on the village: sixty-five young men between the ages of eighteen and twenty-four were enrolled in the national guard, which must have been a nearly complete coverage of this particular age group.[50] More people yet were involved as relatives of the men who were drafted, and everyone also was subject to Revolutionary taxation and voluntary contributions. But there is a difference between mere involvement and active participation, and for that reason, it cannot be said that the French Revolution marks the beginning of the village's immersion in national affairs. Because of the widespread destruction during the Camisard Wars, it is in fact very likely that there was more active political participation in 1702 than in 1792.

This may in part explain the docility of the village population as a whole and the apparent ease with which the notables used the population to their own end. But here it is also necessary to say that the Revolutionaries did not ask for much positive support, especially during the heroic phase of the revolution. The most serious social sacrifice which the Montversois were asked to make was to ratify the new political order by giving out elective offices to the bourgeoisie. Laurent Servière became a deputy in Paris. His distant cousin, Jean Servière, became a departmental administrator, and in June of 1793, he was entrusted with a fairly important mission to Lunel, where he purchased grain probably in order to supply the troops which were fighting the counterrevolutionary insurgents of the northern and western Lozère.[51] At the same time, Rouvière, who had been laconically described in the ancien régime tax list as a "bourgeois," became mayor. Jean-François Boissier, at the age of twenty, was made head of the local national guard.[52] He too was a good revolutionary, and on June 24, 1793, together with 120 men, half of them from the Pont, he went to mount guard on Mont Lozère in order to intercept any fleeing royalist rebels. None of these nominations, of course were in any real sense revolutionary since all of the people involved were eminently respectable. During the Empire, when Jean Servière was named to an administrative post, the subprefect estimated that he had a private income of 2,000 francs a year, and Jean-François Boissier was even richer. With his 3,000 francs, he was admired by all: *"il jouit de l'estime et de la considération générale."* [53]

A not very painful or unusual delegation of political power was thus the first contribution of the less privileged Montipontins to the new order. Initially, very few tangible sacrifices were asked of the villagers. They did have to produce saltpeter, and on 1 Nivose, Year II, the village contributed to the war effort thirteen shirts, fifty-eight pairs of stockings, four vests, six pairs of trousers, and twenty-nine pairs of shoes.[54] Presumably, the Pont must also have contributed other things at other times, but at first it did so painlessly. We do not find between the local and departmental authorities the endless recriminations which characterize the dealings of the state with the Catholic communities to the North. Pont-de-Montvert did its duty and this duty did not appear too exacting.

The one great and conspicuous exception to this was of course the draft and military service generally. But here also it is necessary to make some social distinctions. Characteristically, the Montipontin *volontaires de l'an II* were not typical citizens at all. Once again there are good reasons to suppose that those people who answered the call of *la patrie en danger* were either rich peasants or the sons of rich peasants. The typical Montversois just watched while here, as in the case of municipal office, the rich and the better-off carried through their "revolutionary" program. Unfortunately we do not have a complete list of these volunteers; in a rather macabre way, we only know about those who were wounded or who died for the fatherland, and whose death was listed in the Etat Civil. But there are enough names to make generalization possible.

There is the case, for example, of Jean-Antoine Chapelle, the husband of Marie Roure. The Chapelles of Finiels were the richest peasants there: Antoine Chapelle's widow paid a capitation tax of twenty livres in 1789;[55] in 1793, when Jean Roure of Rieumal married Marie Chapelle, he agreed to give 500 livres to each of his brothers and sisters.[56] Interestingly enough, Jean Roure also had another stake in the Revolution, since his debt to Henri de Pelet, an *emigré*, had just been canceled.[57] There is the case also of Louis Jourdan, *Capitaine de la Compagnie no. 2 du 1er bataillon des volontaires du Département de la Lozère* who signed up on 25 Floreal, Year II: he too was atypical. The Jourdans were actually bourgeois, and his wife Elisabeth Pinet must surely have been related to the "sieur Pinet Bourgeois" since he was the only Pinet in the tax roll for 1789.[58] Jacques Allier of Frutgères was no landless peasant either. His family had been living at Frutgères for centuries, and even owned a seigneury and a farm which was leased out. Louis Molines of Villeneuve was of similar background: there were two Molines families in that hamlet in 1789, and both were listed as landowning *laboureurs* in the capitation tax roll. As for Jean Ayral, "who came home to recover . . . as appears from a certificate which was given to him on 8 Fructidor, Year III," he was the son of François Ayral, one of the most prosperous peasants in his hamlet, where in 1789 he had paid a capitation tax of fifteen livres.[59] The list can likewise be extended to include François Paris, of l'Hopital, who was the son of Jacques Paris, *laboureur* and who later married Marie Viala, also of l'Hopital, the daughter of the very prosperous Marie Viala; and Jean-François Richard "who volunteered for the armies of the Republic at the first call-up," also of landowning peasant stock, since his father François Richard was a m*énager* at Salarial, where François went home to die on 13 Vendemiaire, Year III. Even Augustin Molines, *sergent major du Pont-de-Montvert* and poorest of the lot, came from a family that owned something. He was a Molines from Villaret, and in 1825, his family owned five hectares of land there. In short, then, we know of nine Montipontins who volunteered in 1792 to defend *la patrie en danger;* of these seven were certainly related to the richest peasants of the Pont, and none of them came from a destitute family. The typical Montipontin volunteer was definitely not one of the landless poor. On the contrary, he was the son (perhaps the younger son) of the richest peasant in his hamlet. Very clearly, in military as well as in administrative matters, the Revolution at the Pont was not the handiwork of the humble, but of the rich instead, of the bourgeois and of the better-off peasants.[60]

Given the structure of participation and risks, it may therefore have been fitting and just that the people who should have reaped the greatest benefits from the Revolution should also have been the well-to-do.

As has been seen, jobs, titles and distinctions went to the local notables, who became mayors, justices of the peace, tax apportioners, and even deputies in Paris. But the most substantial rewards were of course the biens nationaux, properties confiscated by the state, usually from the Church, which were sold at very advantageous prices. At the Pont, these *biens nationaux* were quite extensive since the Knights of Malta, from which they had been taken, had owned wide tracts of pasture lands in addition to the feudal rights they held as temporal and spiritual overlord of the village.

The most sizable of these estates to be put up for sale by the state was located on the Mont-Lozère. It consisted of a farmhouse with its stable and barns and more than 100 acres of land. At first it seemed as if this property might slip out of the grasp of local peasants, rich or poor. The authorities had decided not to sell it piece by piece, which usually meant that no peasant could afford to make a bid.[61] But in this instance, the official decision must have been preceded by backstairs intrigue. It had been reached after consultations with two local "real estate experts," Martin, a member of the municipality, and François Guin, who was holding the lease to the estate. It is interesting to note that both of these men turned up as major shareholders in a cartel of rich peasants who banded together to purchase the whole lot.[62] The sale of the property in bits and pieces would have enabled all peasants, including poor ones, to pick up some land. As it was, all of this particular "national property" passed into the hands of some *gros paysans* like Antoine Guin, another former tenant of the Knights, and four other peasants who had been described in 1789 as *laboureurs* and *ménagers*. Two of the purchasers had, it is true, appeared in ancien régime tax rolls as *travailleurs,* but this term did not mean just "laborer" as witnessed by the fact that one of them, also named Antoine Guin, had paid a capitation of eight livres, which implies an income six times greater than that of a real laborer.[63]

Rich peasants had managed to corner a healthy share of the *biens nationaux* directly,[64] and they secured a good part of the rest indirectly. Two other tracts of the Knights of Malta were bought by Jean Benoit, a bourgeois of Viala, a commune fifteen miles to the east of the Pont, and by François Velay, a merchant at Florac. Together these lands were worth about 150,000 francs,[65] but they were immediately resold, those of Benoit to Jean Albaric, a well-to-do peasant, who with his son had managed to buy more than 100,000-francs worth of property,[66] and the rest to Jean Gauch, a *ménager* and landowner, and to David Pantel, a laboureur and the richest man in the hamlet of Finiels.

The most prosperous peasants of the Pont therefore could not complain that the new order had been for them ungenerous. The poor could certainly have done so, since those biens nationaux which slipped out of the reach of the rich farmers went not to their poorer colleagues but to the local bourgeoisie instead, to Jacques Filhon, a local gendarme, and to Jacques Albaric, a merchant, who bought properties in Grizac and in neighboring communes. Another bourgeois, Jean Servière, more cautious perhaps, decided to buy his *biens nationaux* secondhand, mostly from Albaric, who in turn had received them from Benoit of Viala.[67] This made for a safe number of intermediaries between the purchaser and the original owner and possible future claimant. But the largest share of bourgeois purchases went to none other than the regicide conventionnel Laurent Servière. On 22 Prairial, Year II, he bought all of the Knights of Malta's remaining pasture lands, which had been worth yearly 5,000 livres in gold before 1789, and these he purchased for 68,000 livres in assignats or paper money, worth perhaps one-tenth of their nominal value.[68] In essence, he had bought an estate for what it could yield in one year. Theoretically, of course, other people could have done the same, but Servière was able to disburse 42,500 livres only two days after the sale, and this was something that no one else at the Pont would have been able to do.

The quality of participation, the division of spoils and the very nature of the Revolutionary conflict as it was seen at Pont-de-Montvert all point to the deceptive character of Revolution in the village. Before 1789, the gravity of class cleavages at the Pont was undeniable, but ultimately village politics during the French Revolution did not revolve around the problem of social class. Hence the "unrevolutionary" consequences of that hectic decade. After 1789, there was no class lineup at the Pont on political issues. In 1793 as against 1702 the poor did not press for some action that the rich disliked. Nor were the rich of 1793 caught in that conflict of loyalties that had been theirs nine decades before when they feared and disliked the state but had also feared and disliked the poor. In 1793 it was the rich who led the struggle against the state, not the landless artisans and laborers. At this point, the lower classes either watched indifferently or followed passively.

For this reason, the politics of the village during the French Revolution took on a crazy and abstract configuration. Now the enemy was outside the Pont, not inside, and it could not strike back. The rich in 1793 could afford to be demagogic and utopian; they could afford to talk of Brutus and the Great Principles of 1789 because they were safe from the practical consequences of their inflammatory nonsense. In 1703, the rich had been faced with the obvious fact that they should hold the poor in check, for if they did not, they would themselves suffer. In 1793, however, the more incensed the poor would be about the King, the aristocracy, Pitt, and Coburg, the safer they, the rich, would be. Politics had ceased to revolve around the real problems and divisions that existed within the village community. In 1793, the enemies of the Montipontins were not other Montipontins, but other people elsewhere, in Paris perhaps, or abroad, or in the Catholic villages or the northern Lozère, but not at the Pont.

In this way and at this time a most durable discrepancy arose between political myth and actual fact, and this discrepancy is perhaps best brought out by the villagers' ambiguous attitude to the First Empire. Of course, this regime did nothing for the village in the way of education, public works, roads, or schools. It did, it is true, perpetuate the conquests of the Revolution (a more equitable tax system, no tithes, a better organized judiciary and administration). It also paid the stipends of the local clerics, Catholic and Protestants. But these advantages were really in the nature of things twenty years after the Revolution, and they pale into insignificance when offset by the weight of the blood tax.

Military conscription was terribly unpopular at the Pont. It fell on everyone; and, as has been mentioned, military zeal had never been a generalized phenomenon, even in the glorious days of the year II. Conscription was particularly galling also because, unlike death and taxes, it was in 1800 an unusual exaction. It is true that Montipontins had had some experience with this sort of thing before 1789. A few peasants had been called up during the ancien régime, and Antoine Velay had described one such incident in his Livre de Raison:

> the king ordered the soldiers should be called up in all of the kingdom. That began in 1725 and went on until 1735. Taken for the *milice* was one of the Guin sons from l'Hermet, Stephen by name, he was taken to Saint-Ambroix and from there to Marseille and Toulon where he stayed. [Also] Jacques Martin from l'Hermet. That one bought someone to take his place from Mr. Campredon, the subdelegate, for 55 *écus* worth 3 livres each.[69]

In fact, however, conscription before 1789 had been sporadic and avoidable, and the measure of the hatred that the Montversois felt for all things military is that in spite of this, the suppression totale of the *milice* had been one of the demands made in the *cahier de doléance*.[70] How much more hateful, then, the conscription of the First Empire, which was universal and far more difficult to avoid.[71]

It is of course quite true that Napoleon was not the inventor of the draft. The first of the conscripts to leave the Pont, a cavalryman, did so in the summer of 1793; and by 1799 nine men were being called up in a single year. But where the Convention and the Directory had been merely demanding, Napoleon was insatiable: four young men from the Pont were inducted yearly in 1803, 1804, and 1805. Seven more were called up in 1806; another eight in 1807;[72] and in 1812, 1813, 1814, and 1815, a dozen people must have been conscripted yearly.

Theoretically it was possible to buy one's way out of military service, and we do have a notarized contract which explains the modalities of legalized desertion. In 1812 Jean-François Servière, a merchant and a member of the ubiquitous bourgeois family of the same name, made a contract with Augustin Bonnicel of Villeneuve (who may have been a younger son, since his father was a well-to-do peasant and would hardly have agreed to let his eldest son and heir go off in this way). Servière agreed to pay 3,000 francs, a very large sum by local standards and one which even he could ill afford, since he stipulated payment in installments, at an interest of 5 percent, with houses and fields as collateral. In exchange, it was agreed that

> the said Augustin Bonnicel will voluntarily join up and agrees by this document to go as a substitute for Jean-François Servière, who has been drafted with the class of 1807, and belongs to the group of men which the Canton of Pont-de-Montvert must bring forth. Bonnicel will carry out for Servière any and all sorts of military duties in whatever army corps, and will stand in his place wherever need should be as regards his military service, and will leave the Pont from the moment that the aforesaid Jean-François Servière will be called up by the relevant military authorities.[73]

The sums involved, it was stipulated, would be paid to Augustin Bonnicel, or ghoulishly enough, to his representative or *fondé de pouvoir*.

As it happens, Bonnicel did come back, but many Montipontins did not.[74] When the ordinary young villager was called up, he had in the overwhelming number of cases no choice but to go, and his chances of coming back were not too good. In addition to the volunteers who had left the village before 1800, seventeen soldiers of the Pont died before Napoleon was finally trundled off to Saint Helena. Only two fell in battle. One conscript died at *Unskky, dans les prisons de Russie;* but most of them succumbed to fever in the military hospitals of Spain, where most Montversois recruits had been sent since the Lozère was close to the Spanish border. Eight men died in 1813 alone, in Spain and Italy, in Rome and Burgos, faraway places of which they knew nothing.[75]

The unpopularity of conscription grew rapidly. In 1804 the prefect of the Lozère had already had occasion to write about draft dodgers to the mayor of the neighboring village of Fraissinet. Many of them apparently were mutilating themselves in order not to serve, and some had recourse to a

> "widow Jourdan" who had meddled in the art of healing which she applies without sense or reason, and she has even been denounced to me for using certain potions which give false ulcers to the draftees.[76]

Flying columns were organized to catch the draft-dodging *réfractaires,* for whose capture a reward of twelve francs each was promised. Even today local tradition holds that one of the grottoes overlooking the Pont was a refuge for deserters, and it is still known as the "cave of the deserters." But the best overall index of enthusiasm here is probably the records of marriages, for married men were not subject to the draft.

91

In a normal year one could count about ten marriages at the Pont. In the three years 1810–1812, for example, twenty-six couples were united; but there were thirty-two marriages in 1813 alone; in 1814 the number fell to ten, but it went up again in 1815 to eighteen. This made for sixty marriages in three years, more than twice the normal average, and three times as many as were married in 1816–1818.[77]

Yet in spite of these things, in spite of the blood tax, in spite of the fact that the First Empire had done nothing for the village, it was not unpopular. Far from it, Montipontins approved of this regime. They had voted for it in 1800, in 1802, in 1804, and surprisingly enough they voted for it again during the Hundred Days, a period that was marked by a rise in matrimonial fervor as well as by a resounding "yes" to Benjamin Constant's *Acte additionnel aux constitutions de l'Empire*. In the canton of Pont-de-Montvert, 140 citizens went to the polls, 100 of them in the Pont itself.[78] Everyone approved, which is all the more remarkable for the fact that for once there were dissenting voices elsewhere. At Le Bleymard, the Catholic village contiguous to the northern end of Pont-de-Montvert, no one came to vote. In his report, the mayor wrote that "no one came or wanted to vote, despite the announcements and requests,"[79] and he himself did not vote. Since the Bleymardois were antimilitarists, they were quite right to abstain. *L'empire,* after all, *c'est l'épée!* But that was probably not their real motivation, and they were ultimately no more rational than their Montipontin neighbors. It was because they were good Catholics that the Bleymardois refused to support the Corsican ogre, and the coincidence of their material with their ideological interests was purely fortuitous. What matters is that by 1815 political lines in this region and at the Pont were set not on lines of social class, but on issues of ideology which could only accidentally coincide with what the villagers, and especially the poorer villagers, really wanted. In 1815, before Gambetta, before anticlericalism and the verbiage of 1848, politics at the Pont had already hardened in the irrelevant mold that we usually associate with the Third Republic.

Without a doubt, this approach to politics was the most lasting legacy of the Great Revolution at the Pont. This is not to say that the Montipontins derived no tangible gains from the upheaval of 1789. They did: public life was rationalized and their civic dignity was embodied in law. But these and other advantages would have been recognized by any viable regime after 1800, and there is for that reason a great deal that is unwarranted in the Montipontins' zealous devotion to the Principles of 1789. After all, the consequences of the reorganization of French society were not to everyone's liking, and in many ways the rank and file of the Montversois were actually deceived by those few people who really did well out of the Revolution.[80] Who was it that had been drafted and who was it that had gotten the state jobs? And the irony of it all comes out in the fate of those *biens nationaux* which the Montagnard *conventionnel* Servière had bought in 1795. Servière died in 1799 and most of his property was inherited by an illegitimate daughter who married one of Servière's friends, Marcellin Collomb of Les Vans, a town in the Ardèche, in whose family the lands remained for some generations. But in his small way Collomb had already made his mark on history. In 1783, there had been a series of riots in the Ardèche; the *commandant de la ville,* a Monsieur de Dampmartin, was not particularly hostile to the rebels. He knew conditions were bad:

> It is necessary to admit first of all that the first and only causes of the difficulties which took place in 1783 are the misery of the times, the lack of harvests, and the legalistic turn of mind which rules in these parts, as well as the behaviour of the procurators and businessmen who have managed to get rich at the expense of the peasants.[81]

Still, since the rioters had broken into the village and pillaged the houses of the most notorious procurators, "Chambon, Lahondès, et Colomb," they would have to be punished. They were broken on the wheel, before a crowd of 6,000.

> All of the spectators looked sad and dismayed, (but) the procurators and the businessmen from the city who had gone to the place in very great numbers looked quite satisfied.[82]

How unjust therefore that in the end it was this same *procureur* Colomb who became as the heir of Servière the greatest beneficiary at the Pont of a Revolution that had been carried forth or at least supported by the same sort of people whose demise he had cheerfully witnessed only six years before in 1789.

Some consolation it is true can be gotten from the fact that, ultimately, the properties of the Servière-Collombs passed through marriage to a noble-Catholic family, the De Rouvilles, who were active in reactionary Lozerian politics during the Third Republic. Foreknowledge of this unusual sequence might have annoyed Collomb and it would certainly have distressed Servière, the *philosophe-régicide.* But even an awareness of this dismay would have been little consolation for those peasants of Pont-de-Montvert who had wanted these lands for themselves; and it would have been very small consolation indeed for the Montipontine soldiers of Napoleon who died far away in Rome, in Burgos, or *dans les prisons de Russie.*

CHAPTER V   The Breakup of Social Structure

During the eighteenth century the social structure of the Pont did not change much from what it had been at the end of the Camisard Wars. In fact, its increasing rigidity during these decades stands in contrast to the flux that had characterized it during the second half of the seventeenth century. It might of course be argued that the absence of change was in itself a change. Before 1700, Pont-de-Montvert had been constantly growing, shrinking, or adapting itself to new situations. This was not so true of subsequent years, and the stability of the eighteenth century could be seen as an omen of eventual decline. But this fact should not be overemphasized, and one can point to the village's successful absorption of a rising population in the last decades of the ancien régime as a proof of its sustained vitality. From 1700 to 1789 the Pont may not have been as exuberant a community as it had been earlier, but it was still vigorous.

It is not necessary, however, to draw subtle distinctions about the social structure of Pont-de-Montvert in the nineteenth century. The evidence is there for all to see: it collapsed. By 1914, the Pont was a mere shadow of what it had been a century or so before. On the face of it, this did not seem to be so. In 1913 there were still 1,055 people living in the village, about as many as had been there in 1700. But in spite of this, in the age of Loubet and Fallières the whole social and moral structure of the village had already been largely destroyed. In 1900 the Pont was slowly bleeding to death. Since its demographic decline was a consequence and not a cause of this decline, charts of births and deaths are nothing more than a barometer; but they do give us the most obvious proof of the great catastrophe. During the eighteenth century (with only a brief decline in the 1740s) the village population had at first remained steady and then risen sharply. It appears to have fallen somewhat in the 1780s [1] but it rose steadily after that until 1820. Economically, the next twenty years were times of hardship for many Montipontins, and the demographic curve registered that as well. But the village population grew again in the 1840s and 1850s, and at such a steep rate that there can have been very little emigration in these years. The year 1870 was the high-water mark of population growth and the end of an era. The rate of increase had already been slackening in the 1860s, but after 1870 the decline was rapid and nearly unbroken. There were 1,590 Montipontins in 1871, 1,558 in 1877, 1,405 in 1887, 1,287 in 1892, 1,102 in 1907, and 1,055 in 1913.

Emigration was largely responsible for this abrupt loss of one-third of the total in less than fifty years since birth control was probably not practiced in a general way until the 1860s. Before that date, the birth rate in the village stood at approximately 3.3 births per marriage per year.[2] In the 1830s it was set at 3.2; at 3.6 in the 1850s, 3.1 in the 1860s, and 3.4 in the 1870s. In the 1880s, however, the figure falls to 2.7, and in the ten years which preceded the first World War, it sank even lower to 2.3. Clearly, Malthusian practices were contributing to the decline in population of the village, and at an increasing rate; but emigration was by far the most serious and fatal cause of the village's gradual demise.

Paradoxically, one of the causes of the drop in population was prosperity. At first glance, this appears illogical, since it might be expected that the villagers would stay when local wages were high and leave when they could find no work at home. Indeed, this is precisely what happened to the poorest of the village artisans during the 1820s and 1830s when it had become impossible for them to earn their living at the Pont. But in the second half of the century, and especially during the four decades before the Great War, Montipontins emigrated to the mining areas of the Gard, to Marseilles, or Paris not because they were starving at the Pont (wages there were higher than they had ever been) but because they could do so much better for themselves elsewhere. Prosperity at the Pont did not arrest emigration because the new well-being there was largely a reflection of an even greater prosperity beyond the bounds of the village. Wages did rise at Pont-de-Montvert, but only because they had risen more elsewhere, and it made sense to leave.

Emigration and the rise in wages had widespread social consequences in the village. Until the middle of the nineteenth century, the *gros paysans* who needed labor had gotten it on the cheap as they were then competing only with each other. But when the horizon of the poor expanded beyond the limits of the village, the *gros paysans* found that they were now facing not just the Montipontin poor, but the rich everywhere in France. This was an unequal fight. Fortunately (or unfortunately depending on one's point of view) the wealth of *gros paysans* did not progress apace with the wealth of the nation; and the whole social and economic pyramid of Montipontin life, based on inexpensive and plentiful labor, began to sag. Deference, hierarchy, and exploitation: all of these things had presupposed that the rich would be able to squeeze the poor at will. But this was increasingly not the case after 1850. The rising prosperity of the poorest villagers pointed to the end of the village as it had existed for centuries past. It stands therefore as the principal index of social upheaval at the Pont in the nineteenth century.

The betterment of life was all the more deeply felt at Pont-de-Montvert because the starting point had been so very low. In this the village was not unlike other places in the Massif Central, whose poverty had already been mythologized before 1789; Louis-Sébastien Mercier was already appealing to established clichés when he composed his classic description of the Auvergnat, who were, he thought

> like those birds which frost drives to warmer climates. These people flee from the snows that cover the mountains of Auvergne for eight months of the year. The man goes back every year to make his wife pregnant, and leaves her in the hands of old women and of the *curé* while he goes around the kingdom without any fixed domicile.
>
> Each Auvergnat, on the average, brings back four or five louis to his sad homeland. The ten-year-old has earned two louis; they sew them in the belt of their breeches, and children beg along the way.
>
> These hordes have traveled like this since Julius Ceasar, and even before that.[3]

By 1800, however, most Montipontins had a *domicile fixe* and few of them would send their children begging along the king's highway. Some of the old ways did remain, it is true. In 1817 the prefect of the Lozère reported that there were communes in the department where mendicity was a trade, *un moyen d'industrie,* and that there were to his knowledge at least forty or fifty people who owned property but emigrated to beg anyway.[4] At the Pont, however, not much of that was left by the 1820s. In 1809 a prefectoral report indicated that in a population of 1318, there were only fifty-five poor people and four professional beggars (the commune at this point allocated a yearly sum of fifty-three francs twenty-three centimes for the relief of these people and the creation of a departmental poorhouse or *dépôt de mendicité*).[5] Admittedly, more than half a century later, in 1864, the prefect could still report that the number of beggars grew "as winter sets in,"[6] but there are reasons to suppose that beggary was not a serious problem at the Pont even in the earlier decades of the nineteenth century. It was an economic rather than a cultural phenomenon; and economically the lot of the poor by and large has not ceased to improve in the village from 1850 to our own day. Wages are the best indication of this rise in status. In the 1780s landless laborers could expect to make about thirty sous a day—women could earn two-thirds of that, one franc—but of course they could only expect so high a wage for the few months from March or April to August or September.[7] On the eve of the Revolution, in the Lozère the average annual income of a farmhand who received room and board was still little more than 100 francs. In 1853 that had already gone up to 163 francs and in 1871 to 225 francs. At that same time in the 1870s, it was estimated that in the Lozère a weaver could earn two francs a day, or about 600 a year, if he worked endlessly and managed to sell his stuff.[8] Wages at the Pont must have followed a parallel course, and we do have some figures for the village itself. In 1894 during the harvest season, a worker at the Pont received nearly three francs a day; in 1913, a female *domestique* hired from March 1 to September 30 was paid 145 francs in addition to her room and board. By 1914 wages had reached an even more stupendous level. During the harvest, a reaper could ask and receive four francs a day.[9] Wages had doubled in fifty years, quadrupled in a century. Never since the beginning of time had the Pont seen anything like this.

This prosperity had many beneficial effects, not the least of which was the improvement in hygiene and health. Here, the role of the state was as important as the greater well-being of the citizenry. In 1812, for example, the prefect urged all public officials and priests to avail themselves

> of all their prestige and of the means of persuasion which they derive from their function to extend and fortify the trust which should be placed in the use of vaccination.[10]

By 1814 much had been done, and the prefect remarked that parents themselves inoculated their children, and in 1835, when a single case of smallpox broke out at the Pont it occasioned an exchange of views between the mayor and the subprefect.[11] The height and health of conscripts also improved. In 1830 in the canton of Pont-de-Montvert, no more than one-third of the potential draftees were rejected as unfit. The average height of those retained was five feet four, only one inch less than the average for 1930 and a clear improvement over 1792, when only one adult male in seven had been that tall.[12]

The villagers were more healthy and the village itself became a more pleasant place to be in. In 1837 a new Protestant temple was dedicated.[13] In 1839, the village received a post office [14] and it had already purchased a clock. In 1831, *Monsieur le Maire* having made an appeal through official channels about this timepiece,[15] *Monsieur le Ministre* in Paris shortly afterwards graciously agreed to approve this municipal expense. Some years later, in the 1850s, the Pont also received a new Catholic church to replace the old one which had been described by the local *curé* as

> a sad hovel, buried beneath the ground, obscure, stuffy, humid, and, in a word, unworthy of the majesty of Him who deigns to reside there for the love of men.[16]

The tempo of construction was very great, and by the end of the century, one could find at the Pont new schools, new roads, new churches, and even a public fountain.

The diet of the villagers themselves also reflected the wave of prosperity. Chestnuts were now far less important than they had been. In 1852 it had already been noted that this crop was increasingly neglected at the Pont, where the chestnut harvests were declared "detestable"; [17] and in 1905 a member of the Conseil Général from neighboring Saint-Germain-de-Calberte went so far as to claim that it had become uneconomic to gather the nuts. "Chestnuts have so fallen in price," he claimed, "that in many places the value of the harvest does not cover the cost of gathering it." [18] Everyone at the Pont was affected by the new well-being, and echoes of it can be found in the family accounts of the Chapelles and Molines which have come down to us. In his summing up on July 11, 1911, for example, Armand Molines made a list of all the unusual delicacies he had just been able to purchase. "We have just brought back from Fraissinet," he wrote, "a box of sugar, one tomato, two pounds of macaroni, and a piece of chocolate." [19] As for Chapelle, in December of 1907 he found himself so well moneyed that he felt able actually to buy some furniture. His life was becoming nothing less than sybaritic, and in 1913 with the same careful Third Republican hand in which he had noted the sale of oxen and the wages of his shepherd, he too recorded for the month of June the purchase of *"une boîte de sucre et une pièce de chocolat."* [20] Both Chapelle and Molines now began to buy great quantities of wine, with a first purchase of nearly thirty quarts in 1883. Many other Montipontins followed suit. In the eighteenth century wine had been a luxury. In fact it had been *the* luxury that absorbed whatever cash was left after necessities had been purchased, and when the prosperity of the

The town clock.

Pont rose, oenophilia grew apace. There were three innkeepers or *cabaretiers* at the Pont in 1701.[21] None were listed in the tax rolls of the 1780s on the eve of the Revolution, when the profession may have been entered simply as *marchand* (for *marchand de vins*).[22] By 1852, however, these men had come out under their own colors. There were no less than twelve of them—two *aubergistes*, three *cafetiers*, and six *cabaretiers*, a sure sign that there was a market for the precious liquid from the south.[23]

What were the economic bases of the new prosperity? Obviously, to begin with, higher wages elsewhere. Now that urban France provided a market for labor, Pont-de-Montvert entered into the national circuit even if it had to do so backwards and against its will. But in addition to this negative factor, we can also point to some positive ones as well. Of some consequence here were the disappearance of artisan and textile trades (which had supported the poorest elements alive in the village where they depressed local wages); the rationalization of agriculture; and the reversal of the flow of money which in the eighteenth century had drained the village of specie for the benefit of the state and the owners of the tithe.

As for the Lozerian cloth trade, it had already been in a bad way on the eve of the ancien régime. Much of what was made here was low quality cloth, *escots, serges, et cadis* and most of it was exported: "Almost all of the cloth is carried to foreign countries, which is to say, Italy, the Levant, Switzerland, Germany, Spain, Sicily and Malta.[24] Increasingly, however, the local weavers found themselves unable to compete for this trade, either against foreign merchants or against the more mechanized producers of the south and southwest. In 1773 a merchant of La Canourgue, a town to the west of the Pont, wrote that

> our trade, the soul of this region, is being hounded, it has fallen without anyone's condescending to extend to it a helping hand. The sales of woolens which I make force me to attend our markets, which are nothing. Marvejols has no more orders. The Rouergue has taken everything.[25]

For various reasons, not the least of which being that the rough woolens of the region were suitable for military uniforms, the area managed to hold on after 1789 although it had been stagnating or even declining before that.[26] But the end of the empire was also the beginning of the end for Lozerian weavers and carders. In 1810 the price of wool in the Lozére was set at 2.55 francs a kilo. Although it fell to two francs during the hard times of 1811, it had worked its way up again to 2.35 francs in 1815; but after this, its decline was practically uninterrupted. When the wool trade fell off, so did demand, and so did the price of wool which sank to 1.35 francs in 1828.[27] In 1832 an observer wrote that in the Lozére

> artisans and woolen weavers have fallen into a frightful misery. This nation of workers, who used to be clean and even elegant in its attire, today no longer buys anything ... I have seen unemployed young women, poorly dressed, in danger of sacrificing their honor to their needs.[28]

By 1856, it could be said that the Lozerian cloth trade was dead:

> the woolen industry is extinct today, and it is progress which killed it. Indeed, after Jacquard's invention, what could befall the ancient weaver's loom, the hereditary tool of poor families? And after the invention of the Jenney's mule, what are we to do with our spinners' wheels?[29]

What was true of the region was true of the Pont as well. In 1795 more than sixty people in the canton, and more than forty in the village, were weavers, carders or hat makers.[30] In the 1840s, that had fallen by more than one-half.[31] In 1795, there had been eleven hat makers in the canton; in 1846, at the Pont, there were only two left.[32] One of them survived until 1890, but at that date there were all in all, besides him, only one carder and two weavers, all of them rather superannuated types.[33]

To some degree, the decline of the old artisan trades was compensated by an increase in occupations connected with services. By the end of the century, there was, it is true, an expansion in the number of bakers, smithies, tailors, and cobblers as well as of the ubiquitous greengrocers, the small town *épiciers*. But this was a fragile base since it was doomed to fail as soon as communications improved. When Montipontins found that they could buy cheap shoes at Alès, they gave up buying expensive ones at the Pont. In any case, this second wave of artisan trades did not begin to pick up speed until the middle of the century, whereas the old cloth trades collapsed in the 1820s and 1830s. This must surely explain the population decline of that period. There were 1,451 Montversois in 1814, and 1,471 in 1821, but only 1,405 five years later; and an "intercyclical" low was reached in 1841 with 1,372 inhabitants.

Thus in the first third of the century the very poor left the commune, which no longer had the vitality sufficient to absorb them. Their departure was not an unmitigated loss and may even have been a positive blessing since their presence had occasioned both the depression of wages and the high price of grain, two factors which, in turn, had acted as a deterrent to agricultural innovation. Why should the *gros paysans* have bothered with better methods when labor was cheap and when grain could be sold at any price? But now that the poor had begun to leave there was more of an incentive to ameliorate, to rationalize, and especially to take advantage of the opportunities presented by outside markets.

Of course, these changes took place very gradually, but, in spite of this, they did eventually engender a wholesale restructuring of Montipontin agriculture. The details of this conversion are not easy to trace as there are no "hard" statistics before 1880. It appears nonetheless that improvements in techniques were not the crucial aspect of the issue since the yield of the land continued to be on the eve of the First World War much what it had been one hundred years before. More fundamental were the decline in the acreage of land used to grow crops (mostly rye); a decrease in the number of sheep; and, most important, an increase in the number of cattle. More and more, Pont-de-Montvert came to specialize in the fattening of animals which were later sold in the industrial areas of the Gard. In 1833 Jean Boissier, the Pont's leading citizen, had described this trade which he dated back to 1800:

> For the last thirty years or so, the peasants of our mountains have taken to going to the fairs of Cantal from the month of October on. There, in the neighborhood of Aurillac, they buy young bulls which they drive homewards. They train them for labor, they castrate them, and in September these same bulls are sold in the fairs of Vigan, Villefort, and Barre.[34]

Boissier estimated that the Pont's share of this trade came to about 20,000 francs, a sizable sum, which represented a seventh of the village's prerevolutionary income. In the past, the Pont had had a negative balance of trade since it imported grain. Now it found that it produced a valuable commodity, indeed, an increasingly valuable one since the price of cattle rose steadily at the end of the eighteenth century, a pair of oxen could fetch 200 francs, as against 120 thirty years before, and at the end of the empire the price of these animals reached between 500 and 700 francs. By midcentury, the trade was well established. In 1852, the sale of cattle, with that of wool, had become the village's largest source of specie,[35] and in that same year, the prefect of the Lozère reported that a fall in prices due to the importation of cattle from Algeria was much resented in his bailiwick since the sale of these animals was the department's "principal production."[36]

Grain was worth less, and oxen were worth more. The obvious and rational course was to switch from rye to cattle, and this is indeed what happened. The trend was probably well under way by 1800, but it was still visible at the end of the nineteenth century when we can begin to trace it precisely. Between 1888 and 1908, the acreage of rye fell from 1,200 to 750 acres; that of wheat collapsed altogether from 100 to only five acres, and the Pont would never again be the grain factory that it had been before the Revolution. The number of sheep also fell dramatically during these years, from 4,300 in 1891 to 1,000 in 1903 and only a few hundred before the World War.[37] The number of cattle, however, followed an inverse course. It declined slightly in absolute numbers[38] from 778 in 1891 to 610 in 1925, but it must be remembered that in these same years, the population of the village fell by nearly one-half.[39] The number of cows *per capita* had risen sharply, and this remains the most conspicuous aspect of the rationalization of economic life in these years.

Gradually, through emigration, competition with outside entrepreneurs for local labors, and the rationalization of agriculture, Pont-de-Montvert was imperceptibly but surely becoming a more prosperous and less isolated place. From year to year, no one would have noticed the changes that were taking place but they did have a most visible symbol, the roads. In the past, it had been very difficult to go in and out of Pont-de-Montvert. Nor does it seem that Montipontins were much depressed by this state of affairs. If no one needed them, neither did they before 1800 need anyone else. But such was far from the case after that, and during the nineteenth century demands for more and better roads became increasingly frequent.

Theoretically, there had always been some roads, and during the Camisard Wars, as has been said, a real effort had been made to construct better means of communications suitable for artillery. In 1728 we even find a mention of a royal road, a *chemin royal,* which linked Pont-de-Montvert with the southeast.[40] How royal these roads really were is, however, unclear. At certain times and in certain places some of them may have been accessible to ox-drawn carts, especially on the flat plateaus of the Mont Lozère. But as a rule the ascent and descent from the plateaus must have been trying exercises even for men and mules.

This was all the more probably so for the fact that the upkeep of roads was very erratic. Funds were occasionally allocated to widen these paths so that merchandise could be brought to the village in ox-drawn carts as well as on muleback.[41] But the size of the sums involved (never more than a few hundred francs) and the repeated complaints of disgruntled travelers are sufficient proof that communications before 1815 were very primitive. In 1796, the ex-deputy Servière himself recognized this and wrote to Paris that

> the main roads and the municipal ones also have been, I repeat, completely degraded and will become unusable if they are not soon repaired.[42]

Nor was much more done during the First Empire. In May of 1814, when the prefect was told by Paris that he should have the imperial eagles erased from the road markers, he replied that this was not a cause for concern: "Since there are at the moment no road markers at all on the highways of the department, there is no need to carry out this measure." And what was true of the road markers was in large part true for the very roads themselves. As late as 1840 a prefectoral report claimed that even the most important transversal roads like the Mende-to-Villefort highway were impracticable to vehicles of any sort, so that all traffic, including the shipping of wine from the Ardèche, was done on muleback. The same prefect had high hopes for what would come with the new roads. The inhabitants of the northern slope of the Mont Lozère (the Pont is on the southern slope) would henceforth find it easier to carry on their trade

> with more security, and since the new road is not very far from their homes, they will be able to improve their lot and better cultivate their lands.[43]

His optimism was not unfounded as regarded the inhabitants of both the northern and southern sides of the mountain.

After 1840 there was a quickening in the tempo of road building, as there had been for building churches, schools, post offices, and other amenities of bourgeois life. It was given great impulse during the Second Empire, when the locals became nearly shameless with their insistent demands. The municipal council submitted plans which provided for the construction of seventy-four kilometers of roads within the communes, only thirteen of which had yet been completed. These were stiff requirements, but the councillors had high hopes. After all, could it not be said that

> In its constant solicitude for the population of the empire, the government of the Emperor seeks out all possible means to improve the lot of the people and wishes to place it within easy reach of communication? [44]

By 1890 the work was completed, and all the roads which exist today had by then been essentially constructed, and some of them were paved.[45] In fact, it seems that traffic could at times become dense, indeed hectic. In 1906 this very problem even occasioned the resignation of eight municipal councillors. Very sensibly, after the spate of road building, *Monsieur le Maire* decided to change the site of the weekly market. "Velocipedes and automobiles are all using the new road," he argued, "and this could start a panic among the animals." His colleagues, however, did not agree. They were firm in their stand and the prefect's representative who had been sent to report on the situation was forced to conclude that no solution could be found to bridge

> the disagreement that has arisen between the mayor and themselves as regards the municipal order which has relocated the market where cows used to be put on display.[46]

Yet even those councillors who sulked in their tent would not have doubted the usefulness of the new roads, which, like the schools, town clock, and fountains, were conspicuous symbols of the Pont's new prosperity. Nor were these signs deceptive, for Pont-de-Montvert was

104

in fact incomparably better off than it had ever been before. It had more money, and less was taken from it by the powers that be. Its wealth had risen but its taxes and impositions had actually fallen. At the same time, it could now count in its midst a great many people who were paid by the state. In 1890 one could find there one Protestant minister, one Catholic priest, four male and two female school teachers, three *cantonniers*, two tax collectors, one forest guard, three policemen, and two postmen, all of them paid by the state.[47] These twenty-odd people brought into the village far more money than the state took out, and much of this money was spent locally inasmuch as nearly all of the people involved were native Montipontins who improved their houses, bought more food, and generally intensified the economic life of the place by creating a market for local foodstuffs and labor. For centuries, the state had bled the Pont; now the Pont was beginning to live at the expense of the state.

In view of all this, it would seem paradoxical to assert as we have done that the village structure of Pont-de-Montvert collapsed in these same decades. Yet, that is indeed what happened; and, as has been pointed out, the phenomena of decay and prosperity are not unconnected. To begin with, greater national prosperity and the emigration of the poor from the village presented immediate problems for an agricultural system that was inefficient, labor intensive, and wasteful. Indirectly also, emigration and the integration of the Montipontin economy affected the value of land. As the pressure of population fell and as wages rose, land as such ceased to have the intrinsic value that it had had, since it was now valuable only if it could be used and only if it was economically feasible to use it, given the cost of labor and competition from more fertile areas. A farmer who owned a medium-size farm of reasonable quality was now better off than the *gros paysan* who owned wide tracts of marginal lands. Before, land had been the essence of all things: there were those who owned it and those who did not. But now, matters were more complicated. There were those who knew how to use it, and those who did not. There were farmers who would learn how to raise and fatten cattle for the market and there were also their obstinate and old-fashioned neighbors who would persist in eking out a miserable living by growing rye. In itself, land was becoming less valuable than expertise, and the price of real estate declined very rapidly. In the 1850s, a hectare of pasture land went for about 1,400 francs.[48] In the first decade of the twentieth century, land anywhere in the Lozère could not be sold for more than 900 francs a hectare when a half-century before the average price per hectare of first grade land had been 3.348 francs.[49] In these same years, moreover the wage of an *instituteur* went up from 700 to 2,200 francs, just as everyone else's wages went up then. Land was therefore falling in value absolutely, relatively, and by any conceivable standard.

In consequence, the hierarchy of peasant life was truncated at the bottom and at the top. There were far fewer people at the bottom of the scale (only five tenant farmers in 1890, for a population of about 1,300); and at the other end, at the top, the *gros paysans* were becoming perceptibly less *gros*. Unlike the poor and, as we shall see, unlike the bourgeoisie, they did not leave *en masse* during these years. They had a tangible stake in village society and they meant to keep it. But through no fault of their own, this stake shrank before them inexorably and unavoidably.

The economic havoc wrought by emigration and the integration of the Pont in a national market probably would of themselves have laid low the old village social structure, but its decline was accelerated by yet other factors: the spread of education, and the indoctrination of the villagers in Jules Ferry's schools. Of course, schools had not been unknown in the Pont before the Third Republic. Certainly, there had been schoolmasters in the village even before the French Revolution. There are specific mention of *maître d'écoles* in the 1700s at Grizac,[50] and at Grizac again we hear in 1736 of a *maître des petites écoles*. The local ministers before 1685, and the *curés* after that, were also expected to teach at least some children how to read. Indeed, the first nation-wide measures regarding primary education in the seventeenth century were designed specifically to encourage the Catholic clergy to take over the education of children in formerly Protestant villages, and presumably something of that existed in the Pont as well.[51] But still it is very likely that before 1815 children were taught by their own parents insofar as they were taught at all. That is what we know existed at the end of the First Empire and it must also have been so before that.

This dearth of public or even of general education was a conservative and stabilizing social force. Inevitably, very few children learned very much, and those that did came from the village's more prosperous families. Education was a precious quantity, and like land it was passed from father to son. The poor were excluded from this circuit as well, although it is difficult to say where exactly lay the social boundary between the literate and the illiterate. Calculations here are based on an examination of birth and death records, and there is no continuous series for the eighteenth century. For the village as a whole, however, it can be estimated that in 1685, little more than one woman in ten could sign her name, although nearly half of the adult males could do so, a very high figure for the times, due perhaps to a Protestant tradition of Bible reading.[52] One century later, in the 1780s, the figure had risen a little further yet for men, although the proportion of literate women had not changed. Far more interesting than these overall figures, however, are statistics for each social class since literacy varied enormously from one social stratum to the next. In the 1680s, practically all of the poor were uneducated, but all of the notables were able to sign, read, and probably write as well. Some of the letters and accounts of the late seventeenth century have come down to us (namely, the letters of Pons and Servière, the records of notaries, the diary of Antoine Velay). These documents were obviously written by men who were used to writing and to writing intelligibly. Literacy was not so widespread among the women of the notable class, it is true, since only half of them could sign, but then it must be remembered that female literacy in 1680 was practically nonexistent in the lower class. Without a doubt, in the 1680s intellectual knowledge was one of the more conspicuous possessions of the rich, and this did not change until the middle of the nineteenth century.

The years of the French Revolution did not see an improvement in the quality or quantity of education. Admittedly, the new legislators were in this respect filled with good intentions, but it must be said that they had very little to work with.[53] Not surprisingly, the great debates on the fundamental issues of education that were taking place in Paris during this time had only muted echoes in the Lozère. In fact it is difficult to avoid the conclusion that on balance the efforts of the Revolutionary legislators only succeeded in wrecking what little had been accomplished before 1789. The emigration of the local clergy, both Catholic and Protestant, may have been politically desirable, but it was educationally disastrous. To counterbalance this in the regional capital of Mende, a secondary school was eventually created, but this was a unique endeavor, and in any case one that failed rapidly. Servière, who had exchanged his mandate as deputy for the post of departmental administrator, explained that the decline of this experiment in republican character building had been due to "ignorance, prejudice, fanaticism, and the indifference or aversion which is felt for the Republican government, the influence of priests."[54] When it was observed in the Year VI that there were more professors than students, the school was shut down. This left no secondary school at all in the region that Montipontin children could attend unless their parents were willing to defray the costs of their travels and education in Nîmes or Montpellier, and there is no indication that such was ever the case. Moreover, primary education also declined at this time. In the Year VI again, Servière observed that public education of any sort was practically nonexistent in the department. None of the cantons had a primary school, and whatever teaching was being done was in the hands of private instructors.[55]

For the period of the empire, we have conflicting reports, but it does seem that from 1800 on, there have always been some schools in the commune. In 1813, it is true, the prefect wrote that "primary education is practically nonexistent in the department"[56] (this same phrase recurs as a leitmotiv in the administrative reports of the whole period), but we know that in 1809, at least, there were at least four primary schoolteachers at the Pont. Since two of them indicated *cultivateur* as their previous profession, and one of them was described as "without talent—teaches only in the winter," we can perhaps question the devotion of both these men to the life of the mind.[57] But the important thing is that they existed, even though their pronunciation of French was said to be poor and although the highest marks which either of them received was a very tepid *"assez intelligent."* The curriculum in their schools consisted of reading and the "first elements of calculation". One of the pedagogues also declared that he would be willing to become a member of the newly founded imperial university.

The fall of Napoleon marks a break in the history of primary education at Pont-de-Montvert. Until then, it had had its ups and downs, but henceforth it would become ever more a reality and a subject of concern. In 1816, already, an administrator at Florac observed that education was everywhere being revived in his district.[58] In his view the only problem was that no one wanted to pay for it. Although school fees were not very large (the best of the Pont's four teachers charged two and one-half francs per pupil per year), it must be remembered that the Cévennes were a very poor place. In 1821, for example, a prefectoral report suggested that Pont-de-Montvert was populous enough to warrant the hiring of two full-time primary school teachers, but went on to add that the villagers were hardly likely to pay for it:

> the inhabitants are too poor and have too much to do during eight months of the year to pay the school teachers and to devote enough time to the education of their children.[59]

It was in the same spirit that the mayor of the Pont, when asked at this time how many schools his commune was planning to build, replied "zero, for lack of resources."[60] Since the state showed no inclination to make up for the villagers' inability to pay, progress, it can be surmised, came slowly.

It was for this reason perhaps, that in 1823, a "free and charitable committee" was founded at the Pont to encourage primary education. It soon had to report that unfortunately it had not achieved anything at all; but the fact that the four richest men of the village (two of them notaries) were members of the committee shows perhaps at least an awareness of the problem.[61] And by 1831 something *had* been done. There were now sixty full-time students, and even during the snow-bound winter, thirty of them attended regularly. (Not all of them came from the Pont, since the school was technically supposed to accept students from three other communes, but the distances were such that most of the pupils by far must have been native to the village.) The schoolteacher received a subsidy of 120 francs from the town, and there was even a move to open a special and separate school for girls.

Henceforth, the problem would no longer hinge on the existence of schools but on their quality instead. Admittedly, the schoolteachers were now there, but what did the pupils learn from them? Not very much, it seems. It is likely that the novelist Ferdinand Fabre exaggerated when he wrote in 1875 that teachers in the country areas were often the physically incapable scions of rich peasants who saw in teaching a career appropriate to the organically crippled, but it was true that in this period, education certainly was not an attractive or prestigious trade and this reflected on the quality of education.[62] In his report to Cuvier, the subprefect of Florac noted that

> since the career of education offers here so few advantages, school-teachers do not give themselves the trouble, and are not willing to pay to perfect themselves according to the regulations. Teaching is always done in an old fashioned way . . . and children take from two to three years in order to learn, very badly, to read and write.[63]

Another problem was posed by the fly-by-night schools which were opened during the winter months, no doubt by former *cultivateurs*. Since the local notables were keen on education, they did not shut them down, but it was disturbing that much of the schooling was being meted out by

> incapable teachers, who have taken up with the worst methods of education and in consequence are hardly suited to spread knowledge in these parts; but in the absence of better resources, we are afraid that shutting down these schools, however imperfect they may be, would harm the future of our families.[64]

By the time of Guizot's famous education law of 1833, much therefore had already been done at the Pont, but much also left something to be desired. Clearly, the villagers' interest in the matter had preceded the enactment of national legislation, but there were gaps that remained to be filled and these were described at some length in the detailed report on schools that was drawn up in connection with the passage of Guizot's bill. The zeal of one school master was described as deficient, and, in a word, *"triste."* Another unfortunate pedagogue, who incidentally did come from a well-to-do peasant family, was said to have no qualifications at all, beyond that of getting along with the Protestant minister. He had never been to a normal or teacher's training school, he did his job very badly, and even his conduct was *pas trop régulière.* The report is also particularly interesting in that it indicates that only ten of the sixty pupils did not pay the school fees, which shows quite clearly that education in 1830 was still, as it had always been before, the prerogative of the local bourgeois and of the richer peasants. Moreover, education was no more disruptive intellectually than it was socially, since most of the reading was done out of the Bible, the New Testament and the Psalms. Nothing else was taught there, not even, as had been true in 1809, "the basic elements of calculation." [65]

This state of affairs certainly did not disappear overnight. But gradually, during the next four decades, the intellectual content and social extent of education continued to develop. In 1835 the wage of the official communal *instituteur* or schoolteacher had already gone up to 400 francs a year, which was a respectable sum for Pont-de-Montvert.[66] Unofficial schools continued to thrive (one of them was run by the wife of a former *instituteur*), but the official ones began to outstrip their rivals since they now began to receive official subsidies. Indeed, it is in connection with this that we find the first direct lobbying of a ministry by a deputy on behalf of the village. Admittedly, Meynadier's plea at the ministry of the interior only brought to the village a subsidy of one hundred francs "for the furniture of the school" [67] but the sum by local standards was not a negligible one, and the precedent is striking. Official schools were henceforth located in better locales, and the quality of teaching also rose. After 1839, as was pointed out by the sub-prefect to the mayor, schoolteachers would be eligible for a subsidy if they decided to come to Mende *"pour perfectionner leur instruction et leur méthode d'enseignement,"* [68] and in 1856, this same official estimated that in his district, sixty-six of the eighty-eight schoolteachers were *capable.* Admittedly, only two were *distingués* (in what sense of the word we do not know), but then only three of them were "distinctly feeble." [69] In fact, most of the teachers at the Pont were by now reasonably competent and far more sophisticated than their predecessors of Napoleonic times. When they were not, and if the standards of teaching declined, the villagers would themselves complain, something which would have been quite unthinkable even twenty or thirty years before.[70]

By the 1860s most of the work had been done, and just as it would be wrong to think that the Guizot law of 1833 had marked the beginning of primary education at the Pont, so would it be wrong to think that it was the Ferry laws of the 1880s that made primary schooling a concrete reality. Certainly, for a long time the physical plant remained very rudimentary. The girls' schoolteacher, for example, complained that access to her classroom led through her husband's bedroom; this was, she thought, an inconvenient arrangement and one that would not be suitable for another schoolmistress.[71] But the important thing was not that her school had been so haphazardly set up; a more just sentiment would be that of Dr. Johnson on hearing a woman preach, amazement that it had been done at all. Henceforth, there would be schools for girls and schools in the outlying hamlets.[72] More money would now be earmarked for teachers' salaries and in 1859 no less than 2,490 francs was set aside for that purpose.[73] After 1856 books and paper were also given to the poorer students, and in 1859 Ernest Atger, a native of Grizac, received a scholarship that enabled him to further his classical studies at Marvejols.[74]

Much had been done for the Pont by Napoleon III and his minister of education, Duruy, and it is only because their expectations had risen so quickly that Montipontins could dare to think that more yet should be done for their schools. For they did think this, and one of the first acts of the new and republican municipal council of 1871 was to request that "free primary education should be given to all of the children of the commune."[75] Nor were the Montversois to be disappointed, as the Third Republic proved to be very generous in this respect. In 1877, the prefect himself requested that a dossier should be drawn up to study the possibility of building five new schools; and in 1880 the Republic gave to the commune the huge sum of 35,000 francs for that very purpose. By 1882, one could find schools not just at the bourg, but in Grizac, Finiels, Prat Soubeyran and Villeneuve as well. The apotheosis of the whole process came in 1895 when the mayor dedicated the new school buildings of the bourg itself, and this most imposing *groupe scolaire* survives to our own day as a reminder of the Third Republic's and Pont-de-Montvert's belief in the amelioration of man through knowledge and industry.

Important as this great spate of building was in and of itself, it derives its real significance from the fact that it was the visible symbol of a great intellectual revolution. Education before had been a privilege. Now it was a right, so that, roughly speaking, from 1880 onwards everyone at the Pont received some sort of schooling. In 1867, 30 percent of the village's conscripts were still unable either to read or write,[76] and although this was a sizable improvement over what had existed before the creation of public education forty or fifty years earlier, the figure nonetheless indicates the fragility of pedagogic efforts before the Second Empire. Twenty years later, this had changed radically. It would be difficult to overestimate the importance of this fact which quite conceivably was the single most important event in the moral life of the Pont during the nineteenth century.

Most obviously comprehensive education made for some social leveling: before 1850, only the rich could read and write. In 1900 everyone could do so, and one of the most conspicuous differences between the life-styles of the rich and the poor had irrevocably fallen. More important than this, however, was the fact that education was now genuinely universal. Before 1850 there probably had been many Montipontins who had lived their lives far removed from any collective institution. The well-to-do, it is true, did stay in the same hamlets for generations and centuries. But many Montipontins floated about. They were not a part of the feudal system. They were landless laborers and did not pay homage to their feudal overseers. In fact, they had no guidance of any sort. Before 1720 they had had no religious direction, and even during the Revolution their participation and commitment had been shadowy. As has been seen, the officials and volunteers of 1792 had not been typical citizens. Indeed, the only collective and universal phenomena in which all Montipontins had been involved at some time or another before 1850 were the draft and taxes. With the creation of schools, this changed. For the first time, all Montipontins would henceforth be involved in some positive collective action. This was a very important change, and the impact of educational reform would be incomprehensible if we did not bear in mind the amorphous, uneven, and nongeneral effect of all institutional *encadrement* before the Third Republic.

This question is all the more important for the fact that what was taught in Jules Ferry's schools was not ideologically neutral. To the religious books of the 1820s and 1830s were now substituted republican and lay works, which although they were certainly unrevolutionary, did not serve to bolster the social status quo. From the first, republican education in the village was slanted to present the libertarian and positivist thought which is so characteristic of the period. In the Pont as everywhere, this new ethos was typified by Bruno's celebrated book, the *Tour de France par deux enfants,* which was already used in all of the progressive cantons of the Lozère in 1883–1884 although it had only been written in 1877. There one can find the real face of *la France nouvelle,* which was far from what had been awaited and desired by Prévost-Paradol. The past does not exist in this book. The children, whose voyage serves to show what France then was or ought to be, come from Alsace but there are no echoes of the defeat of 1870 and no call for *revanche*. There are no priests, no kings, no battles. Nor for that matter are there any factories or smokestacks. But what can be found on every page is honesty, justice, morality, and the virtues of rural democracy. A leveling of sorts, where there are no Frenchmen that are very poor or none that are very rich, and where hard work and honesty are the good and rewarded values that all must try to reach.[77]

Thus by 1900 the social and ideological impact of education on the village was far different from what it had been. To the few children who had learned in the Good Book respect for their elders, or indeed, had learned nothing at all, there was substituted a general, lay, and republican education which served to destroy social barriers just as the old system of nonschooling had sustained them. It destroyed the village structure intellectually by substituting for the prestige of inherited wealth and status the prestige of work and achievement, and it destroyed it even more directly through a direct attack of the old social bases. This was the inevitable consequence of republican reforms since most schoolteachers, nearly all, in fact, were hardly sympathetic to the overtly hierarchic village structures. Their training and politics predisposed them to a very different sort of thinking. Although Jules Ferry's cohorts did not have much sympathy for the idle and shiftless, they did dream of emancipating the talented poor from their low village status, of lifting them from poverty, and of providing them with the scholarships that would send them to the departmental normal schools, in short, of wrenching them from what the author of the *Communist Manifesto* had described with characteristic gentleness as "der Idiotismus des Landlebens." *

Even more destructive than this, perhaps, was the example that was set by the *instituteurs* themselves. The very career of schoolteaching now afforded an obvious and simple path for social ascent. In 1911, for example, no less than twelve Montipontins had become schoolteachers, some of them in the Pont (where one could also find *instituteurs* who came from other parts of the department) and most of them in nearby communes.[78] Of course, it could be argued that this inflow had served to bolster the sagging ranks of the village's bourgeoisie; and indeed one of Jules Ferry's aims had indeed been to give the new teachers prestige by giving them a salary which would set them on a par with the local notables. But the end result here was quite different. For after all, if a poor landless peasant child could be-

* Professor A. J. P. Taylor concurs; he, too, is of the opinion that "rural life cannot survive the impact of rationalism" (*The Habsburg Monarchy* [London, 1960], p. 30).

come through education almost a *Monsieur,* what did it now mean to be a *gros paysan?* Who was better off, the young scholarship student at Mende, or the forty-year-old dependent son of some village patriarch? The old social hierarchy suffered grievously from the rise of *instituteurs.* Previously it had provided the only path of social ascent, but by 1900 it had lost not only its monopoly but its usefulness as well. In 1820 the choices of the landless laborer were harsh in the extreme. In essence he could stay in the village or in another like it, and if his lot was to be improved there, it could only be through constant effort within the system. Or he could leave and try his luck as an unqualified and illiterate worker in the industrial cities of the south and north. But now, an alternative was offered to him. Through education, available to all, he could perhaps cushion his departure with a minor post as teacher or postman or gendarme in the tentacular bureaucracy of the state. Armed with his basic degree, his *certificat d'études,* his horizons were unlimited by the standards of his grandfather and even of his father. Drained of prestige at the top, the sytem was also being drained of labor at the bottom, and it is fair to say that education had much to do with this.

But Pont-de-Montvert's traditional structure had been more than a purely agricultural affair. Beside and above the peasant, there had also been artisans and a rural bourgeoisie. By 1900 they had gone also. The traditional artisan crafts had disappeared first, and the local notables did so later. The most important branch of the Servière family died out when Laurent Servière's daughter left for Les Vans. The Pinets and the Velays, descendants of Velay of Grizac, had also left, and shortly after the French Revolution, François Velay, *marchand, demeurant à Florac* sold his properties at the Pont for 90,000 francs.[79] Two families, it is true, did come to the Pont from smaller communes to the east and west. The Boissiers came from Fraissinet in the first decades of the nineteenth century, and the Pantels from Viala. But neither struck root. The heir of the Boissier fortunes left in 1832 to become a sub-prefect at Florac. When Albin Meynadier married into this same family, he used his inheritance to further his flight from the Pont, and in 1913 he lived with his wife at Digne where he was *directeur de l'enregistrement.*[80] As for the Pantels, two of them did become mayor of the village, in the 1860s and 1870s, but the family did not renew itself.

Nor did the local bourgeoisie as a whole. No one joined it from below. Those people in the Pont or the hamlets who aspired to bourgeois status went directly from the peasantry to the middle or lower middle class of the cities. Since the families that had been at the top also died out or left, the result was that by 1914, there was no local bourgeoisie in the sense that there had been even in the 1820s. Of course, some class differences remained. Some people were still more *considéré* than others, and some names remained more prestigious than the rest. But the criteria of *considération* were increasingly personal ones. Any capable and hard working person could become well thought of, if he set his mind to it. All that was needed, really, was to do well in school. This was a very different sort of *considération* from what had existed a hundred years before, in the last decades of the ancien régime. Then it was land that mattered, but that was no longer true in 1914.

The old village structure was now being sapped from every side, and the very people who stood to gain most from it were eventually amongst those most eager to leave. Small wonder, then, that the old communal customs should have disappeared as well. Common lands, common agricultural rights became less important and sometimes vanished altogether. In 1844 they had still been quite extensive. At that time, both *vaine pature* and *parcours* were practiced within the hamlets of the Pont, and the rights which governed the wanderings of common herds on common and private lands were closely defined. Communal lands were also widespread, and the way in which they were used (according to the wealth of the inhabitants or sometimes on a purely democratic basis) was regulated by immemorial customs. The municipal council at that time was keen on preserving these rights, and it "demanded the maintenance and preservation of these apportionments, since their abrogation would be irretrievably prejudicious to the interests of our agriculture." The councillors even asked for the abrogation of the law of June 10, 1793 that had provided for a distribution of communal lands, which division, they thought, "should be prohibited in the most absolute manner." [81]

By the end of the century, however, attitudes had changed greatly. In 1917 only one of the village's hamlets had a communal shepherd, and he did not watch over more than 150 sheep. The only lands that were still open to *parcours* were the now largely unused pastures of the Mont Lozère. The size of communal plots had also shrunk drastically. Those belonging to the inhabitants of the bourg itself went from 207 to 111 hectares; at Grizac, the figures are 372 and 102 hectares. Nothing at all was left of the 181 hectares of commons in the hamlet of Frutgères. They had been sold to individuals, and more often to the state, for reforestation.[82]

In short, on the eve of the World War the Pont had ceased to be the hierarchic, self-contained, and "organic" community that it once had been. The communal links between inhabitants were now far fewer than they had been, not only in that Montipontins depended much less on each other than they had before, but also because they depended less on the village. Before they had been villagers first, and then Protestant, Languedocien, and French. Now they were French first, republican next, and the village was low on the list as a matrix of life.

In this way, Pont-de-Montvert had become on the eve of the First World War a perfect example of that France which Montipontins had read about in Bruno's *Tour de France par deux enfants*. The Montversois were patriots now, and they lived in an essentially classless society where the deserving and hard working poor could really better themselves. Thanks to Jules Ferry's schools they were now thoroughly socialized and *embourgeoisé*. They could all read and write; they spoke French. They were no longer mystics as their forbears had been, and although they seldom went to Church, they were very moral. They lived peaceably with their parents, wives, and children; and in the seventy years that followed the legalization of divorce, only two couples availed themselves of that antisocial right. Pont-de-Montvert in fact was nearly perfect, and it had become what Clemenceau had wanted the whole of France to be, *"une démocratie rurale."* All should have been well here, but alas it is perhaps a sad reflection of the radical-socialist dream that the politics of this ideal society should have been something of a joke.

CHAPTER VI Politics Since 1815

The political life of Pont-de-Montvert at the beginning of the eighteenth century was deeply marked by the Camisard Wars, and the French Revolution at the end of the eighteenth century had a similarly serious effect on politics. But there is no such cataclysmic phenomenon for the hundred years that stretch from the fall of Napoleon to the outbreak of the First World War. Events were less dramatic in those years, and politics then were more a matter of trends than of sudden breaks with the past.

Participation is one of these trends. One of the great constants of Montipontine political life for decades and centuries had been the relative noninvolvement of the villagers in political matters. Some of them, the rich, had always been concerned with public matters; indeed, one of their principal social functions had been to act as intermediaries between the poorer villagers and the public authorities. But for most Montipontins, the state and its workings had remained a great mystery with which they had no positive contact at all before the creation during the Third Republic of a comprehensive network of primary schools. During the 1830s and 1840s, the police continually congratulated themselves on the "perfect peace" that reigned in the Lozère where most people, they thought, were not interested in politics.[1] In their opinion, this was what had always been and always should be.

Yet there were signs that after 1815 popular indifference to politics was less great than it had been. Although many Montipontins had abstained during the elections of the Revolution and the Empire, there had nonetheless been in the later years of even this period a fair number of active voters; and, as has been said, the choice that was made during the Hundred Days in 1815 was a particularly important one with definite political and even ideological implications. Of necessity, however, there was less of this after 1815 when participation in national elections was artificially circumscribed since only the richest taxpayers were entitled to vote. In the whole canton of Pont-de-Montvert, there were only three "censitary voters," and one of them usually resided at Florac. From our point of view, therefore the elections for the regional Conseil Général are more interesting since they were based on a larger franchise: fifty of the canton's inhabitants could vote here. Thirty-three of them did so in 1833; and in 1841, there were forty-six voters. Of these, the least wealthy paid a land-tax of seventy francs.[2] This meant that the poor were still excluded but it also implied that most of the *gros paysans* had in some way been enfranchised even before 1848 and universal suffrage.

It is true that the visible manifestations of popular involvement in politics were sometimes hard to see. In 1871, for example, there was only one newspaper subscriber in the whole of Pont-de-Montvert;[3] but the reports of observers at this same time do indicate that there was a continuous politicizing of the electorate. In 1869 the *procureur général* of the Lozère could write to Paris that the legislative elections of that year had caused more "agitation" then the preceding ones.[4] Twenty years later, the subprefect of Florac felt that the process had been completed:

> In this region where most people are Protestants, political education is generally well developed and has given rise, as regards public matters, to habits of electoral discipline which guarantee a republican victory in this district.[5]

There never were actual party cells:

> the republican party is not organized in the countryside, and there are no committees to back up the efforts of the deputies,[6]

but by the 1880s political consciousness was fully developed.

Together with this increasing involvement, another and perhaps more conspicuous trait of the political life of Pont-de-Montvert from 1815 to 1914 was the unending drift to the left, from a deep republican blue to increasingly dark shades of red. Since the end point of this evolution brought the village well into the camp of Marxism-Leninism by 1914 already, it can be seen that this was a most profound change from what had been true in the reign of Louis XVIII in 1814; but it is also true that even then, the Pont was well to the left. During the Hundred Days, the radicalism of the place was well established, and Napoleon's "liberal" prefect of the Hundred Days had noted that even the most prosperous and conservative Montversois notables were "very attached to the government."[7] After Waterloo and the return of reaction, the village was therefore duly occupied by Austrian troops, and the rerestored legitimist subprefect directed that all the communes of the canton of Pont-de-Montvert should be disarmed. "It is important," he concluded, "that this lair of insubordination should be reduced and made harmless."[8] His fears, however, were quite superfluous for there was never to be any open resistance to the rule of the Bourbons at Pont-de-Montvert. Quite conceivably, the regime may even have been popular at first, since in February of 1815 the local Protestant minister saw fit to write a very touching peroration on the return of Louis XVIII, which he concluded by thanking heaven "for the notable favor which he made to our dear homeland by restoring Louis the Desired One on the throne of his fathers."[9] Be that as it may, the Catholic excesses of the *ultras* must soon have disconcerted the Protestant Montipontins: in June of 1816 one of them was condemned to nine months in jail for shouting *Vive l'Empereur,*[10] and in 1821, when money was collected all over France to purchase the estate of Chambord for the posthumous son of the Duc de Berry, Pont-de-Montvert was conspicuously absent from the list of donors.[11]

From 1815 to 1830 the villagers were to the left. But how far to the left? Probably as far as one could go, which was not very. Opposition to the legitimism of the Bourbon did not imply socialism, jacobinism, or even republicanism, and the progressivism of Pont-de-Montvert was easily reconciled to the *juste milieu* of Louis-Philippe. The bourgeois rule of the citizen-king was not unpopular, and in the elections of 1833 for the Conseil Général twenty-five of the canton's thirty-three voters opted for a pro-government man; three others chose another person also sympathetic to the *juste milieu,* and only four Montipontins sided with the candidate of the "moderate democratic opposition,"[12] that is to say for a man who was in sympathy with the moderate reformism of Odilon Barrot, whose father incidentally, had been a *conventionnel* from the Lozère in 1793. History also records that the Duc d'Orléans, son of the King and heir to the throne, came to Florac in 1831 and was cheered by the National Guard battalion from the Pont, "whose patriotism was well known." Not irrelevant to the blossoming of this era of good feelings was the fact that Guizot's father's mother was a native of the Pont, a most exceptional circumstance which gave Montipontins an *entrée* in Paris. No surprise, then, that when construction of the new Protestant church was held up for lack of funds, Guizot should have seen fit to intervene. Dutifully, the austere statesman wrote to his *cher collègue,* the Minister of Educa-

Town buildings at Pont-de-Montvert. *Below left,* the entrance to the Protestant church; *below right,* an example of eighteenth-century architecture.

tion and Religion, to inform him that he would learn with pleasure that the request of the villagers had been granted. In his opinion,

> in view of the poverty of these people, of their habits of work, of order, and of obedience to the law, the request which they have made seems to me definitely worthy of consideration.[13]

For Montipontins, Orleanism was an adequate and progressive regime. Indeed, if they resembled the other Protestants of the Cévennes, they may not have seen much difference at all between Orleanism and republicanism. Local officials were surprised by this, and the Bonapartist subprefect of Florac wrote in 1852 that

> there is a fact which it is rather odd to see and it is that among the Protestants, Orleanism and republicanism often went hand in hand. They often regret the past when they remember the protection which was afforded to them during the reign of Louis-Philippe.[14]

Seen from Paris, this confusion was, it is true, distressing; but seen from the Pont, the amalgam of the two doctrines was really quite sensible. Did they not both embody the Great Principles of 1789 and were they not both symbolized by the tricolor of the Revolution and the Empire? In the Lozère, those were the issues that mattered.

In any case, Pont-de-Montvert's drift to the left before 1848 had remained within the bounds of propriety and order; interestingly enough, the same was true during the Second Empire, which was seen in the village as a regime of the left. There were difficulties at first, echoes perhaps of the serious disturbances that had taken place in the Gard when the Second Republic was overthrown. In April of 1852 the prefect of the Lozère was forced to admit that Louis-Napoleon's coup d'état had been accepted only with "some hesitation." But the inception of a virile state, of a *pouvoir fort,* he thought would be sure to win over the heart of the masses.[15] This, alas, was not inaccurate, and one year later the subprefect of Florac after visiting all the communes of his district, including the Pont, reported that he was pleased with the welcome he had received and that "everywhere, the populations welcomed with gratitude the representative of His Majesty." [16]

The results for the imperial plebiscites also reveal a gradual but decided acceptance of the New Order at Pont-de-Montvert. In December of 1851, 307 Montipontins had voted for the Empire, but more than a hundred people must have abstained. In 1870 there were many fewer abstentions.[17] There were 469 eligible voters, 391 of them cast a ballot, and there were only 14 *nons.* (See Table 2.) Since a participation of 80 percent is all that can ordinarily be expected at the Pont,

Table 2. Plebiscites and elections

Years	Registered voters	Voting	For the Empire	Against the Empire	Blanks	Abstaining
Plebiscites						
1851	—	308	307	0	1	(about 120)
1870	469	391	377	12	2	78
Legislative elections						
1857	429	320	300 (Chambrun)	20 (Desmolles: right opposition)	0	109
1863	428	342	172 (Barrot)	143 (Chambrun: moderate opposition) / 26 (Roussel: republican opposition)	0	86
1869	468	383	324 (Barrot)	59 (Chambrun: now outright right opposition)	0	83

Source: For plebiscites AN B II 1092 and ADL IV M2 5; for legislative elections ADL IV M4 13, ADL IV M4 14, ADL IV M2 5.

where many people must walk for miles to reach the polls, it follows that there was in the last year of the Empire practically no opposition to the regime. With varying degrees of enthusiasm the Montversois eventually accepted the rule of Napoleon III, which seemed to them far more reassuring than the alternatives proposed by the left or the right; the local chief of police was not far off the mark when he described their reactions to the Emperor's proclamation following the plebiscitary triumph of the Liberal Empire in May of 1870. "It had had a very good effect in the area," he reported, "and especially in the hamlets where revolution is generally feared. What the Montversois prefer is a progressive sort of liberty."[18]

This gradual acceptance of the Second Empire at the Pont is all the more curious for the fact that it was in contrast to what took place elsewhere in the Catholic and conservative areas of the northern Lozère. At the beginning, Napoleon's rule, it is true, was acceptable everywhere, north and south, to both the left and right. In the 1850s, the emperor had not yet antagonized the clericals with his antipapal policies, and there were many people like the Catholic noble de Chambrun, the official Bonapartist candidate in the Pont-de-Montvert district, who were willing to compromise initially with this occasionally leftist but essentially authoritarian government. This was a convenient arrangement since the right received a guarantee of social order from a government that could still be seen by the left as an heir of the Revolutionary tradition of 1789. The Italian war, however, ended this period of harmony in the northern Lozère. The left was not hostile to this venture, and the Protestant Montipontins must have been quite pleased to see the Pope become a prisoner of the House of Savoy. But after 1860, the Catholics were less pleased and Chambrun in particular fell out of step with the regime.

Pont-de-Montvert, by contrast, remained increasingly loyal to the regime of *Napoléon le petit*. In the national context, the Second Empire was in many ways quite reactionary and some observers have even seen it as incipiently fascist, but that was not the way it was perceived by the Montversois. Within the framework of Lozerian politics, the men who were consistently favorable to the Emperor were well to the left. For many years, in the 1860s the "official" candidate who received the help of the prefects was Joseph Barrot, and his progressivist credentials were unimpeachable since he was the son of Odilon Barrot, the moderate leftist of Louis-Philippe's day, and the grandson of a Republican deputy of 1793. Moreover, Barrot's opponent in the 1860s was no other than the former "official candidate," Chambrun, whose devotion to the Great Principles of 1789 was often tenuous. Clearly

123

since Joseph Dominique Adalbert, comte de Chambrun was by birth and religion to the right, Barrot and the Second Empire were *ipso facto* on the left.

The political life of the Pont in the 1850s and 1860s was played out on this background, and it is a measure of the political sophistication of the Montversois in these years that they were quite able to see why it was they should vote for Chambrun in the 1850s and why it was they should vote against him in the 1860s.[19]

The support given by the authorities in the 1850s to this Catholic aristocrat must have been galling for the Montipontins. But out of loyalty to the nephew of Napoleon I, they accepted the choice that had been made in Paris.[20] They voted for Chambrun when the prefect asked them to do so and the evolution of this candidate's popularity at the Pont is a good indication of the Montipontins' attitude towards the Second Empire, republicanism, and the left. From 300 votes in 1857, Chambrun fell to 143 in 1863, and to only fifty-nine in 1869. This decline parallels Chambrun's own doctrinal evolution. In 1863, he had done badly, but not too badly, probably because he was at that time only moderate in his opposition, and in any case more opposed to the Italian policy of the Second Empire than to the Second Empire itself. The Montipontins of 1863 may also have had some sympathy for the noble count's (opportunistic) antimilitarism. Chambrun often quoted Berryer's famous retort to the Minister of War who had claimed that France did not count her dead, and at Pont-de-Montvert people were likely to agree with the legitimist who had replied, "Yes, but mothers do count them." In 1869, however, Chambrun did very poorly. Pont-de-Montvert did not want to vote for a man of the right. That is why the Montversois chose Barrot in this last legislative election of the Second Empire. But neither did they want a government of the extreme left, and that is why the Republican candidate of 1863, Théophile Roussel, did so poorly with only twenty-six votes. At the Pont in the 1860s, republicanism was still a leap in the dark. The right was rejected; but before 1870, as far as the Montversois electorate was concerned, a vote for the left was still a vote for Napoleon III.

As it happens, however, the Republic that was created by Adolphe Thiers, the comte de Chambord, and the Paris Commune (each in their own way) did not turn out to be overly revolutionary. In the Pont as elsewhere, the *campagnes* quickly rallied to the new system. By 1873 the village had even managed to convince Thiers' new republican prefect that it had always remained "faithful to its republican traditions,"[21] a statement which can be euphemistically described as being at odds with the facts. The political conversion of the villagers from Bonapartism to republicanism was however quite swift. Indeed, it was already completed in 1877, and during the 16th of May crisis, Roussel, who had secured the support of twenty-six voters in 1863 now polled 353 out of 459 Montversois.[22] From the first, the Pont was securely anchored to the Republic and the drift to the left was henceforth no longer characterized by allegiance to one regime rather than another (there were no alternatives to republicanism) but by a gradual drift from one party to the next. In 1881 the prefect reported that Pont-de-Montvert was "the most advanced district in the Lozère,"[23] and in 1893 it was said to be

> one of those areas, where the republican leanings are the most progressive; in a legislative election, the radical candidate is sure to win.[24]

In 1893, the subprefect could similarly write of the local deputy Jourdan that, at the Pont, he was able to accentuate the radical character of his program "without fear of arousing the timidity of his voters" since the intransigeance of the region's principles drove the candidates ever forward towards the "most excessive political programs."[25]

Yet even the most cursory look at the "excessive programs" of the republican, then radical, and later socialist politicians shows that this drift to the left was clearly circumscribed. In fact there is underlying all of the debate an unending search for order. The reluctance of the villagers to opt for republicanism during the Second Empire is in itself a proof of this. As long as republicanism remained an unknown quantity, they would not drift that far, and the debate of the 1870s is particularly revealing in this respect. Immediately after the fall of the Empire, the republicans had appeared to be in favor of "disorder" since they were in favor of continuing the war. Léon Valéry, the republican candidate, who had been imported from the outside the Lozère, proclaimed loud and clear that he would prefer a "war to the finish"[26] to a peace which would have been disavowed by honor. But six years later the local republican candidate, Bourillon, at Mende, was less bellicose. Quite to the contrary, he claimed, the Republic was peace. "The Empire means war with Prussia; it's despotism, disorder, invasion." As for monarchy, that was not much better he thought. That meant "war with Italy, government by the Priests." How much better the prospects offered by the Republic: "tranquility, peace, liberty, law." "So," he concluded, "vote for the Republic. Vote for Monsieur Bourillon."[27]

In the neighboring district, which included the Pont, Roussel was equally forthright. A vote for the Republic was a vote for order: his was not an adventurous republic, but a *République constitutionnelle,* which would defend those "fundamental institutions"

> on which rest not only the safety of our hearths, but the very progress of human morality, which is the best guarantee that one could have of social order.[28]

It was difficult to be more explicit, or, as it happens, more successful. The right, which recognized the deep-seated desire for order that lurked behind the claims of all political families, tried as best it could to dispel the view which now held *it* to be a source of disorder. It had secured a popular mandate in February of 1871 by opting for peace but it had lost this advantage in the years that followed by arguing for papalism and the *gouvernement des curés.* This was an unenviable development, and there were those on the moderate right who would have disavowed clerical extremism in order to regain the conservative dominance of 1871. The candidate of the party of order in the Mende district for the elections of 1877 was particularly scandalized by the current slander of his leader, Marshall MacMahon. He wrote that

> It has been said that the Marshall is the head of a clerical government. What a joke. He just does not want that the ministers of religion or religion itself should be insulted; and he's right.[29]

An old soldier, he declared, was *ipso facto* incapable of being a clerical. Republicanism he warned was disorder, and the victory of that pernicious doctrine would involve France in a war with the other European powers, keen on stamping out a hotbed of revolutionism. He concluded,

> We will all vote for MacMahon, which is to say for order, for peace, for the public works (that have just been decreed), for the universal exposition, and in order to keep what we have for fear of worse things to come.[30]

This was not an inspiring program, but it was explicit; in the northern Lozère, Catholic voters responded. At the Pont, however, an appeal of this sort was bound to fail. Both the right and left had gone to great pains to show that they believed in social order. But through a set of unusual chances, the left could offer both order and a revolutionary mystique. This was an unbeatable *mélange.* Henceforth, the Montversois could have their cake and eat it too. They were grateful, and their adhesion to the Third Republic was both massive and durable.

126

It could of course be asked why it was that the villagers did not see through the transparent and facile progressivism of Republicanism. And how did they manage to double-think for so long, to be both unchanging and revolutionary, at peace with themselves but at war with the "system"?

The answer here is a very simple one. Throughout the nineteenth century, Montipontins followed the lead that had been given them during the revolution from 1789 to 1815. They were able to be conservative people addicted to revolutionary politics because the political debate continued to be ideological, abstract, and remote. Those issues which did face the people of Pont-de-Montvert (such as, for example, tariffs which would protect them from foreign competition and eventual economic extinction) did not form a bone of contention between parties since all groups whether of the right or the left were united in their determination to preserve, to conserve the thousands of villages like the Pont. This left as the substance of political debate those issues which were of no real consequence to the people of the Pont, and on those it was easy for them to adopt extremist and radical stands. Since the debate was irrelevant, it did not matter where they stood.

In the first half of the nineteenth century and indeed in some ways until the 1890s, the abstract issues which fascinated Montipontins were the questions of regime. What type of government would France have? This could pass as a serious issue, but there was less to it than met the eye, since in the end all governments had behaved in more or less the same way. Admittedly the town council had been unusually successful in blackmailing the Empire for roads and subsidies, but the July monarchy had itself begun to build roads, and the Third Republic was also a most generous institution.

But however much substance these questions of regime may have had, the issues which replaced them after 1870 as the focus of politics were without a doubt very ideological and quite devoid of practical import. Even before the fall of the Empire, there had been some indications that there would be a shift of this sort. In 1869, for example, the Catholic candidate Chambrun had laid much stress on the problem of religion, although the official candidate Barrot (for whom the Pont had massively voted in 1869) had tried to steer away from this. All that he had to say about the Roman Question was that in his opinion, the "civil element" in society should not impede on the "religious element" and vice versa.

But after 1870, however, ideological problems like religion became most popular, and parties of the right and left flooded the village with

127

great conceptual schemes. The French Revolution became the touch-
stone of political debate. Candidates were for it or against it. Thus,
Henri Belon, a Protestant and Opportunist, declared himself

> a passionate admirer of our glorious Revolution of 1789 which has
> placed rich and poor, bourgeois and peasants, on the same footing of
> equality by abolishing privilege.[31]

Belon it is true received only 153 out of 470 votes at the Pont, but that
was only because his opponent added to his own love of the Revolution
an anticlericalism which was very much to the taste of the Montversois.
But no one questioned the Great Principles of 1789, and in 1898 Louis
Jourdan, the local deputy, could still summarize his program as the
"completion of the work of the Revolution." [32]

Given this frame of mind, it was tempting for candidates to become
more and more outrageous in their offerings to the voters. Since plat-
forms were essentially irrelevant, the natural way for newcomers to
replace the old war horses was by appearing more intransigent, more
pur et dur than the incumbents. In 1906, for example, the established
candidate at the Pont was named Louis Dreyfus. Naturally, his opponent, Rolland, clearly placed himself to the left of Dreyfus. They
met at the Pont to argue things out; and the subprefect reported that

> the two opponents said about the same thing, but M. Rolland was
> somewhat more progressive and declared unrelenting war on capital-
> ism and the bourgeoisie.[33]

All of which becomes somewhat grotesque if we remember that
Louis Dreyfus was a very rich man, a Parisian and a banker who had
probably decided to carve himself an electoral fief in the Lozère, a
region that was so backward, so poor, but also so republican, since it
was, in an official's words, a place where "public administrators receive the most obliging deference from the inhabitants and the elected
bodies." [34]

Even apparently substantial issues became unreal in the Lozère. It
is often said that the whole of the French body politic during the
Third Republic was deflected by anticlericalism from the consideration
of such concrete issues as social legislation and the income tax. But
even the income tax was unsubstantial in the Lozère and at the Pont.
It was first introduced as an issue in the Florac district (which includes
the Pont) in 1893 by a minority candidate. In 1898 it was picked up by
the majority candidate Jourdan who wanted both a progressive income tax, a two-year draft law, and the separation of Church and state.
From then on, it was always to be found in the program of republican

candidates, but everyone could read between the lines of manifestos like those of Georges Paraf, who pointed out that "this tax will only hit those people who make more than 5,000 francs a year. In our Lozère, people so favored by the fates are very few." [35] Nor was the left alone in its determination to obfuscate and avoid all serious issues. In 1893 the conservative de Colombet, who ran in a neighboring district, explained, for example, that yes, he had voted for a colonial army, but no, his antimilitarist constituents should have no fears. If he had voted for this colonial army it was only to keep the conscripts of the regular army from being sent abroad. All that his supporters had to do was to remember that black was white, and everything would be all right. Jacques Piou, in the same district only twenty years later, also conformed to local mores. Certainly, he declared, there should be an income tax, but the new levy would have to include

a set of immediate reductions for small farmers and tradesmen, and this can be done by taxing foreign bonds. [36]

In short it would have to be an income tax that did not tax income. Piou was in any case ill at ease with such mundane themes. He preferred to dwell on the Jews, on the *judéo-maçonnique* conspiracy that had for years been attacking the faith. That was the real problem: the choice was not really between a tax or no tax, a three-year draft or a two-year draft (Piou favored the longer stretch, so of course did not talk about it). The choice facing the Lozère was this:

Do you want the Lozère to demand respect for its old religious belief or do you want it to fall once again under Jewish and masonic influences. [37]

Everyone always believed in lofty abstraction and ideological premise. Or nearly always, for at times, the attention of Lozerians and Montipontins did wander a bit. As a rule, because of their post-revolutionary political past and because of the absence of social conflict within the village, the Montversois did put up with this sort of debate, and even cheered the contestants to ever greater heights of oratory. But at the same time their common sense told them that politics was more than this. Since what we might call middle-level issues did not exist, however, the concomitant of ideology proved to be only pettiness, personal favors, and small time spying. The politics of Pont-de-Montvert did in spite of everything have a material and nonideological content, but of a very small sort.

Deputies to begin with were not only expected to defend Great Principles; they were also required to secure favors for their more loyal constituents and to satisfy what a prefect euphemistically described as

> unceasing demands, often excessive, of a needy electoral *clientèle* which is greedy for jobs and small favors.[38]

All of them did their best. Naturally the deputies of the left were able to point out that, in a republic, nonrepublican deputies would not have much pull: "A reactionary deputy will not be able to secure your rights."[39] Republican deputies had more connections. In 1889 Bourillon asserted that in order to secure favors for their constituents, deputies would have to appeal to the republican ministers who headed the administration; but his opponents would not be able to do this: "He alone," ran his posters, "will be able to go see all of the ministers. HE KNOWS THEM."[40] There was no limit to electoral demagogy. The right wing Paulin Daudé, who was born in neighboring Fraissinet, was perhaps the worst of all since he was by his origins closest to the voters. In 1898 he emphasized the fact that the debt conversion of 1894 had not been used to lower the land tax, which in the Lozère fell largely on peasant owners. Had this been done, he pointed out, those who paid one hundred francs would only have had to pay forty-five francs. To make matters clearer, he then added that those who had paid twenty francs would only have had to pay nine francs. He concluded,

> Peasants, since 1894 you have paid one million extra francs. Who has forced you to take this enormous sum to the tax collector? It's Bourillon's vote."[41]

Personal favors were the concrete results which voters expected from their political representatives. Naturally enough, this in turn led to petty quarrels and intrigue. It was now important to ask who deserved these favors, who was most loyal to deputy x; and as a *quid pro quo,* deputy x could also ask if those who had been rewarded had loyally performed their electoral duty. At the Pont, regular lists were drawn up of all the voters, on which the political opinions of each citizen was neatly labeled. In 1889 we find, for example, that there were in the village six people who were "notoriously antirepublican," all of them apparently *légitimiste-clerical,* two of them stonemasons, and one of them a day laborer. They, however, were relatively innocent. Far more culpable was the local priest, who egged them on, Pierre Malafosse, aged sixty-three, a "fanatical Jesuit."

> All of these voters would support the Republic if they were not held in check by the priest Malafosse.[42]

130

Right on through until 1914, and perhaps later, reports of this sort were filed for everyone who applied for any state job. Those who did not qualify as "Good Dreyfusard," or as "Republican—was educated in lay schools," had little chance of getting a state job.

The right replied in kind. Since they were unable to use the state to beat the electors, they used the Church instead. Instances of clerical involvement in Lozerian politics go back at least to 1848, when it was so flagrant that an election to the National Assembly was declared null and void. During the Second Empire, Chambrun did not hesitate to appeal directly to the priests for support. His missive to them was full of nuances.

> I do not come at this time, Monsieur le curé, in order to ask you to give to my candidacy a support whose nature might not be suited to your particular mission and to the sacred character of your office. But . . .[43]

After 1871, however, there were no limits to clerical pressures. Parishioners who voted the wrong way were denied Holy Communion, and wives were instructed to rebuff the sexual advances of their republican husbands. At the Pont, there was of necessity very little of this pressure, since there were so few Catholics, but this pattern was rampant in neighboring communes. In 1889 the prefect reported that the behavior of priests at Mende had been inadmissible:

> Priests and *curés,* vicars, clerics of all sorts, with some rare exceptions carried out an unbounded propaganda. By day and night, they went in every house of the district in which they lived, arguing about the candidates . . . defending step by step the candidacies of the opposition; and they did not even shirk what is for the people of the Lozère a decisive argument: the moral issue . . . They said and wrote that it was a mortal sin to vote for the Republican candidate.[44]

In short, it was proper for the prefect to interfere but not for the bishop. Still, it is difficult to take sides. At Clochemerle-Pont-de-Montvert, there is not much to be said for or against either side.

By 1914, there was little left of the Pont as it had been two centuries before. And where is the greater difference: between the radical-socialists of 1914 and Esprit Séguier who died on the stake, mutilated and content; or between Esprit Séguier and his tormentor du Chayla? Whom would the Protestant martyr have preferred? His equally fanaticized Catholic enemy or the jolly, anticlerical republicans of 1914? It is hard to say, but it is less hard to see why the politics of the village had degenerated so badly.

Pont-de-Montvert

It might be argued that in the late nineteenth century, Pont-de-Montvert was the way it was because it was reflecting what was going on in the rest of France. In a way, this is quite true. The debate at the Pont was about Dreyfusism and anticlericalism because those were the issues elsewhere. After Gambetta had declared that clericalism was the enemy, Pont-de-Montvert was bound to follow suit. But it would have been just as docile if Gambetta had latched onto some other issue such as antinationalism, trade unionism, or zoroastrianism. Pont-de-Montvert would have accepted and absorbed those, too. What the subject of politics was did not really matter, and this was so because politics itself was now irrelevant to the real concerns of the villagers.

Therefore it should not be thought that the village was making some great sacrifice in accepting the word handed to it from Paris. The ideological twists of national politics after 1870 were not some sort of Procrustean bed on which a reluctant Pont-de-Montvert had been bound and fettered. At the time of the French Revolution, it is true, the shift in politics from substantial to ideological issues had gone against the grain. In 1789 the Pont was a class society that ought to have had class politics, but it did not. Quite the contrary, the Mont-versois committed themselves after 1789 to a new and anomalous political structure whose ambiguity was evinced by the villagers' reaction to Napoleon's regime. In practice, they hated it, but they approved of it in theory and at the polls; and by 1914 this sort of double-think had become the normal situation of politics at Pont-de-Montvert.

Conceivably, the Montipontins' concern for ultimately irrelevant issues would not have lasted throughout the nineteenth century if the old class structure of the village had survived intact. Eventually, both the poor and the rich might have gone their own way as they had in 1702, and the lower classes might in the end have rejected the leadership of the bourgeoisie. After all, they had accepted it only because of common but temporary enmities: the state, the "They," the outsiders, the clericalists. But this parting of ways never took place. When the poor became less poor and more bourgeois, when the rich began to be less rich, the class structure of the village collapsed. Attacked ideologically and economically, after 1820 it was too weak to reassert itself politically, and the pattern that had been abnormal in 1789 had become perfectly normal in 1914. Since there were no forces that militated against what had originally been an artificial pattern, the pattern gradually became an established norm. The Pont by 1914 had become a classless society. It is therefore no surprise that it should have had antipolitics. Of course, between Esprit Séguier and his radical-socialist heirs there stands a decline of religious fervor, decades and centuries of socialization, and education. But more important, perhaps, there stands also the collapse of the old hierarchic class structure of village life.

Emile Molines, Eugène Molines, Marcel Molines, Paul Molines: *"mort au champ d'honneur," "mort pour la France,"* Lovely words, these. But for a population of one thousand, thirty-three deaths is too much. The Pont had deserved better than this from the Republic. It had been loyal; it had always supported good republican candidates. In exchange, it had asked for nothing of much substance: a few jobs here and there were enough to make the people of the Pont feel that they were being justly ruled. The hecatomb of the First World War was cruel payment for the deference they had always shown the authorities.

In truth, it must be said that in some ways the Montversois must bear some of the blame for this. In 1939 they heard of war with a sinking heart, but in 1914 there was at first great enthusiasm. Montipontins had not sat in Jules Ferry's schools for nothing and now they were all good patriots. In 1870, pro-war sentiment in the Pont and throughout the Lozère was minimal, nonexistent in fact. But 1914 was different, and the Montversois left for their *dépôts* with good cheer. Yet it is obvious also that four years later, they were right in thinking that they had somehow been deceived. Before 1914 public life and politics had been something of a farce. Labels were meaningless, parties nonexistent, and in the end, even that persecuted and horrid Jesuit, Malafosse, did not suffer all that much at the hand of his tormentors. But in 1914 suddenly politics were no longer a joke. The point was unexpectedly driven home that politics could kill.

For that reason, the electoral debates of the 1920s and 1930s do not arouse the same amused detachment as did those of the 1880s and 1890s. What was funny before 1914 was not comic after 1918. But in spite of this, the political life of the village went on much as it had before. The candidates continued to make the same preposterous claims, and with the same cynicism. In 1932, for example, Pomaret, an independent socialist who was the local deputy and the mayor of Pont-de-Montvert, could still argue that he differed from his rival in that he was

skeptical—skeptical and indifferent to the honors of power. The deputy and the cabinet member have only been a man, simple and devoted, using his activity and influence for the service of his compatriots alone.[45]

And some Montipontins probably believed him although Pomaret's scepticism was perhaps best evidenced by his participation in a rightist government which was also supported by the deputy from the northern Lozère whose constituents were as determinedly right wing as the Montversois were left wing.

But indeed, how could the nature of politics have changed in the village after 1914? The population decline continued from 1055 inhabitants in 1913, to 843 in 1926, and 728 in 1936. Increasingly, those who remained were the old, the incapable, the apathetic whose ability to exert some sort of change economically, socially, or politically was usually negligible. A pattern had been set early in the nineteenth century; it had become perfectly visible before 1914. It did not change after this. And since the village remained unchanging in a society which was increasingly transformed, it appeared increasingly backward, and even impotent. In this light, the old slogans of liberty and especially progress to which Montipontins continued to subscribe (and do still subscribe today) became less comic and more pathetic. The people of Pont-de-Montvert were everyday more than the last the prisoners of a political tradition that bore no relevance to them or to the sort of life they led in their village.

Yet it may well be that we should not mourn these changes, however sad they may seem at first. Certainly we can regret the fact that the Montversois were in the end deceived and even decimated. It is also easy for us to suppose that it would have been a "good thing" if the villagers had been able to resist the wiles of bourgeois politicians who have at different times led them to *les prisons de Russie* or who have simply used them for their own purposes and remained indifferent to the real problems that have faced Pont-de-Montvert. But for that to have been, the Pont would have had to remain the village that it had been before the Revolution. Certainly then it was a vigorous community in which the poor had a life and a mind of their own. But it was also a cruel place where most people were ground down by poverty and where the conflicts of politics were born ultimately of social oppression and of the robbery of the many for the benefit of the few. In the end, it is hard to say who was better off: the Montipontins of the generation that was marched off to Verdun or those of the generation who propelled the Servière family to fame and fortune.

It is not unreasonable to lament the end of the Pont as it was before

The Pont in winter.

1789. Bound together and united by common ends, many of the villagers may not in fact have been too unhappy there. It is also sad to see the way in which their descendants have been unable to resist and have indeed applauded at their own political exploitation. But it is also true that very few of us would want to find ourselves in the Pont of Louis Servière. Life there was most certainly nasty, short, and brutish. It is indeed a world we have lost and since our roots are in the Pont and in villages like it, we should not disown it. But neither is it, I think, a world that we should regret. It would have been better, certainly, if the last days of Pont-de-Montvert had been less bloody and if its inhabitants had been better able to resist outsiders. But that should not obscure for us the terrible hardships which have been the lot of nearly all those people who have lived there. Their descendants, wherever they may be, have gone a very long way, and it would be folly to see their flight as some tragic loss. We should perhaps remember that Pont-de-Montvert is part of our past, but we should not regret that it is no more than that.

AFTERWORD: Village Studies and the History
of France

Briefly summarized, the social history of Pont-de-Montvert was characterized by the simplification, decline, and eventual demise of a tripartite class structure based on the subsistence economy of a closed village. The political consequences of this evolution varied between 1700 and 1914. In the beginning, during the reign of Louis XIV and the Camisard Wars, there were marked differences between the political behavior of peasants and notables. The rich were collaborators; the poor were rebels. But this distinction waned during the eighteenth century so that by 1789, both rich and poor were now united in their detestation of the central government. This, it can be added, was a state of affairs that was much to the advantage of the bourgeois notables, since their exactions both direct and indirect were on the eve of the Revolution more of a burden for the peasantry than had been true eighty years before.

The end of the eighteenth century, therefore, marks a political turning point; and the same is true economically and socially for the beginning of the nineteenth century. It is during these years, in the 1820s and 1830s that one can see at the Pont the first indications of the collapse of the old class structure. The forces which made for this varied from time to time, but we can at any rate list them in order of appearance: the extinction of rural industries, the absorption of the village into the national economic and social structure, the inception of generalized primary education, and a fall in the price and relative value of land.

How much of these social and political developments were typical of France as a whole? To our way of thinking, a great deal. The question of class conflict during the reign of Louis XIV has, for example, pro-

137

vided one of the most interesting points of modern historiographical controversy. Some years ago, a Russian historian, Porchneev, relying on unpublished French documents and also, it must be said, on Marxist abstractions, argued that France in the seventeenth century had not known a social revolution as England did in those same years because the French bourgeoisie had not carried out its "objectively correct" role.[1] Had it conformed to the Marxist model, Porchneev argued, the French bourgeoisie would have utilized peasant discontent in order both to overthrow the feudal, aristocratic order and to establish its own predominance. Many objections were raised against this theory. Some historians, Edouard Mousnier among them, argued that this was a very schematic view of the problem.[2] They were not prepared to accept the idea that the bourgeoisie, or even the aristocracy, had methodically abandoned the peasants to the mercies of the feudal state. Many instances of collaboration between bourgeois and peasants were brought forward. It was even suggested that such collaboration was usual and unexceptional in a society which was not yet nationally homogeneous. Since France in the seventeenth century was still a conglomeration of small and distinct units, it was not surprising that the lords, bourgeois, and peasants who inhabited some small region might feel closer to each other than to a distant and exacting royal government. Moreover, Mousnier also argued, the collaboration of the bourgeoisie with the feudal state, such as it may have been, had not resulted in the feudalization of the bourgeoisie but in the *embourgeoisement* of the state. The bourgeoisie may have become more sympathetic to a government whose authority they were able to usurp through the purchase of public office, but this had its counterpart in the rationalization and moderation of a theoretically absolutist monarchy.

Much of this discussion, of course, goes far beyond the limits of Pont-de-Montvert, but the debate as a whole does have some bearing on the history of our village. Admittedly, there is little for us to say as regards the consequences for the state as a whole of the purchase of feudal seigneuries by the Montipontin bourgeoisie in the last decades of the eighteenth century. Much of Mousnier's argument is not applicable to the setting of this book; but Porchneev's reasoning, however, is of great relevance here. Certainly what happened at the Pont during the Camisard Wars fits neatly into his point of view. In those years, the local bourgeoisie which had bought seigneuries and served the interests of absentee clerical landowners refused to side with the peasantry against a regime which was both persecuting them and doctrinally repulsive. There are many reasons that can serve to explain the stand of the Montipontine notables in 1702. Some of them of course have nothing to do with politics: differences in style of life, or fear of material reprisals, the natural distaste of the educated for the un-educated—these things could have existed in any political context. But neither should it be overlooked that thanks to the seigneurial system and to intermarriage with its betters, the Montipontine bourgeoisie was closer to the establishment at the end of the seventeenth century than it would be in 1789, when it was better off and no longer persecuted. Hence perhaps the fact that in 1702 it collaborated when it ought to have rebelled and that in 1789 it rebelled when it ought to have collaborated.

Like the events of the reign of Louis XIV, the history of Pont-de-Montvert during and after the French Revolution can also be inserted in the general historiographic debates that have been waged of late. It would be futile here to trace the successive interpretations of the Great Revolution. Suffice it to say that this upheaval was for France an event of such magnitude that it has been constantly reinterpreted, and that historians have quarreled about its origins and nature with as much acrimony as did the participants themselves. Explanations have ranged from the famed *"c'est la faute à Voltaire, c'est la faute à Rousseau"* to Marxist theories of class war and sociological specula-tion on the political consequences of social and economic dislocation. Most germane to our problem is the debate which opposed Alfred Cobban's revisionism to the "official" French and Marxist school of Jaurès, Mathiez, Lefebvre, and Soboul.

For many decades, the accepted trend of interpretation saw the cause of the French Revolution first in the disaffection of the peasantry (less poor however than Michelet had thought) and more particularly in the growing expectations of an increasingly prosperous bourgeoisie. Before 1700, as Mousnier had shown, the bourgeoisie had been able to buy a share of public authority. This had reconciled it to theoretical, political absolutism. But in the course of the eighteenth century, just as it became, thanks to the growth of trade, more prosperous, better educated, more aggressive and self-aware, the paths of social ascent one by one were cut off. No longer was it possible in the 1780s for a bourgeois to become a bishop like Bossuet, or a marshall like Catinat, or a minister of state like Colbert. This was intolerable, and profiting from the financial distress of the monarchy which was unable to pay its way after the very costly war of American independence, the bourgeoisie rose up against the state. In 1789, with the help of the peasants, it overthrew absolutism, feudalism, and exclusive aristoc-racy, and brought to a close one phase of that cycle which Marx assumed would end with the creation of a classless society. Variants were subsequently added. It was shown that the plight of the peasants had become more acute in the few years which preceded the Revolution. Evidence was garnered to highlight the existence of a feudal reaction during the eighteenth century with a revival by landlords of forgotten feudal dues. Within the context of established canons, the events of the period were clarified. Georges Lefebvre insisted on the fact that there had been in 1789 four distinct revolutions: aristocratic, bourgeois, peasant, and popular, all of which had momentarily coalesced to shatter the absolutist monarchy. Much interesting material was also unearthed by Albert Soboul about the Paris mobs, about the *sans-culottes,* on their goals, methods, and thinking, as well as on the differences which separated them from moralizing bourgeois revolutionaries like Robespierre. But the kernel of the argument remained as Jaurès had presented it: The French Revolution was a social revolution with political consequences rather than vice versa. It was carried out by a clearly delineated class, the bourgeoisie, with the help of another class, the peasants, against yet a third social class, the aristocracy shielded by the clerical and feudal state.

Recently, however, this interpretation has been challenged by the English historian, Alfred Cobban, in his *Myth of the French Revolution* and in *The Social Interpretation of the French Revolution.* The author of these two short works argued that the Jaurès-to-Soboul interpretation was overly schematic and was perhaps less warranted by a strict interpretation of the facts than it was by Marxist orthodoxy. The inevitability of class conflict, the unavoidable tension between bourgeois and aristocrat, the existence of two social classes with different economic bases, these things were for Cobban so many myths or *vues de l'esprit.* They were hardly warranted by what we knew about the eighteenth century, meager though our knowledge was, since so much of it had been elaborated with an eye to the preconceived model. In fact, Cobban argued, the French Revolution cannot have really been meant as a social revolution since France in 1815 was socially similar but politically different from what it had been in 1788. Nor should it be thought, he argued, that the French Revolution opposed the bourgeoisie as a bloc to the aristocracy as a bloc. Indeed, how could this have been since the bourgeoisie in France had remained overwhelmingly rural. Like the aristocracy, the bourgeoisie in 1788 was essentially made up of landowners, many of whom owned feudal offices and had therefore a vested interest in the perpetuation of the status quo. The real social enemies of the bourgeoisie were, as far as Cobban could see, not the nobles but the peasants. Insofar as the French Revolution was a social conflict, that was where it lay. Hence

Cobban's conclusions: the French Revolution was not a social revolution engineered by the bourgeois class against its noble class enemies. It was instead a political and intellectual movement, a defensive reaction of the literate professional bourgeoisie, of the officials and owners of feudal office who felt threatened not only by a reactionary state but by the new bourgeoisie, which was increasingly orientated to commerce, colonial trade, and industry.

Whatever the merits of Cobban's interpretation at the national level, it must be said that it has value as a framework for the understanding of events at the Pont from 1789 to 1815. Admittedly, we cannot lightly dismiss the older Marxist view of the problem. There were indeed at the Pont in the eighteenth century many of the objective preconditions of social upheaval: poverty, population pressure, a concentration of leaseholdings, and the exploitation of the many by the few. That there were therefore social antagonisms at the Pont in 1789 must be true. It is impossible to suppose that so much misery should not have led men with a tradition of revolt to reflect on the nature of their grievances.

But in the end, at Pont-de-Montvert, the French Revolution was not about these complaints at all. The peasants did not rise up against the nobles (there had not been any at the Pont since 1700) or even against the bourgeoisie. They rose up against the fiscal exactions of the state. Nor was the Revolution there a bourgeois one in the sense that Jaurès had thought, for although the local notables never lost control of it, their purpose cannot originally have been to overthrow the feudal order. They had all of them become rich by using it to exploit their poorer neighbors, and it would have been folly for them to have wanted to destroy it. Hence the conclusion that at the Pont, the French Revolution was a political and an intellectual movement rather than a social one. That must surely have been the *conventionnel* Servière's view of the problem. His family, after all, had become very rich thanks to the workings of the system. Since he also read Voltaire, Holbach, and La Mettrie, the inference is clear: he became a republican because he believed rather than because he hoped to gain, although, as it happens, he did that too.

Beyond this, Cobban's interpretation is all the more interesting from a Montipontine point of view in that, at the Pont, the French Revolution was indeed in many ways a "myth." In 1815, for all practical purposes, life at Pont-de-Montvert was very much what it had been thirty years before: hierarchical, conformist, family oriented, unchanging. The great transformations which remolded Pont-de-Montvert from the time of the Revolution down to 1914 began after 1815 and were not political ones at all. The succession of regimes was really quite meaningless, and regardless of who slept in the Tuileries, the same bureaucrats continued to enforce in the Lozère the same rules in the same trivial and self-satisfied way. It was during the nineteenth century that the conditions of social life in the village began a complete mutation, and this had practically no relation to the political debate which was increasingly ideological and pointless.

This transformation, indeed destruction, of Pont-de-Montvert as it had been was not of course an isolated phenomenon, and it may well be at this very point that the history of the Pont and of France most clearly overlap. The destruction of rural industries was a generalized phenomenon, as was the emigration of the poor to the factories and of the medium rich and rich to the bureaucracy. The competition for labor, the rise in wages, the spread of education, all of these things had everywhere combined to destroy the framework of *la Vieille France*. In 1900, the shell everywhere remained: there were still millions of peasants left, but the glory of rural France was long since gone. Péguy may have been thought unduly pessimistic when he wrote before 1914 that old France was nearly dead [3]—that may have seemed a bold thing to say in a country that would remain predominantly rural until the 1930s—but we can see now how right he was.

The social history of the Pont in the nineteenth century was therefore not exceptional, and the same can be said, but in a more interesting way, of its political life as well. This may seem rather paradoxical, for it is clear that in a country where the tone of politics was always set in the capital, any provincial debate must appear in some ways futile. This is obviously all the more so for a small community like Pont-de-Montvert. But in spite of this there are many valid and important points of contact between the politics of village and nation.

Our point of departure here is that French politics have been unusually sterile, perhaps, as Michel Crozier explained in his *Bureaucratic Phenomenon,* because of the bureaucratic nature of French society. France is a community which is at once very stable and very divided. It is hierarchical but controlled; and this enables the great to be great, but it also protects the small who are never hopelessly oppressed. In this system, political revolutions have few lasting social effects, and this is not surprising since they are intended to be mere corrective measures. They aim to resolve technical dysfunction and are not really concerned with basic justice or injustice. Thus most French politicians are verbal revolutionaries and in practice conservatives who are only interested in readjusting the rules of a game whose principles they do not dare to question. France has been described as

142

a nation of tranquil people with agitated legislators. But the claim here is that even the legislators are not altogether excitable. Their politics are noisy but not dangerous.

This holds true generally and especially during the fading years of *La Belle Epoque,* but it is also true for Pont-de-Montvert from 1815 to 1914. Nor is this similarity altogether surprising. There were of course in nineteenth-century France many differences, some of them very great, between social groups and classes. But with the exception of urban workers, a small and perennially repressed and decimated group, few Frenchmen seriously questioned the fundamental bases of their society. There was broad consensus as to what its principles should be: social hierarchy, political order, commercial autarchy, the preponderance of country over city, and the pursuit of moderately nationalistic goals. Occasionally bloody and invariably acrimonious political debates did not really matter very much, since the argument was about details rather than about the game itself.

This is not very different from what was to be found at Pont-de-Montvert. Like France itself, the village was afflicted in the nineteenth century with many problems, some of them born of new expectations and some also from the perennial misery that had always been the lot of the people who lived there. But few of these questions were settled and the causes of this inactivity are not unlike those which held true for France as a whole. Profound as they may have seemed to the foreign observer, the divisions within French society were in fact too weak to carry the country beyond the brink of sustained social disorder. There were of course great doctrinal gaps between the *petits bourgeois,* the peasants, and the urban elites. But these could always be composed in the face of a real threat to social order. Similarly, within the infinitely smaller compass of our village, the gaps that subsisted between rich and poor peasants, between the educated and the uneducated, the agricultural workers and the remaining notables, were never so great as to bring about a fundamental parting of ways. With the emigration of both the local bourgeoisie and the *braccianti,* what remained of the population of Pont-de-Montvert was in the nineteenth century too homogeneous to undo the political consequences of 1789.

Thus, although the artisans of the village's political system (that is to say, Servière and his fellow notables) had disappeared, their handiwork remained. Just as they had been the disciples of the *philosophes* before 1789, so it was that the attention of all of the Montversois after 1815 was riveted to the great intellectual problems of the day. They did not care so much about their own practical dilemmas as they did about Church and state, Republicanism and Bonapartism, capital-ism, and socialism. Moreover, although the hatefulness of royal and Catholic tyranny in 1700 had been variously interpreted in function of its practical effects by the various social groups which cohabitated in the village, there was no such division in 1900. Everyone approved of the new ideological messages, and in the same way. It is hard to avoid the conclusion that this doctrinal unanimity was due to the attenuation of social distinctions within the village, and this, writ small, is what was true of nonindustrial, nineteenth-century France.

Nor was the ordering of political priorities at the Pont made more palatable by the course of events at large. The hecatomb of the Great War was too much and showed how flimsy some of the Montvertsois' beliefs had been. After the slaughter of Verdun, of the Somme, of the Chemin des Dames, *"unsere grosse Siege,"* the grand illusions of radical socialism did not look too good. The people of the Pont were doubly cheated, by themselves and by the course of their national history, and there again the story of the people of the Pont is not very different from that of many Frenchmen in the interwar years. It is true that after 1920 the Pont was too weak to react as violently as did the rest of France in the 1930s. There were no local echoes to the riots of February 4, no Cagoulards, and no denunciations of either *métèques* or bolsheviks. But the lassitude and passivity of the villagers during these decades stands in contrast to their prewar enthusiasm and is eloquent enough. The denouement of nineteenth-century politics was harder to see at Pont-de-Montvert than elsewhere, but the path which the nation had followed to the disaster of 1940 was also the path which the Pont had cheerfully and irresponsibly traveled.

The history of Pont-de-Montvert does therefore have many points of contact, some negative and some positive, with the history of France as a whole. It can also be asked how similar the village has been to other villages in France.[4] There is no simple answer to this question, however, largely because the methods that have been used by village historians have been so different. Most serious village histories, for example, have emphasized the importance of the structure of landownership and have seen this as the determinant of political behavior, although that certainly has not been our own view of what was true for Pont-de-Montvert.[5] Others again have emphasized the importance of political and even intellectual factors, like the creation of schools as the mold of village life and politics,[6] and again this does not concur with what appears to us to have been true at the Pont. It is therefore impossible to compare the *whole* history of Pont-de-Montvert with the *whole* history of other communities—the frameworks in which they have been set are too dissimilar to allow continuous comparisons. But we can look at certain aspects of the history of Pont-de-Montvert and juxtapose those with what has been found to be true in other village communities.[7]

Although the area around Pont-de-Montvert and in the northern Cévennes generally has not been methodically studied, there are many reasons to suppose that the Pont was not altogether unlike its neighbors. The structure of the ownership of land, for example, was not unusual at Pont-de-Montvert. It is well known that there were many more peasant proprietors in southern France than in northern France, and Pont-de-Montvert was quite typical in this respect. There are other similarities as well: in preindustrial times, rural industries were extremely common throughout the region, and again that was true of the Pont.[8] The population curve of the village is likewise quite in the order of things. It is characterized by a steep rise on the eve of the French Revolution and an accelerated decline in the second half of the nineteenth century. Within the curve, it is true, there are some anomalies. Pont-de-Montvert was slower to decline, since it reached its maximum population in 1875 some thirty years later than was true for rural France as a whole, and the fall in its population, when it finally came, was more accelerated than was usually the case outside of the Lozère. The great rise in prosperity during the second half of the nineteenth century, however, was not in anyway anomalous. This development was everywhere present, although its impact may have been greater at the Pont, which had been much poorer to begin with; and everywhere also the consequence of higher wages and emigration was a weakening of the old social structure.[9]

The great trends in the economic life of Pont-de-Montvert are not therefore very different from what has been found to be true in other villages all over France. The political history of the Pont is, however, less typical if only because the village was a Protestant community in a country where nearly all peasants are Catholics. On the surface of things, this might seem to have been a crucial factor since rural Protestantism and left wing politics were so often found together in southern France, in the Gard, the Ardèche, and the Cévennes generally. But at the same time, in a more fundamental way, the fact that Pont-de-Montvert was a Protestant village in a Catholic country does not invalidate comparisons between its politics and those of other villages like the Catholic communities of the northern Lozère. There too, politics were abstract and irrelevant, and the particular hue of a political stance is not of much consequence if all politics are meaningless. The anomalous Protestantism of Pont-de-Montvert therefore does not set it apart from the Catholic villages, and there is no reason to suppose

Afterword

that its politics were fundamentally very different from those of other small French towns of the same period.

That the Pont should have crystallized its particular opinions during the French Revolution is likewise quite in the order of things. It has been shown that for many French communities, rural and urban, contemporary political traditions have their origin as far back as the last decades of the eighteenth century. That has certainly been true of the villages in the Vendée and the Sarthe that have been studied in some detail.[10] Admittedly, the original cause of allegiance there was not religion, as was true at the Pont. In the Vendée what mattered most may well have been the prerevolutionary dislocation of peasant life by bourgeois merchants from the outside. But although the origins of political prejudice may not have been the same in the Vendée and at the Pont, it was indeed at the same moment in history that the pattern jelled in both places; and the Pont is certainly representative of many French villages in having political roots which reach back to a distant past.

The perpetuation of the Pont's political stance also has counterparts in many other villages, for not only did the Pont begin its political career two centuries ago, but it has persisted in this same tradition unswervingly since that time. On the whole, French historians have not been as interested in the durability of political traditions as they have been in their origins; but in those places where the perpetuation of political opinion has been studied in some detail—by Edgar Morin, for example, in his *Commune en France*—the parallels with Pont-de-Montvert are very striking. In his book, Morin describes the political continuity that links the communist and socialist present of his small Breton community with the past of the Third Republic and of the French Revolution; and he shows for Plodemet what also holds true for Pont-de-Montvert, namely, that the parties of the left and of the extreme left have come to embody the Great Principles of 1789, justice and liberty, by becoming in fact the party not just of the working class or of upheaval, but of order and of the small bourgeoisie as well.[11] If the communist party at Plodemet or at the Pont had remained thoroughly revolutionary, it would also have remained suspect to many. But by espousing the cause of the small against the outsiders, the great, and the rich, communism at Plodemet has become the party of the ordinary Frenchman who identifies his own private interests with the principles of the Great Revolution. Thus, in Morin's village, a political tradition born in the eighteenth century perpetuates itself today thanks to a political party which claims to be revolutionary but which is in fact a bulwark of some aspects of the status quo, and this of course is very reminiscent of what was true at Pont-de-Montvert. In both communities, the French Revolution, radical socialism, socialism, and communism are often seen as many facets of the same doctrine, and this because most of the people who live there have amalgamated or confused libertarian principles with the defense of a threatened popular and petit bourgeois social order. The origins of this state of affairs, it is true, are quite different in the two places since Plodemet is a Catholic community. But the more important thing is that regardless of the paths they have traveled, both villages have come to the same end. In both places, an essentially irrelevant political tradition survives today because it serves to defend what is in fact a socially static, uniform, and outmoded way of life against threats from the outside world.

All in all, therefore, it is no exaggeration to see in the history of our village many reflections, some clear, some muted, of the history of the *Grande Nation*. In the story of this small Cévenol community, we can find echoes of the great problems which France has faced in the last three hundred years: why there was no bourgeois revolution in the seventeenth century, why there was a revolution in 1789 and what it was about, and why nineteenth-century French politics should have been so strange.

Of course, it is not surprising at all that Pont-de-Montvert should have in many ways resembled other villages or even the image that we have of the French Nation. How indeed could it have been any other way? The people of the Pont are Frenchmen, and with varying degrees of success, admittedly, they have lived as Frenchmen in France. Their view of themselves has been colored by what they think of France, just as the "certain idea of France" which has guided them has also been in part at least a reflection of their own idea of Pont-de-Montvert.[12] Indeed, the links between the Pont and France are not encompassed just by those events or situations which have been similar in the Pont and in other communities in France. The representativeness of the Pont lies also in its individuality. There is no one typical, archetypal French village that other villages approximate more or less closely. There are thousands of unique villages, all of which together were at one time France, just as millions of unique beings together form a nation or a race. That may well be why "man likes to enter into another existence . . . to touch the subtlest fibers of another's heart and to listen to its beating."[13] We can understand because of the similarities, and we are curious about the differences. And that may also be why the history of Pont-de-Montvert can both be written within the limits of the village and at the same time remain meaningful historically within the context of the history of France.

Afterword

It is perhaps no accident that in French the word *patrie* has two meanings: the nation at large surely, but also and for every Frenchman his own commune. And if the perspective of the greater whole is necessary to make sense of its parts, it may also be true that a real perception of the history of France can begin with an understanding of some of its villages.

APPENDICES

APPENDIX 1 Family Landownership

In Villeneuve, in 1631, we find that the land belongs to a few families, the Andrés, the Combes, the Albarics, the Pelades, the Pons, with the Molines and the Pantels trailing behind them.

In 1700, landownership has not changed much, although the Combes and Pons family have left Villeneuve and now live at the Pont, where the Andrés had already been living in 1630. In 1789, 150 years later, we can still find a great deal of continuity in both ownership of land and actual physical presence. The Albarics are still the largest landowners. And remaining also are the Pantels and the Molines, both families more prosperous. By leasing land in addition to what they owned originally, they are much better off than they used to be and are now landowning *laboureurs* instead of tenants or *rentiers* as they had been at the beginning of the century. Of course, some families had by then moved out or disappeared like the Jourdans or the Bondurants, who went to Génolhac but retained an interest in the region and bought some *biens nationaux* there in 1795. Others have moved in, like the Servières who originally came from another hamlet, l'Hopital. But even there, one finds continuity, because David Servière in 1789 was the son of Jean-Antoine Servière, himself the son of David Servière (born in 1673) and of Jeanne Rouvière, who was the daughter of Jean Rouvière and Jeanne Quet of Villeneuve, who were married at the Pont on July 7, 1673. In other words, in 1789, the Albarics, Pantels, Molines, and the Servière family were descendants of the original owners of 1631. Many other people came and went. Some, like Aaron Bonnicel, who had leased the Combes property in 1701, founded families which remained. Others like Pierre Martin who had at the same time leased the André lands did not. But the important point is that there remained in the hamlets in the seventeenth and eighteenth centuries a nucleus of landowners whose status and geographical positions changed somewhat, but not much.

Table 3. The inhabitants of Villeneuve

1631	1661 (Villeneuve and Rieumal)
Marie Molines, widow of Antoine Pantel	Moyse Molines
	Margueritte Pantel
	Heirs of Jean Pantel
Heirs of David Albaric	Alexandre Albaric, husband of Jeanne Pelade
Jean Pelade, husband of J. Pons	
Pierre Pons	
Jean Pons	
Jean Jourdan	Jean Jourdan
Jean Combes	
Heirs of Maurice Combes	Jean Combes
Jeanne Combes	
Jacques Roux	Jacques Roux
Jean André	Demoiselle Margueritte Dandré
Jacques André	
	Jacques Rouvière
	Antoine Quet
	Jeanne Quette
	Jacques Bondurant
	Jean Roure
	Madeleine Roure

1696–1701	1750	1789
Jacques Molines (tenant of Pierre Albaric)	Jacques Molines	Jacques Molines
	Jacques Molines	Jacques Molines
	Jean Molines	
Antoine Pantel	Pierre Pantel	Jean Pantel
Pierre Pantel		Pierre Pantel
	Pierre Albaric	Jean Albaric
Marc Antoine Jourdan	—Jourdan	
Aaron Bonnicel (tenant of Jean Combes)	Aaron Bonnicel	Jean Bonnicel
André Mazoyer Rouvière	Antoine Servière	David Servière (grandson of Jean Rouvière of Villeneuve)
		Louis Rouvière
David Rouvière	Pierre Allier	Jean Allier
		Pierre Allier
Jean Pelat		
	Jacques Pucheral	Jean Pucheral
		Pierre Pucheral
Pierre Martin (tenant of Mme. Dandré)	Pierre Perrounende	
		Jacques Richard
		Jean Roure

153

APPENDIX 2 Cahier de Doléances de la Paroisse de Frutgères pour Présenter à l'Assemblée du Diocèse*

1. Cette communauté située sur un sol très rude et très âpre n'offre de tous côtés qu'une chaine de montagnes dont la stérilité s'étend sur chaque individu, la rapidité des terres augmente infiniment les travaux nécessaires à la culture et les torrents qui sont très fréquents dans cette communauté entrainent le plus souvent les récoltes ou les fumatures et obligent les propriétaires à des travaux très couteux et presque toujours continuels, les impôts sont si excessifs qu'ils éxèdent le tiers des revenus.

2. Que Sa Majesté soit suppliée d'accorder une protection spéciale à l'agriculture et en déchargeant tous ses fruits des péages, leudes et impôts quelconques; lui accorder toutes les prérogatives que doit et peut exiger la mère nourricière dans un état bien conçu.

3. Supplie également Sa Majesté de vouloir supprimer toute gabelle; par ce moyen le sel dont le prix est exorbitant devenant à meilleur compte, le cultivateur pourra en faire une consommation plus considérable, alors leurs troupeaux et engrais se multiplieront et donneront plus de ressources aux agriculteurs; les laines en acquérant la qualité augmenteront en quantité ce qui produira un bien considérable pour tout le pays.

4. Qu'il ne fut jamais permis sous aucun prétexte de faire aucun défrichement dans tous le pays des Cévennes ou la rapidité du dit pays et la légèreté des terrains que les ravines emportent plus facilement; qu'elles soient surtout défendues dans les bois parce que les rompues qu'on y fait nous mettent dans le cas d'en manquer au premier jour, comme aussi il ne devrait pas être permis de se servir du bois pour la fonderie des mines dans un pays ou il est si rare, mais bien du charbon de pierre qui est commun et a portée soit pour la mine de Villefort ou autres qu'on se propose d'établir aux environs.

* The draft of this cahier was never presented to the wider assembly of the bailliage. For this reason, it cannot be officially labeled as a *cahier de doléances*. A copy of this draft is in the papers of the Chapelle family of Pont-de-Montvert.

154

5. La communauté de Frutgères supporte depuis un temps immémorial toutes les contributions de la province que du diocèse pour l'ouverture de routes de la province [et] réclame en son particulier un chemin du Pont-de-Montvert à Mende, ou du moins l'entretien d'icelluy qui existe; cette route est absolument nécessaire pour le Haut et Bas Gévaudan, elle est même beaucoup plus courte qu'aucunes de celles qui ont déjà été pratiquées et plus abondantes en fourrages. Les vins, hiles, et charbon de pierre seraient exportés à moindre frais et beaucoup plus facilement dans le Haut-Gévaudan.

6. Supplie Sa Majesté de rapprocher autant que possible la justice des justiciables afin de la rendre plus courte et moins couteuse. La supplie surtout de fixer le sénéchal de Mende en telle ville que bon lui semblera afin qu'il ne soit plus ambulant et d'en fixer les limites.

7. Supplie encore Sa Majesté d'accorder à la province du Languedoc une constitution libre et entière ainsi qu'Elle l'a accordée à la province du dauphiné.

8. Demande la suppression totale des milices comme étant très onéreuse pour les communautés et agriculteurs ou dans restreindre la levée dans les villes.

9. Que tous les biens fonds du Royaume soient sujets à l'impôt tout les biens nobles que possédés par la Noblesse et le Clergé que par le Tiers-Etat—qu'il en soit de même des biens francs ou qu'ils soient situés dans le Royaume, distraction de ce que les dits biens payent déjà sous le nom de décimes, ving-tièmes, ou franc fief.

10. Le Bas-Gévaudan eyant été lésé dans l'administration municipale par le Haut-Pays, la communauté réclame une administration distincte et séparée et qu'il soit permis au Bas Gévaudan de se nommer des commissaires ou son syndic particulier pour la répartition égale des impôts.

11. Que les quatre communautés prétendeus chefs lieux composent le colloque du Bas Gévaudan, mais que toutes, les communautés assemblées ayant le droit exclusif de nommer leurs commissaires pour travailler de conni-vence avec le Syndic du Haut-Gévaudan pour la répartition de l'impôt, lequel commissaire sera tenu de donner tous les ans copie à toutes les communautés du procès-verbal des Etats du diocèse.

[unsigned and undated]

APPENDIX 3 French Passages Translated

in the Text

Page 1   Le 17 août 1697 à deux heures de nuit après avoir bien plu tout le jour, il fit de si grands éclairs, tonnerres et pluie qu'il emporta tous les moulins de Pont-de-Montvert avec six à sept maisons sans y rien laisser et notamment de M. Pons, mon beau-frère, qui avait épousé ma sœur Cassandre, en nombre de quatre moulins à blé et à foulons, emporta une partie des ponts, tous les jardins . . . emporta beaucoup de terres et surtout celles qui étaient près de la rivière, n'y ayant laissé ni prés ni arbres.

qui emporta beaucoup de terres, et notamment les moulins de mon dit beau-frère qu'il avait fait reconstruire, après quoi ma sœur mourut de chagrin y ayant employé une partie de sa constitution.

Page 2   venant de Trèsme, mourut à l'entrée du Villaret, à cause de la neige et mauvais temps, même la, jument qu'elle menait mourut aussi étant restée deux jours et trois nuits dehors, aprés le mardi 15 fut portée aux Bondons, par ordre de M. le Curé comme étant de la paroisse.

Page 13   droits et facultés qu'ils possèdent (de tenir) un marché tous les mercredis de chaque semaines ou il se débite bled, chastaigne, du bétail, sans payer aucun droits de lods ni péage sur les marchandises qui entrent et sortent du marché et ont jouy du même privilège de toute ancienneté.

Page 17   Chez M. Campredon, subdélégué de Monsieur l'Intendant (chercher) douze couvertures petites pour les donner aux gens qui n'en avaient point pour couvrir les soldats.

156

Page 36 On en condamna plusieurs à la question. On donna la géhenne à cinq hommes en un jour, et deux jours après à trois autres. On voulait leur faire découvrir ceux qui avoient assistés à ces assemblées, mais surtout ceux qui y avoient fait la fonction de ministres. Quels maux qu'on leur fit souffrir, ils ne voulurent déclarer qui que ce fut.

pour obliger les habitants d'aller à la messe, ceux qui ne le fesoient pas étaient condamnés à dix sols d'amende ou recevoient logement chez eux à discrétion.

Page 37 aagé de 10 ans, fils de feu Jean (Malachane) et d'Elisabet Quin . . . La mère est remariée, et a abandonné ce garçon qui n'est point instruit et deviendrait vagabond.

Page 38 On l'exécuta au Pont-de-Montvert, le mercredi 25 janvier 1702. Elle marcha avec fermeté au lieu du supplice, repoussant avec une douceur pleine de modestie, le missionaire qui l'accompagnoit et l'exhortoit à changer de religion. Quatre tambours ne cessèrent de battre la caisse depuis le moment qu'elle sortit de prison jusqu'à son dernier soupir.

Page 40 Il y eut beaucoup de maisons conservées comme celles des anciens catholiques et autres qui avaient des amis auprès des puissances, du nombre desquelles fut celle que nous avons ici à Grizac quoi qu'elle me coutât plusieurs voyages à Montpellier et ailleurs.

Page 41 tous les troupeaux furent rassemblés, sous la promesse que le sieur Viala de St. Jean de Gardonnenque et sur l'assurance que l'intendant nous faisait de les payer, ils les firent prendre par les soldats du régiment de Hainault qui vinrent et les fit emmener, le bandit, sans rien donner à personne et nous réduisit à la mendicité.

Je suis tellement foulé par le logement des troupes, que je ne puis tenir. Outre deux lits et deux couvertes que je fournis aux casernes, j'ai chez moi 2 capitaines, 2 lieutenants, et six soldats. Je dois encore de 5 en 5 jours deux livres d'huile et 2 quintaux de bois . . . mon valet peut-il à peine nous tenir de bois à la maison . . . il me faudra vendre mon mulet faute de foin, quoy que j'en eusse recueuilli plus de cent quintaux . . . Mais les soldats nous prennent tout sans payer; quelques uns ont été payé à 3 sols par place. Demain, nous attendons ici de couchée M. de La Lande et sa suite qui est de 900 hommes. Je me verrai à la fin obligée d'abandonner tout. Dieu est toute ma consolation.

Appendix 3

Page 42   apprendre à la postérité le grand crime que c'est de se rebeller
            contre son souverain. La rebellion des atroupés n'estant que du
            bas peuple, cela n'empêche pas que les plus relevée et les plus
            sages ne souffrent de ce terrible châtiment.

            une vie abominable, les filles couchant librement et sans honte
            avec les garçons qu'elles aiment, cela est notoire.—A Esclopier
            (paroisse de Saint-Etienne), une se mit au milieu de deux et à
            Saumanes, deux filles se mirent avec quatre garçons, soutenant
            qu'ayant parlé à Dieu, il n'y avoit pas de mal.

Page 49   la faculté de semer des pommes de terre à un petit coin de terre
            qu'il voudra.

Page 50   communément malsaines et peu commodes . . . le trou à fumier,
            ce cloaque fangeux qui semble en défendre l'approche, y répand
            continuellement des miasmes putrides.

Page 56   les habitants du Gévaudan sont pauvres et misérables, leur misère
            est connue dans tout le Languedoc et dans les autres provinces
            voisines aux quelles ils fournissent une grand nombre de servantes,
            de valets et bergers, de bouviers, et encore, beaucoup de men-
            diants.

            l'abandon de ce pays, que font les trois quarts de cette paroisse
            qui sont obligés d'aller dans le bas Languedoc, le Vivarais et le
            Gévaudan pour gagner à la sueur de leur front de quoi payer leur
            taille.

Page 57   il s'y fabrique [at the Pont] des cadis qui servent à habiller les habi-
            tants du pays: et chacun en fait un peu pour son usage quelques
            pièces pour vendre et ces pièces n'ont aucune longueur ni poids
            fix.

Page 60   à la cotte onzième de tous les grains en gerbes, et à la même cotte
            pour les agneaux, percevant en outre un sol pour chaque toison de
            brebis et de moutons.

Page 65   modique jardin, si ce sacrifice eut pu contribuer au bien être et au
            bonheur d'un peuple naguère doux, paisible, et débonnaire, qu'il
            affectionne de tout son cœur. Mais il ne peut être qu'indigné contre
            les malintentionnés qui corrompent et fomentent ce pauvre peuple
            sans utilité ni profit.

Page 72   Vers le mois de Juillet 1729 Mgr l'évêque de Mende, voyant une
            disette générale dans tout le pays et particulièrement dans son

158

diocèse, sollicita la province pour avoir du blé éstranger, ce qui lui fut accorder, on fit voiturer une grande quantité de blé à St Jean de Gardonnenque et on le distribua aux paroisses suivant leur population . . . Il n'y eut pour la paroisse de Grizac que 10 sacs de tuzelle qui furent distribué aux plus pauvres.

sur un sol très rude et très âpre (qui) n'offre de tout côté qu'une chaine de montagne dont la stérilité s'étend sur chaque individu.

Page 73   en déchargeant tous ses fruits de tous péages, leudes et impôts quelconques, lui accorder toutes les prerogatives que doit et peut exiger la mère nourricière dans un état bien conçu.

ayant rompu toutes sortes de commerce en occupant tous les passages ou ils ont égorgé plusieurs muletiers, sestant mesme porté à cette extrémité de deffandre le payemant de la taille et de la capitation, et de menacer de tuer ou de brusler ceux qui en feroient le payement et la levée; sy bien que presque touses les communautés des Cévennes, par lappuy ou la crainte de ces scélérats ont refuzé et refuzent encore de payer la taille et la capitation.

Page 76   jusqu'en 1702, il adressa des exhortations aux fidèles, s'élevant beaucoup contre les prophètes qui couraient le pays, prêchaient la guerre, ordonnaient de tuer les prêtres et de brûler les églises. Mais les passions étaient déchainées; on le traita d'incrédule.

Nous ne souffrons ni fanatiques, ni piétistes, ni anabaptistes; la parole de Dieu est seule reconnue pour règle, et plut à Dieu que vous vissiez régner l'ordre et la règle que nous y tenons.

des prophètes ignorants, que le peuple suivoit avec zèle, à défaut de pasteurs éclairés, et dont les absurdes prédictions étoient reçues avec une pleine confiance et une dangereuse docilité. Ainsi, la vive lumière dont les églises réformés avoient brillés dans le XVIIe siècle, s'éteignit peu à peu et fit place à une longue obscurité.

Ne pouvant plus se nourrir de l'Evangile et de la vérité, l'esprit se repait de rèveries et de chimères. La guerre des Camisards en fournit une preuve sans réplique.

Page 77   au lieu de travailler à m'expulser du royaume (devrait travailler) à m'y retenir, persuadée que je luy rendois d'utiles services en formant des bons sujets.

Appendix 3

Page 77   Je les détournay par mes avis, aymant mieux donner des martyrs
à l'Eglise que d'attirer des troubles dans la province ou de blames
sur la religion.

Les églises de Lozère, du Pont-de-Montvert, de Castagnol, de
St-Juilhan, de Florac firent de grands progrès et se relevèrent par
une merveilleuse assistance de Dieu, étant favorisé par la con-
tagion [the plague of 1721] qui avoit fait retirer toutes les trouppes
de nos montagnes et des Cévennes.

Le lendemain matin, jour de dimanche, furent convoquées les
églises de Genolhac, Frutgères, et du Pont-de-Montvert, et où
assista encore l'église de C . . . L'assemblée fut très-nombreuse.
On y vit ce qu'on n'avait peut-être point vu depuis la Révocation,
cinq enfants baptisés à la tête de l'assemblée. Cette cérémonie
attendrit le cœur de tous les assistant. Que de larmes furent ré-
pandues pendant la prédication! La pluie nous incommoda, non-
seulement pendant cette cérémonie, mais encore après. L'exercice
achevé, la pluie ayant cessé, les uns se retirèrent et les autres
prirent une réfection sur le lieu. Là, se virent un grand nombre de
cercles de personnes assises sur le gazon qui avec simplicité prirent un sobre et simple repas composé des aliments que chacun a
soin de porter de chez soi, et qui se termina par un chant d'un
sacré cantique. C'est ainsi qu'on en use ordinairement dans les
assemblées de ce pays. Avant de quitter la place je bénis cinq
mariages.

Page 78   Le pauvre Bonnicel du Pont-de-Montvert qu'on avait fait étudier
pour être abbé, mais qu'ensuitte prit le party de marchand, était
garçon de boûtique à Montpelier . . . fut aussi condamné à la
corde.

Page 79   les personnes même qui n'y auraient jamais voulu paraître: procureurs, notaires, marchands, bourgeois, notables, le gentilhomme
même, seigneur de place; on y mène jusqu'aux enfants qui com-
mencent à marcher . . .

Quand on demande aux gens d'une certaine sorte qui avaient
jusqu'ici méprisé les assemblées pourquoi ils y vont aujourd'hui,
ils rèpondent qu'ils ne croyent pas contrevenir aux ordres du roi,
parce que le roi le sait bien et qu'il le souffre.

Page 80   est pleine de misérables depuis quelques années, les récoltes ont
manqué, il y a actuellement une grande mortalité dans les bestiaux.

Les mauvaises récoltes qu'il y a eu depuis quelques années dans cette montagne a mis les habitans dans une extrême misère et il est à craindre qu'ils ne fassent une grande sottise s'ils se trouvaient dans l'impossibilité de payer, si l'amende était sy considérable.

Page 84   le peuple paroit sensible à la privation des messes et nous pensons que ce mécontentement est seul capable de le porter à quelque insurrection.

Page 90   Le roi ordonna de faire des milices dans tout le Royaume. Cela commença en 1725 et continua jusqu'en 1735. Furent pris dans ces milices un fils Guin, de l'Hermet nommé Estienne, il fut conduit à St-Ambroix, de la à Marseille et Toulon ou il est resté;— Jacques Martin de l'Hermet. Celui-ci acheta un remplaçant à Mr. Campredon sub-délégué de l'Intendant pour 55 écus de 3 livres.

Page 91   que le dit Augustin Bonnicel s'engage volontairement par le présent acte à partir pour la cohorte en remplacement du dit Jean-François Servière conscrit de 1807, faisant parti du contingent des hommes que doit fournir le Canton du Pont-de-Montvert, de faire pour ce dernier toute espèce de service militaire dans quel corps d'armée que ce soit, de le représenter partout ou besoin serait, en fait des services militaires, de partir pour le compte du dit Jean-François Servière du moment qu'il sera appelé par les autorités compétentes.

Qui se mêle d'exercer l'art de guérir, qu'elle applique des remèdes à tort et à travers, et on me la dénonce comme ayant même employé certains remèdes pour donner des ulcères factices aux conscrits.

Page 93   Il est nécessaire de prévenir que la misère des temps, le manque de récolte . . . l'esprit processif qui règne dans ce pays, la conduite des procureurs et des gens d'affaire qui ont réussit à s'enrichir aux dépens des paysans, sont les premiers et seuls motifs des troubles qu'il y a eut en 1783.

Tous avaient l'air triste et consterné, les procureurs et gens d'affaire de la ville et des environs qui s'y étaient rendus en très grands nombres avaient l'air de la satisfaction répandue sur leurs visages.

Page 96   semblables aux oiseaux que le froid chasse dans une plus douce contrée, ce peuple fuit la neige qui couvre huit mois de l'année ses montagnes. Il y retourne tous les ans pour faire un enfant à sa

161

femme, la laisse entre les mains des vielles et des curés, et parcours ensuite le royaume sans avoir de domicile fixe.

Chaque Auvergnat, l'un portant l'autre, remène quatre ou cinq louis dans sa triste patrie. L'enfant de dix ans en a gagné deux; ils les cousent dans la ceinture de leur culotte, et les enfants mendient le long des chemins.

Ces hordes voyagent ainsi depuis Jules César et plus anciennement encore.

Page 98   triste réduit, enterré sous le sol, obscur, sans air, humide en un mot, indigne de la majesté de celui qui veut bien y résider par amour pour les hommes.

Page 100   Presque toutes les Estoffes se transportent dans les pays Etrangers, scavoir l'Italie, le Levant, la Suisse, Lallemagne, la Poulogne, Lespagne, La sicile et Malte.

notre commerce, l'âme de cette contrée, est aux abois, qu'il tombé sans que personne daigne luy tendre une main secourable. Le débit que je fais de laines m'oblige à fréquenter nos marchés qui ne sont rien. Marvejols n'a plus de commission. Le Rouergue les a toutes enlevées.

Des artisans, tisseurs de laine, sont tombés dans une affreuse misère. Ce peuple d'ouvriers, jadis propre et même élégant dans sa mise, n'achète rien aujourdhui ... J'ai vu des jeunes filles inoccupées, mal vêtues, en danger de sacrifier à des besoins leur honneur.

Cette industrie des laines est morte aujourd'hui, et c'est le progrès qui la tuée. Que pouvait devenir en effet l'antique métier à tisser, meuble héréditaire des pauvres familles, après l'invention de Jacquard? Et que faire du rouet de nos fileuses depuis l'invention des Mules-Jenny?

Page 102   depuis une trentaine d'années nos paysans des montagnes sont dans l'usage de fréquenter dès le mois d'octobre plusieurs foires de Cantal aux environs d'Aurillac où ils vont acheter des jeunes teaureaux qu'ils conduisent chez eux; ils les y élèvent au travail après les avoir domptés, les font châtrer et au mois de septembre ... ces mêmes bœufs sont vendus aux foires du Vigan, Villefort, et Barre.

Page 104   le gouvernement de l'Empereur dans sa constante sollicitude pour la population de l'Empire cherche tous les moyens pour améliorer le sort du peuple, pour lui faciliter des voies de communications?

les vélocipèdes et les automobiles passant tous maintenant par la nouvelle voie pourraient produire une panique sur les animaux.

le désaccord intervenu entre eux et Mr. le Maire, au sujet de l'arrêt qui déplace le marché ou l'on exposait les vaches.

Page 109   la carrière de l'enseignement offrant parmi nous si peu d'avantages, les instituteurs ne se donnent pas la peine ou ne font pas la dépense de se former aux bonnes méthodes; c'est toujours un enseignement routinier qu'on suit. . . . et deux à trois ans sont employés par eux à apprendre très mal à lire et à écrire.

des instituteurs sans capacité, imbus des plus mauvaises méthodes d'enseignement et peu propre par conséquent à répandre l'instruction dans nos contrées; mais en l'absence de meilleurs resources, on craint de nuire à l'avenir des familles en provoquant la suppression de ces écoles, toutes clandestines et très imparfaites quelles sont.

Page 118   L'éducation politique des habitants de cette région qui en grande majorité professent la religion protestante y est très généralement développé et a donné naissance, pour l'esprit public a des habitudes de discipline électorale qui assurent la représentation républicaine de cet arrondissement.

Page 121   la pauvreté des habitants, leurs habitudes de travail, d'ordre et de soumission aux lois, me paraissent rendre tout à fait digne d'intérêt la demande qu'ils forment . . .

il est un fait assez curieux à constater, c'est que parmi les protestants, l'Orléanisme et le républicanisme s'alliaient fréquemment . . . Le souvenir de la protection dont ils ont joui sous le règne de Louis-Philippe leur fait souvent regretter ce passé.

Page 125   L'Empire, c'est la guerre à la Prusse, c'est le despotisme—c'est le désordre, c'est l'invasion. La Royauté, c'est la guerre avec Italie, c'est le gouvernement des curés—C'est encore l'invasion. La République, c'est la tranquillité—c'est la paix—c'est la liberté—c'est la loi. Votez donc pour la République. Votez pour M. Bourillon.

Page 126   sur lesquelles repose avec la sécurité de nos foyers, le progrès même de la moralité humaine c'est à dire la meilleure entre toutes des garanties de l'ordre social.

163

Appendix 3

Page 126   Nous voterons tous pour MacMahon, c'est à dire pour l'ordre, pour la paix, pour les grands travaux, pour l'exposition universelle, pour le maintien de ce qui est de peur d'avoir pire.

Page 128   un admirateur passionné de notre glorieuse Révolution de 1789 qui en abolissant les privilèges a placé sur un même pied d'égalité riches et pauvres, bourgeois et paysans.

les deux adversaires ont fait un exposé à peu près identiques mais plus avancé chez M. Rolland, qui déclare une guerre acharnée au capital et à la bourgeoisie.

les administrations publiques trouvent auprès des corps élus et des habitants le plus d'obligeante déférence.

Page 129   cet impôt ne frappera que ceux qui ont plus de 5000 francs de revenus. Dans notre Lozère [Paraf was also a Parisian] ces favorisés de la fortune sont très peu nombreux.

un ensemble de dégrèvements immédiats au profit des petits agriculteurs et des petits commerçants et cela par des taxes sur les valeurs étrangères.

Voulez-vous que la Lozère fasse respecter ses vieilles croyances religieuses ou retombe sous les influences juives et maçonniques?

Page 130   Paysans! depuis 1894 vous avez payés 1,000,000 de plus. Qui vous force de porter au percepteur cette somme énorme? C'est le vote de Bourillon.

Tous ces électeurs voteraient pour la république s'ils n'étaient bridés par le desservant Malafosse.

Page 131   bon dreyfusard . . . républicain—à éte élevé dans des établissements laics.

Je ne viens point en ce moment auprès de vous, Monsieur le curé, pour vous demander de prêter à ma candidature un concours dont l'activité et la nature pourraient n'être pas conforme à votre mission particulière et au caractère sacré dont vous êtes revêtu. Mais . . .

les prêtres et les curés, vicaires, desservants, hormis quelques rares exceptions se sont librés à une propagande effrênée. De jour et de nuit, ils sont allés dans toutes les maisons de la circonscription de leur desserte, ne se rebutant même pas devant un mauvais accueil, discutant les candidats, défendant pied à pied les candidatures opposantes et finalement ne reculant pas devant l'argument décisif pour les populations de la Lozère, *du cas de conscience* ... Ils ont dit et écrit que "voter pour un candidat républicain c'était commettre un pêché mortel."

Page 133   sceptique; sceptique et indifférent aux honneurs du pouvoir— le député et le ministre n'ont été qu'un homme, simple et dévoué mettant au seul service de ses compatriotes son activité et son influence.

Notes

1. See, for example, *Journal de la Lozère,* 15 November 1828, and *Délibérations départementales de la Lozère* III, 702.

2. Paul Joanne, *Dictionnaire Géographique et Administratif de la France* (Paris, 1899), p. 2336.

3. Antoine Velay, "Livre de raison de Antoine Velay, originaire de Racoules," unpublished. A copy of this work is in the possession of M. Albin Pantel, of Pont-de-Montvert.

4. *Ibid.*

5. Winter sets in early at the Pont, often by mid October. Hence the proverb: "Per san Luc/la néou per truc." St. Luke's Day is October 18.

6. "Livre de raison de Antoine Velay."

7. Robert Louis Stevenson, *Travels Through the Cévennes on a Donkey* (New York, 1911), pp. 129–131.

8. ADL G 2097. (See "Manuscripts and Documents" in this volume.)

9. To illustrate the uniqueness of conditions at the Pont, it may be of use to compare rainfall there and at Le Bleymard, the next village to the north. Total average yearly rainfall is nearly the same in the two places, but in July it rains twice as much at Le Bleymard as it does at the Pont, where in turn precipitation is one third higher in January, February, and March. It would be most difficult and hazardous therefore to assume something about weather at Pont-de-Montvert on the basis of what could be found out about weather elsewhere. Monsieur Leroy-Ladurie has worked out the dates of climatic cycles for the Languedoc, but conditions there are so different from the ones at the Pont that his conclusions cannot help us very much. Observations about Pont-de-Montvert itself would be needed, and even different observations in different parts of the Pont. Rainfall, to take that example again, is far more likely in the valleys than on the hilltops, so that cyclical changes in precipitation would have more obvious effect in the bourg than in the hillside hamlets. See Société des Arts et Lettres de la Lozère, *Chroniques et Mélanges* (Mende, 1940), IV, 288.

10. See Emmanuel Leroy-Ladurie, *Les Paysans du Languedoc* (Paris, 1966).

11. Albert Grimaud and Marius Balmelle, *Précis d'histoire du Gévaudan* (Mende, 1925), p. 110.

12. Indeed, the Lozère had achieved some territorial unity by 800 B.C. and the beginning of the iron age. See Michel Lorblanchet, "Les Étapes de peuplement sur les Grands Causses des origines à l'époque Gallo-Romaine," *Revue du Gévaudan*, 13 (1967), 214.

13. *Le Monde*, 27 November 1968.

14. Charles Morel, "Fouilles et recherches inédites," *Revue du Gévaudan*, 7 (1961), 103–136.

15. Charles Camproux, *Etude syntaxique des parlers Gévaudannais* (Paris, 1958), p. 512.

16. This is not surprising since the Cévennes have been continuously and densely populated since 2000 or 1800 B.C. It has been estimated by some that the population of the area was as dense then as it is today. See Benjamin Bardy, "Notes et comptes rendus: Géographie préhistorique, protohistorique, et Gallo-Romaine des Cévennes méridionales et de leurs abords," *Revue du Gévaudan*, 13 (1967), 209.

17. See Marius Balmelle, "Iconographie du Pape Urbain V," *Revue du Gévaudan*, 10 (1964), 73–88. Since Pont-de-Montvert is today a protestant community, it derives little satisfaction from this singularly unusual event. Although collateral descendants of the pope still do own forests in the village, they play no role whatever in village life and there is nothing much left there to remind us of Urban V. His ancestral home, the Château de Grizac, was itself burned down in 1713: "Le mardi 2 octobre 1713, à minuit, Jeanne André, veuve de David Rampon, habitant Grizac, faisant lessive, mit par mégarde feut à sa maison qui brûla entièrement et fit brûler la grange de Claude Boyer qui joignait la sienne, et la bise s'éleveant porta le feu au Château où restait Antoine Atger qui brûla tous ses effets, ayant été obligé de sortir ses enfants tout nus, et il ne resta rien dudit Château ... ce fut un terrible spectacle comme on peut le penser" ("Livre de Raison de Antoine Velay").

Today, *mutatis mutandis,* the chateau belongs to Amélie Chantegrel, of Fraissinet. She inherited it from its previous owners, whom she had served for some years as a maid. She is in consequence affectionately known to her neighbors as "la châtelaine."

18. See Jacques de Font-Réaulx, "L'exemption fiscale de la seigneurie de Grizac," *Revue du Gévaudan*, 8 (1962), 137–139.

19. The aggressiveness of feudal nobles at the Pont in this period is all the more likely in view of the fact that nobles were generally turbulent in the Gévaudan of the thirteenth and fourteenth centuries. Professor J. R. Strayer has even suggested that the bishop's treaty of *paréage* with the French crown in 1307 was designed to reassert episcopal authority in the face of seigneurial threats. See J. R. Strayer, "La noblesse du Gévaudan et le paréage de 1307," *Revue du Gévaudan*, 13 (1967), 66–69.

20. Leroy-Ladurie, *Les Paysans*, p. 215.

21. George de Burdin, ed., *Documents historiques sur la province de Gévaudan* (Toulouse, 1846), II, 161.

22. Compoix of Frutgères 1631, Municipal archives of Pont-de-Montvert.

23. Wheeled traffic was practically unknown until the middle of the nineteenth century. Although we do find at the Pont frequent mention in eighteenth-century tax lists of both *muletiers* and *bastiers, voituriers* by contrast

are almost nonexistent. Everything that went in or out of the Pont in those years did so of its own accord, or else was carried on the backs of men or animals. Sheep and cows were no problem, but grain traveled on mule back only, and tradition has it that men carried even the dirt that was used to make the terraces along the hillsides. In that sense, it might be said that Pont-de-Montvert was literally created from the void by the men who lived there, and few things there are more moving here than the contrast between the abandoned and sometimes hardly visible terraces of today with the image of the back-breaking, ant-like labor which went into their construction.

24. ADB-du-R HOM 1944.

25. Technically, five of these hamlets were not part of Pont-de-Montvert at all. Originally, since the parish of the Pont had had its seat at Frutgères, the hamlet of Grizac, which is close to the bourg but not to Frutgères, was institutionally linked with another parish, Fraissinet. In the eighteenth century, in spite of the fact that it was then thoroughly a part of the Pont, Grizac still had its own tax lists, separate from those of both the Fraissinet and the Frutgères–Pont-de-Montvert parishes. In 1790 this anomalous situation was resolved. Grizac was fused with the parish of Frutgères, now become the commune of Pont-de-Montvert. This was indeed as it should be, since the Grizacois had been Montipontins in all but name since at least the seventeenth century.

26. Albin Pantel and Emile Servière, "Seigneuries cévenoles," *Revue du Gévaudan,* 12 (1966), 13–65, 48.

27. That is, the mill was not common property under the feudal system. ADH C 2969.

28. We do not know very much about the way in which the tithe was collected. From a series of acts in the records of the notary Folcher in July of the years 1684, 1685, 1686, 1687, and 1688, we can reconstitute the amount of the tithe for these years—or at least an approximation of it, for although all of the village's hamlets are accounted for in the notarial acts, not all of the communities are accounted for in any one year. Since the size of the harvest varied a great deal from year to year, so did the amount of the tithe collected. This could explain in part why the bourg as a whole paid a tithe of only fifteen setiers of grain in 1684, although the hamlet of Montgros had to pay as much as ten setiers some years later when its population in 1700 comprised no more than five families. Some of the disproportion can be explained in this way, but it is also quite likely that regardless of fluctuations in the size of the harvest, some of the hamlets at the Pont always paid more than others.

29. There was, it is true, a continual lend-lease of females for matrimonial purposes. Although our information is very sketchy, it seems that females tended to move to their husbands' place of residence rather than vice versa, but even this involved only a few families.

30. ADL C 55.

31. A detailed description of familial stability and a table of continuity for the rich in the hamlets can be found in Appendix 1.

32. ADH C 2969.

33. AN F20 349.

34. ADH C 2969.

35. The only record of criminality in the grand style for the years before 1700 dates back to 1626. In that year, the Estates of the Gévaudan decreed

the destruction and "rasement de la maison dite Villeneuve, située près de Pont-de-Montvert et de la Lozère, dans laquelle s'étaient retirés et fortitiés les fils et complices du brigand Combes" (Burdin, *Documents historiques sur la province de Gévaudan* I, 151). It is interesting to see that these particular criminals had ceased to function within the community and had withdrawn literally as well as figuratively from the society of their fellow villagers. Their case, therefore, is not unlike that of another criminal, J. P. Devèze, in the 1790s. At that time, we are told, there lived in the hamlet of La Veissière, together with his two sons a sinister man named Devèze. His record was bad, since he had been "pendant toute sa jeunesse la terreur de la contrée" (ADL II U 118). For many years, he terrorized the local population, but was finally apprehended and executed on 18 Frimaire, Year V. Like the "brigand Combes," Devèze was a totally antisocial type, who had nothing in common with his law-abiding neighbors. There are, of course, many other instances of crime in the history of the Pont. We can cite cases of adultery, thievery (ADL II U 21 B 1–11), assault and battery (ADL II L 253 72), poisoning *(Archives de la famille Pantel)*, murder (ADL III E 8642), and even infanticide (ADL IV M 8 115P). Precise statistics are not to be found, but our impression is that criminality was not rampant at the Pont. Criminals were deviates, and they were shunned by all Montipontins, rich and poor alike.

36. *Village in the Vaucluse, Village en France,* these are titles that are ideally suited for histories and descriptions of French villages in our own time. It does make sense that in order to understand what villages are about today we should begin by explaining where it is that they are, and of what region they are a part. These villages exist in their own right, but at the same time, in present circumstances, they cannot be understood if they are removed from their regional or national context. That would not have been at all so true of Pont-de-Montvert in 1700, or even in 1800. At that time, the Pont was more of a world unto itself than it was some part of a greater whole. It was not Pont-de-Montvert in the Lozère, or in France. It was, more plainly, Pont-de-Montvert.

I. SOCIAL CLASS ON THE EVE OF THE CAMISARD WARS (1702–1704)

1. The use of the word "class" presents complex historical problems, not all of them semantic. It is not my purpose here to imply that there existed at Pont-de-Montvert in 1700 clearly defined social classes as Marx thought of them with different economic bases, fated to oppose each other. Nor do I mean to suggest that there existed some necessary connection between the existence of Montipontins social classes and the political life of the village. Indeed, the thrust of my argument is that although connections did exist, they were not necessary and varied widely from time to time. If I were to be facetious, I could conclude that I have defined and used "class" in a zoological rather than a sociological sense. This is not altogether satisfactory, but the concept of class is too useful to be discarded even by non-Marxist historians. Fernand Braudel has resolved the same problem in the following way. He writes of social conflict in the Mediterranean world of the sixteenth century. "Dirons nous qu'il s'agit d'une lutte des classes? J'imagine que B. Porchnev, l'admirable historien des troubles populaires de la France du XVIIe siècle, n'hésiterait pas devant l'expression. Après tout, historiens, nous employons

bien des mots que nous avons forgés, *féodalité, bourgeoisie, capitalisme,* sans tenir un compte toujours exact des réalités différentes qu'ils recouvrent, selon les siècles. Question de mots ... Si par lutte *des classes* nous désignons, sans plus, ces vengeances fratricides, ces mensonges, ces fausses justices, alors va pour la lutte des classes! L'expression vaut bien celle de tensions sociales que nous suggèrent les sociologues. Mais si le mot implique, comme je le pense, une certaine prise de conscience, la lutte des classes peut être claire pour l'historien, mais il contemple ce passé révolu avec des yeux du XXe siècle; elle n'a pas eu cette netteté pour les hommes du XVIe, assurément peu lucides sur ce point" (Fernand Braudel, *La Méditerranée et le mond méditerranéen à l'époque de Philippe II* [Paris, 1966], I, 78, 79).

2. Pantel and Servière, "Seigneuries Cévenoles," p. 48.

3. *Ibid.,* p. 50.

4. Pierre Pons, "Extraits des mémoires de Pierre Pons," *Bulletin de la Société de l'Histoire du Protestantisme français,* 32 (1883), 224. Hereafter *BSHP.*

5. "Livre de raison de Antoine Velay."

6. The practice of these loans, although very frequent, was not so widespread, however, as to affect even in the long run the economic structure of the village. The proof is that the number of small landowners did not change appreciably from the seventeenth to the twentieth century. It is hard to say in what light these loans were seen by those who had to borrow. Perhaps they were more grateful for having been bailed out than resentful at the interest and burden they had to bear.

7. "Livre de raison de Antoine Velay."

8. The earliest known case of such a migration is that of Antoine Roux, who was born in the Mazel, a hamlet on the northern slope of the Mont-Lozère. It is known to us from a renunciation of proprietary rights dated 1538. Out of gratitude to his uncle who had educated him, Antoine Roux, who now lived at Nîmes, gave up his claims to whatever inheritance he might have had. Antoine had no intention of ever going back to the Lozère, which he described as "pays aut, montahnes froit infertile et malvays et qu'il n'avoit que fère de demeurer ni fère résidence auculne à sa maison et pays de la où il est natif sestoit délibérer demeurer dorésénavant au pays bas pource qu'est bon pays fertil et abondant en biens" (Archives Départmentales du Gard, E 761, fol.73).

9. The deaths of very small children were apparently not always recorded, hence the persistent discrepancy between births and deaths. For that reason we do not really know if there was a surplus of births or not, but we can infer one from the size of the gap. Unfortunately, we cannot infer for this period information based on subsequent patterns. The appearance of good statistics, with complete registration of all births, coincides with the spread of vaccination in the first decades of the nineteenth century. We know therefore that there was a large surplus of births in the earlier decades of the nineteenth century, but we cannot assume that this was also true two centuries before since hygienic conditions were widely different before and after. Generally speaking, all life statistics, official or unofficial, which were drawn up before 1820 must be considered with circumspection. In 1800, the prefect Jerphanion had this to say about them: "Il est d'autant plus difficile de constater d'une manière exacte la population de ce département, que dans le nombre des

autorités constituées chargées de la rédaction des tableaux particuliers, il était à craindre que les une n'apportassent la plus grande tiédeur ou de l'inexactitude dans ces opérations importantes, et que d'autres, ne voyant dans ces renseignements qu'un nouvel impôt à établir, n'atténuassent la population de leurs communes respectives" (Jerphanion, *Statistique du département de la Lozère* [Mende, 1802], p. 17). At other times, in order to become the seat of some administrative organism, communes were also known to pad the number of supposed residents.

10. Robert Gagg, *Kirche im Feuer* (Zurich, 1961), p. 124.

11. ADL C 377.

12. Jean Chaptal, *De l'Industrie française* (Paris, 1819), II, 124.

13. The coincidence in the rise of population and in the rise in the number of artisans, together with the incidence of intermarriage and the fact that artisans were the poorest of the poor in the village, strongly suggests that artisan crafts were in some sense an overflow due to excessive crowding on the land. It is difficult to substantiate this statistically, since we do not know the names of most of the artisans or landless laborers. Tradition, however, has it that the two roles were not distinct. During the winter months, agricultural laborers would come to the bourg where they would work as weavers and carders. Likewise, many weavers would go off to the south as seasonal laborers during the summer months. All in all, therefore, there are many reasons to suppose that artisan crafts and rural overpopulation were intimately linked through the 1820s when competition from abroad and from French manufacturing concerns brought the rural crafts to ruin. But this relationship cannot be proved, for the Pont at least, in a strict historical sense.

14. Population count for 1701—Pont-de-Montvert, ADL C 55.

15. In 1789 her descendant Jean Albaric was the richest peasant in the whole commune. He profited from the Revolution by buying large tracts of *biens nationaux;* today there are still some Albarics in Villeneuve, large parts of which still belong to them.

16. ADL III E 8639, Folcher, 19 April 1700.

17. "Livre de raison de Antoine Velay."

18. The Albarics, for example, rented out their Villeneuve farm for at least one generation to the Molines. Indeed, although the fortune of the Albarics weathered this storm, it enabled the Molines to prosper and to approach the lower rungs of the notable class. In 1661, Moyse Molines owned one-thirtieth of what belonged to Alexandre Albaric, and in 1701, Jacques Molines "*rentier*" was still quite poor, barely above the level of the landless laborer. But through marriage, diligence, and by renting the Villeneuve farm from the Albarics (who some decades earlier had moved to another hamlet), the Molines worked their way up in the world. By 1750 there was a Jacques Molines, "*laboureur.*" In fact, by 1789, we find two Molines at Villeneuve who are *laboureurs,* but significantly they were now making less money than before, obviously because the Albarics had returned to manage their own farm. There were only a few ways of making money in the Pont, but the one which the Molines had followed was one of the best: they managed someone else's property. Although this may have enabled them to rise later, what matters here is that in 1700, the Molines were marked by the fact that they rented land to live. In and of itself, this placed them in a dependent and inferior relationship to their landlords.

19. In 1747, the bishop of Lodève noted that "les Cévenols sont peut être

de tous les françois ceux qui se persuadent le plus aisément qu'ils sont nobles
. . . et de se créer des seigneuries." (ADH C 47).

20. The source, ADL G 63, is undated. However, from the names of the beneficiaries it can be said to have been drawn up after 1686, the year of the death of the sieur André, and before 1693, the year that the Demoiselle des Portes died.

21. Not all of these aristocrats had actually inherited their rights. Indeed, the first sale on record reaches back to 1229, when the commander of the Knights of Malta had begun to round out his domains. In similar fashion, if the rights of the barony of Florac were in the hands of the Grimoard de Beauvoir du Roure family, which had originally sprung from the Pont itself, it was only because a member of the family had bought them back in 1642 for 124,600 livres from François Mirmand, treasurer general of the kingdom and Intendant des Gabelles in Languedoc.

22. François Escalier, notary at the Pont who paid a capitation of 15 livres, Bonnet de Combes, the heirs of the sieur André, the sieur Dussau, Molines of Finialettes and Allier at Frutgères. Molines and Allier were peasants. Most of these men were rich. Allier, however, was not well off. His father, Pierre Allier, had been put down in the cadastre of 1631 for very little. He was therefore not a *gros paysan* and his position seems to have deteriorated further by 1661, judging from the value of his land at that time.

23. In 1730, the nonnoble fiefs were worth less than 100 livres a year. See also Pantel and Servière, "Seigneuries cévenoles," p. 18.

24. ADL G 63.

25. Compoix of Frutgères 1631.

26. Cadastre of 1661.

27. Pont-de-Montvert. *Municipal Archives*. Etat civil Protestant.

28. Cited by Frank Puaux, "Origines, causes, et conséquences de la Guerre des Camisards," *Revue historique* 129 (September 1918), 211.

29. "Livre de raison de Antoine Velay."

30. *Ibid.*

31. I am indebted for the details of the text to the genealogy of the Servière family which was drawn up by M. Emile Servière of the Pont.

II. POLITICS IN 1700: PONT-DE-MONTVERT AND THE CAMISARD WARS

1. The description of the Camisard War which I present here is based on numerous and largely overlapping accounts that have been written since 1710. The most famous contemporary accounts are perhaps those of Abraham Mazel and Elie Marion, published by Charles Bost and the London Huguenot Society. The Catholic account of Father Louvreleuil, *Le Fanatisme renouvellé*, is also very interesting. The recent books of the author Marcel Pin (*A Côté des Camisards, Un Chef Camisard: Nicolas Jouany, Jean Cavalier, Chez les Camisards,* and *Mme. de Maintenon et les Protestants* are popular and interesting works. Much can be found about the Camisards in the standard histories of Protestants and Protestantism, notably in the works of Emile Léonard. Finally, novels have been written about the Camisards. Jean-Pierre Chabrol is the author of *Les Fous de Dieu* (Paris, 1961) in which much of the action takes place at the Pont. Max Olivier-Lacamp's *Les Feux de la colère*

(Paris, 1969) deals with this same period. Charles Alméras' *La Révolte des Camisards* (Grenoble, 1960) is a more classic, historical interpretation.

2. There is one exception to this on record, but of a special sort. In July of 1772, the subdelegate Lafont sent a circular to the parishes of the Cévennes, including Pont-de-Montvert, to inquire about the disputes which had arisen between shepherds and landowners about their respective rights along the *drailles* (for a description of these paths, see chapter III). But the quarrel here was one which did not interest the state, since it opposed some locals to other locals. When the state itself was involved, it ordered and did not consult.

3. We have on record one case of Montipontin emigration to England, but for a somewhat later date. It is that of John Pain (probably Jean Pin) who was naturalized as a British subject on May 1, 1713. He is described as the "son of John Pain by Simmone, his wife. Born in Pont-de-Montvert, Province of Cévennes, in France" *(Publications of the Huguenot Society of London* 27 [1923], p. 115).

4. "L'on abattit et l'on brula tous les moulins et les fours de la compagne . . . On proposa de couper tous les bois chataigniers, d'arracher les vignes, et de bruler tout le païs ouvert, c'est à dire tout ce qui se trouvoit hors des places murées. On n'exécuta pas ces dernières propositions, mais le brûlement feut exécuté en partie" (Charles Bost, ed., *Mémoires inédites d'Abraham Mazel et d'Elie Marion sur la guerre des Cévennes,* p. 53).

5. See Père Louvreleuil, *Le Fanatisme renouvellé* (Avignon, 1868), *passim.*

6. See "Documents. La Persécution dans le diocèse de Mende d'octobre 1685 à mars 1688," *BSHP,* 40 (1906), 417, for a description of the refugees from the diocese of Mende. This was low by any standards, since in the province as a whole, 8 percent of the Protestant population decided to emigrate. See Paul Geisendorf, "Recherches sur l'émigration huguenote du Gévaudan avant et après la revocation de l'edit de Nantes," *Revue du Gévaudan,* 6 (1960), 110–120. Geisendorf quotes a contemporary source to explain this low incidence of departure: "comment perdre de vue ces champs," he writes, "ces vignes, ces douces retraites où l'on mangeait son pain en paix sous l'ombre des figuiers."

7. In 1706, another Pierre Vignes of Salarials was tried and executed at Montpellier for his role in the murder of the abbé du Chayla. Elie Marion, however, describes him as a *"cardeur de laine"* which implies that the two Pierre Vignes were related rather than one and the same person. But it is suggestive that the one prosperous peasant whose relatives were involved in actual resistance after 1702 belonged to a family which twenty years before, in 1685, had already been unusually committed to religious intransigence. For Vignes' income see ADL C 72.

8. The expression is to be found in Antoine Velay's "Livre de raison." Velay himself says nothing about this *"changement."* He himself obviously went through the motions of conversion, and his children were even married in church, which was unusual. Baptism by a Catholic priest was easily accepted, but a Catholic marriage was a great concession to the status quo.

9. Other people were more fortunate. Pinet, the notary of the Pont, had been warned in advance and fled to Toulouse, where he died three years later. M. de Laurent, Chapelle of Finiels, and Talon were also implicated. Of course, since only notables attended the meeting, only notables were persecuted for having been there.

10. Jean Nissolle, "Récit manuscript de Jean Nissolle, marchand de Ganges, réfugié en Suisse. 1685," *BSHP,* 10 (1861), 454.

11. Pierre Pons, "Extraits des mémoires de Pierre Pons, natif du Pont-de-Montvert, réfugié à Genève, où il est mort," *BSHP,* 32 (1883), 218.

12. Their departure did not please the local official persecutor, a missionary named Moutet. In order to provide the intendant with a *casus belli,* Moutet organized surprise searches of houses for arms and books. On Friday he searched for meat. But this was a luxury which Montipontins could ill afford, and the abbé did not succeed in apprehending any violators of the Church's dietary laws.

13. Charles Bost, *Les Prédicants Protestants des Cévennes et du Bas Languedoc* (Paris, 1912), p. 204.

14. *Ibid.,* p. 347.

15. *Ibid.,* p. 222.

16. I have pieced together the information for this meeting from ADH C 181 and ADL C 72.

17. "Documents. Les Enfants des nouveaux convertis," *BSHP* 31 (1882), 110.

18. Gagg, *Kirche im Feuer,* p. 121.

19. Antoine Court, *Histoire des troubles des Cévennes* (Alais, 1819), p. 160.

20. Bost, *Mémoires inédites d'Abraham Mazel,* p.3.

21. ADL C 72.

22. Bost, *Mémoires inédites d'Abraham Mazel,* p. 4.

23. ADL C 72.

24. ADL C 73. The Montversois who joined the rebels after 1702 were also from the lower class. When the farm of Jean Velay (who was rich) was raided by the local Camisards (who were poor) he listed among the attackers two landless tenants and an artisan, "le nommé Pelatan" who was a blacksmith at the Pont. The women who followed the Camisards also had similar social backgrounds: Suzanne Chabrol was a native of Grizac, and all the Chabrols who lived there were landless, or artisans, or just "poor." Jeanne Jalabert, who was especially inspired and reputed to possess the "gift of preaching," came from Champlong where the Jalaberts were laborers or stonemasons. Jeanne Combes, finally, who was derisively described by the bourgeois Pons as "a so-called Combesse of Felgerolles, near Pont-de-Montvert" was no better off. The Combes of Felgerolles were in a bad way. The widow of Tristant Combes was unable to support her children, who were away, "servants des maîtres," and the only other Combes in the hamlet was a landless laborer.

On the whole, women fared better than men at the hands of royal justice. Most men who were arraigned, especially when found to be in the possession of arms, were put to death. But women were more often released. Jeanne Jalabert was allowed to go and returned to the Pont. Suzanne Chabrol went into exile in Geneva, and Jeanne Combes was not killed but sent to prison instead, in that Tour de Constance at Aigues Mortes, which since the seventeenth century has been famous in the annals of Protestant martyrology.

It should be said, however, that exceptions were made for men who were willing to join the royal army. They too were spared. Many suspected Cévenols were also conscripted in the army, like the Pons brothers or Mallet-Higonnet and Mallet-Jean de Toine who were the sons of Jean Mallet, an accomplice of Jeanne Cobes (*BSHP*, 32 [1883], 228).

25. There were at the Pont two exceptions. The first, André André, has already been mentioned. The other was Jean Vierne, whose case would be comical if it had not ended so badly. Vierne was a notary at Felgerolles. In January of 1703, although age eighty, he set off from the Pont to Alès, leading some oxen that he wanted to sell there. On his way, at Génolhac, he fell in with a stranger to whom he confided his admiration for the Camisards. This was an error, for, as it happens, the stranger in question was a Catholic priest in disguise. To make matters worse, on his way back to the Pont, Vierne happened to be in Génolhac again when the town was attacked by a Camisard band. Vierne urged them on and was accused of having shouted "Courage mes enfants! Bannissons l'ilolâtrie! Ville Gagnée! Feu et sang!" These were serious offences. He was arrested, tried, and on June 28, 1703, broken at the wheel. See Pin, *Chez les Camisards,* p. 112.

26. One of the few exceptions to this rule is a very perspicacious essay by Louis Mazoyer, "Les Origines du prophétisme cévenol" in the *Revue historique,* 197 (January–March, 1947), 23–55. The same idea has also been taken up by Emmanuel Leroy-Ladurie in his *Les Paysans du Languedoc* (Paris, 1966), pp. 626–629.

27. Protestant writers like Charles Bost, Marcel Pin, and Emile Léonard have throughout laid stress on the mystical and prophetic qualities of the Protestant Cévenol mind. But in Pont-de-Montvert, at least, such a theory would leave too much unexplained. In his essay, Louis Mazoyer, however, has stressed the fact that of the thousands of prophets, not one was a notable; to this it can be added that of the rebels as well as the prophets, in the Pont, not one was a truly "respectable" individual, by peasant or by bourgeois standards.

28. Mazoyer, "Les Origines du prophétisme cévenol," passim.

29. Antoine Velay, "Livre de raison."

30. "Extraits des mémoires de Pierre Pons," p. 222.

31. Antoine Velay, "Livre de raison."

32. *BSHP,* 32 (1883), 153.

33. *BSHP,* 31 (1882), 110.

34. Antoine Velay, "Livre de raison."

35. Lise Dupouy, "Les Protestants de Florac de la révocation de l'edit de Nantes à l'edit de tolérance," *Revue du Gévaudan,* 11 (1965), 152.

36. Charles Bost, ed., *Relations d'Abraham Mazel,* Publication de la Société Huguenote de Londres 34 (Paris, 1931), p. 4.

37. Burdin, *Documents historiques sur la province de Gévaudan,* p. 323, "Accounts of the Estates of the Gévaudan, 6 August 1704."

III. SOCIAL CLASS IN THE EIGHTEENTH CENTURY

1. Emile Servière, "Commanderie de Gap-Français, Ordre des Hospitaliers de St-Jean de Jérusalem," *Revue du Gévaudan,* 10 (1964), 54.

2. Liste nominative, Archives municipales du Pont-de-Montvert: Etat Civil, 1921.

3. More exactly it went from 1163 (829 for Frutgères and 334 for Grizac

which is suspiciously high) to 1338 (1063 and 275). The source is ADL G 1005, cited in Achille Foulquier's *Notes historiques sur les paroisses des Cévennes* (Mende, 1906), p. 71. See also Société des Sciences, des Arts et des Lettres de la Lozère, *Documents antérieurs à 1790* (1889), IV, 345.

4. See J. Sentou, "La Lutte contre la vie chère dans la généralité de Languedoc au XVIIIe," *Annales du Midi,* 66, pt. 2 (1954), 155–170; and J. Sentou's "Impôts et citoyens actifs à Toulouse au début de la Révolution," *Annales du Midi,* 61 (1948), pt. 2, pp. 172–173. This proportion can also be derived from a comparison of the capitation paid by certain landowners with the incomes estimated in the cadastre of 1825. There it can be seen that the capitation represents about 3.5 percent of the estimated income which in turn was set at one fifth of actual income. It follows therefore that the capitation represents about 0.7 percent of personal income in 1825. But since the Pont was more prosperous in 1825 than in 1789, we can still operate on the assumption that the capitation of 1789 does represent one percent of personal income at that time.

5. Jan Marczewski, ed., *Le Produit de l'agriculture française de 1700 à 1958.* Institut National de Science Economique Appliquée (ISEA), (Paris, 1961), p. 81.

6. Commerce and Industry: Maximum for the Lozère, AN F 12 1544-15.

7. *Ibid.*

8. ADL M 12264, and Albert Fayet, *Usages Locaux* (Mende, 1885), p. 20. In the earlier part of this century, when chestnuts were less important, these customs were much simplified; it was then decided that all chestnuts, ripe or not, belonged to the owner of the land on which they had fallen (see ADL Q 1937).

9. Cadastre of 1825, Service Départemental du Cadastre, Mende. Today there are no more chestnut trees at the Pont, and tradition now has it that there have been none since the great frost of 1709. The cadastre or platt-book of 1825, however, allows for no ambiguity on this score, and there must have been producing chestnut trees at the Pont well into the nineteenth century at least. It is very curious to see how important the frost and famine of 1709–1710 have become in the French rural popular mind. At the Pont, there are only a few dates that everyone remembers: 1702, the Camisards; 1709, the frost; 1789, the Revolution, and most awesome, 1914, *la Grande Guerre.* As a rule, the people of the Pont use private or local events to date public happenings: e.g., the February riots (of 1934) took place when Jean-Paul was doing his military service, but some dates like 1709 or 1914 are so important that they do escape this rule of private thumb.

10. ADL L 141. My italics.

11. ADL VI M2-2. My italics.

12. ADL III E 8690, 8 May 1787.

13. ADL III E 8694, 4 April 1793.

14. ADL III E 8686, Molines notaire, 11 May 1781.

15. Private papers of the Molines family, Pont-de-Montvert.

16. M. Benoit, "Notice sur la culture du chataignier," *Revue des Sciences des Lettres et des Arts de la Lozère* (1830), p. 190.

17. *Ibid.*

18. ADL L 225.

19. ADL VI M2-2.

20. Jerphanion, *Statistique du département de la Lozère,* p. 77.

21. AN Flc III Lozère 6.

22. ADL L 167.

23. Burdin, *Documents Historiques,* II, 375.

24. ADL III E 8698, Rouvière notaire, 16 Floréal An VII. Servière was a precursor in this respect, for as late as 1837, in a report to the local agricultural society, an observer noted that plows were largely unknown in the Lozère: "le seul (instrument de labourage) qui soit en usage dans le pays, c'est l'araire des Romains" *(Bulletin de la Société d'Agriculture, des Sciences, des Lettres et des Arts de la Lozère* [1837], p. 42).

25. AN F1c III Lozère 6.

26. The return journey took place in two shifts. The weaker, less healthy sheep, together with the new-born lambs would begin the return journey in mid August. The rest of the flock would start down the mountain in the second half of September. The sheep were grouped in herds of 3000; they would travel about fifteen miles each day.

27. ADL H 416.

28. ADL III E 8694, Molines notaire, 11 Brumaire Year III.

29. Nicole Feneyrou, "Contribution à l'histoire de la transhumance au XVme siècle," *Revue du Gévaudan,* 9 (1963), 123.

30. E. Fages, "Notes d'histoire Gévaudannaise," *Bulletin de la Société des Sciences, des Lettres et des Arts de la Lozère* (1907), p. 5.

31. ADL C 486.

32. ADL J 259.

33. *Ibid.*

34. Jules Barbot, "Les Anciennes Drayes de la Lozére," *Bulletin de la Société des Sciences, des Lettres et des Arts de la Lozère* (1902), p. 1. Barbot suggests that the number of transhumants declined steadily after 1789 from 300,000 to 150,000 in 1902.

35. ADL C 486. Pont-de-Montvert covers an area of 8,500 hectares (about 20,000 acres), and it was then estimated that one hectare of average land could sustain one cow or two sheep. AN F12 1346.

36. ADL C 52.

37. *Documents relatifs à l'histoire du Gévaudan.* 3e partie. *Documents antérieurs à 1790* (Mende, 1885), I, 436–441. See also ADL C 36 and Jerphanion's *Statistique du département de la Lozère* of 1800, where this seasonal emigration is described in some detail. Indeed, the prefect saw it as fundamental to Lozérian economy: "Il est certain," he wrote, "que sans ces émigrations périodiques et annuelles, les habitants des Cévennes n'auraient pas de quoi vivre chez eux" (pp. 22–23).

38. ADL C 55.

39. ADL C 73.

40. ADL C 377.

41. *Ibid.*

42. AN F12 1346.

43. *Ibid.*

44. ADL C 478.

45. The problem of nomenclature is very complex and even confusing. At the end of the eighteenth century, although *mesnagers* were slightly more prosperous than *laboureurs,* all of them were landowners. This was not true at

the beginning of the century, when *laboureur* was similar in meaning to *rentier* or tenant. In the 1690s, a landowner is a *mesnager,* but in 1789, he is sometimes called *mesnager* and sometimes also *laboureur.* The complexity of the whole problem is shown by the fact that the same terminology was not used in Pont-de-Montvert proper (parish of Frutgères) and in the hamlet of Grizac (parish of Fraissinet). Grizac and Frutgères actually did have similar social and economic structures, but that would not appear to have been so at first glance, again because of the imprecision of the words *rentiers, laboureur, mesnager.* In Grizac *in 1789,* there were eleven *laboureurs* and only two *mesnagers;* in Frutgères, the proportions were reversed: there were only fourteen *laboureurs* for twenty-four *mesnagers.* But, in fact, there was no difference at all between the two communities, because in 1789 *laboureur* and *mesnager* had the same meaning although that had not been true in 1696. Alfred Cobban has discussed similar problems of historical nomenclatures in his perverse and stimulating book, *The Social Interpretation of the French Revolution* (Cambridge University Press, 1965), p. 17.

46. ADL C 377, Capitation lists for 1750 and 1789.

47. See, R. Cuche, *Le Conventionnel Servière* (Mende, 1955), p. 178.

48. At first, Servière did not use his seigneurial title because he had agreed not to do so when he bought it, the former owner and his wife Elizabeth de Parlier having stipulated that they would keep it for their lifetime. Servière did not mind. His family had been moving forward for ten generations and perhaps that had given him a familial and secular frame of mind.

49. The exact amount of the seigneurial dues (as distinct from the tithe) which were paid to the Order of Malta, in their capacity as temporal lords of the village, are hard to establish. The dues, consisting of "plusieurs censives et rentes seigneuriales et foncières sur les villages et terrains de Gap Français et ses dépendances qui sont la paroisse de Frutgères, celles de Fraissinet, Grizac, Saint-Maurice de Ventalon, Saint-Frézal, Maslong, Cambonnas et autres" were never itemized for the Pont alone. But for the wide area described above (seven parishes) they amounted to about 250 bushels of grain, worth about 5,000 livres. If we add this sum to the other dues (fifty-two livres in cash, seven and a half pounds of wax, and sixty-two chickens) and divide it by seven, we can conclude that the seigneurial dues for the Pont as a whole were on the order of less than 1,000 livres, which comes to less than one livre per person per year. It is only fair to point out, however, that some people (landowning peasants) would pay more, and that others (artisans) would pay less.

50. ADB-du-R HOM 1944.

51. ADL H 416.

52. Two and a half setiers, or about twelve bushels, is the figure given by both Vauban and Lavoisier in their estimates of national production and consumption. (See Jan Marczewski, *Le Produit de l'agriculture française de 1700 à 1958,* I.S.E.A. (1961), p. 81. At the Pont itself, the *donations partage* usually indicate a consumption of three setiers per year, but these donations were made by rich peasants. Fernand Braudel provides estimates for the level of consumption of wheat in various European countries during the sixteenth century and discusses the difficulty involved in determining this figure. See Fernand Braudel, *La Méditerranée et le monde méditerranéen,* I, 384, n.4;

385–386. G. Lefebvre in his *Etudes orléanaises,* CNRS (Paris, 1962), p. 241, gives similar figures.

53. Contemporaries were well aware of the fact that the village produced less food than it consumed as witnessed by an undated complaint drawn up by some Montipontin, probably in the second quarter of the eighteenth century: "A messieurs les commissaires du diocèze de Mende. Les habitans de la paroisse de frutgères et le pont de Montvert ont l'honneur de vous représenter très humblement que leur paroisse est situé dans les plus mauvais pays du diocèze et le plus cazuel pour les glaces ou les fréquentes grelles ou il est expozé ou par la mortalité des bestiaux . . . le travail de la terre y estans extrèmement pénible par les rochers desquels elle est presque couverte n'y pouvant semer que du seigle qui ne produit pas dequoi nourrir les habitans de ladite paroisse ce qui les a réduiz à une grande misère" (ADL C 376).

54. ADL III E 8659. Folcher, notaire. 23 March 1779.

55. ADL M 3036.

56. ADL M 3036.

57. The figures for 1684–1688 have been reconstituted from minutes entered in the records of the notary Folcher—for Frutgères, the Pont, and l'Hopital: 27 July 1684; for Montgros: 27 July 1684 and 14 July 1686; for Salarials and Le Cros: 27 July 1684 and 14 July 1686; for Finiels and Prat Souteyran: 27 July 1684 and 14 July 1686; for Champlong de Lozère: 27 July 1684, 8 August 1688, and 25 July 1691; for Villeneuve: 27 July 1684, 14 July 1686, and 26 July 1684; for Mazel and La Veissière: 27 July 1684; for Felgerolles and Le Merlet: 27 July 1684; for La Cépedelle: 27 July 1684; for Rieumal: 27 July 1685 and 28 July 1688; from the records of the notary Daudé —for Grizac le Villaret: 15 March 1757; for l'Hermet: 18 May 1757; for Champlong du Bougès: 12 March 1757. For the 1780s the figures can be found in ADL H 416.

58. ADL III E Grégoire notaire, 29 September 1762.

59. Shortly afterwards, Louis Servière also became the collector of feudal dues for the barony of Florac. He agreed to pay over 3,825 livres a year for the right to collect the dues on the baron's behalf. See Lise Dupouy, "Les Protestants de Florac," p. 97.

60. ADL G 2097.

61. ADL C 377.

62. ADL C 376.

63. Pantel and Servière, "Seigneuries cévenoles," p. 53.

64. This contemporary verdict is quoted by Fages, *Les Anciennes Justices de la Lozère* (Mende, 1903), p. 86.

65. J. Bouret, *Dictionnaire géographique de la Lozère* (Mende, 1852), p. lxxiii.

66. AN F1c Lozère 6.

67. *Délibérations du Conseil Général de la Lozère* (Mende, 1845), p. 177.

68. ADL III E 8698, Rouvière notaire, 16–19 Floréal, Year VII.

69. ADL Q 205. See also ADL III E 8686, Molines notaire, 17 July 1782.

70. J. B. Delon, *La Révolution dans la Lozère* (Mende, 1922), p. 42.

71. ADL Q 205.

72. Capitation lists for Frutgères for 1750 and 1789, ADL C 377.

73. In the middle decades of the eighteenth century, we do find at the bourg

members of the Richard and Velay de Marueilhac families. They indeed had not been there before. But by 1789, the Velay de Marueilhacs were gone and the Richards were back in Rieumal. It is likely therefore that the elders of these to families had only come to the bourg in order to spin out their old age rather than to found new dynasties.

IV. REVOLUTIONARY POLITICS

1. The expression is Robert Gagg's, who has very aptly described this movement in his *Kirche im Feuer,* pp. 104–130.

2. Because of the administrative confusion created by the pooling of Fraissinet and Grizac, the amount of taxes paid cannot be ascertained precisely. According to the *Procès Verbaux d'Assiette,* these rubrics included all the moneys paid to the state, but something must nonetheless be missing. Since the taxes set for 1790 in 1789 were supposed to be commensurate to those paid in 1789, we know that the village was thought to have disbursed in 1789 9,805 libres (*Délibérations Départementales de la Lozère,* IV, 64). This is nearly 3,000 livres more than what can be estimated from the Procès Verbaux ADL C 854). Taxes, tithes, and dues can therefore be conservatively estimated to have represented at least 12 percent of total village income and perhaps as much as 15 or 16 percent.

3. In 1789, the *curé* or vicar of Frutgères and his *vicaire* or curate were both of them on the *portion congrue.* The *curé* received 400 livres and his subordinate 250. This was not much money. The income of these people was theoretically supplemented by the *casuel* or fees for baptisms, marriages, and burials; but in a Protestant community this did not mean much, and after 1787 it meant nothing at all. *Curés* were also expected to pay something for taxes, the "décimes, dixièmes, et dons gratuits." They also had to pay the running expenses of their church. At Grizac, the curé paid thirty livres a year for "pain, vin, cierge, blanchissage du linge de l'église, huile de la lampe, et l'entretien d'un clerc." There was not much left over, and his lot was quite miserable, as is witnessed by a very pathetic letter addressed in 1765 to his bishop's *vicaire général* at Mende by Bros, *vicaire* at the Pont: "Monsieur, Je viens par la présente vous demander avant le temps mon semestre des missions, mais vous devez, monsieur, être persuadé que c'est la nécessité qui m'y oblige. La providence dans moins de sept mois m'a affligé de deux maladies très dangereuses qui m'ont beaucoup coûté. La dernière que je viens d'essuyer m'a entièrement obéré. Vous n'ignorez pas qu'on est obligé de payer les médecins et apothicaires bien grassement, et ce qui achève de m'écraser: c'est que de cinquante livres que vous avez la bonté de me donner, Mr. Bonnicel marchand de Mende qui vous remettra la présente doit en retenir vingt huit pour toile que je lui dois depuis un an. Ainsi, monsieur, j'implore votre charité si elle veut bien me faire la grace de m'augmenter les missions de quelques chose pour cette fois; et je ne manqueroy pas de prier le seigneur de vous récompenser pour vos bienfaits à mon égard. J'ay l'honneur de me croire avec le plus profond respect votre très humble et très obéissant serviteur. Pont de Montvert ce 9e May 1765" (ADB-du-R. HOM 1944; ADL G 2097; ADH G 1883).

4. ADL C 377.

5. "Livre de raison de Antoine Velay."

6. This draft is unpublished, and the reader will find it reproduced *in extenso* in Appendix II. Since it was never officially presented to the *assemblée du diocèse,* it cannot officially be described as a *cahier de doléances.* It is merely the draft thereof. A manuscript of this draft can be found in the private papers of the Chapelle family. It bears the title "Cayer de Doléances de la paroisse de Frutgères pour présenter à l'Assemblée générale du diocèse."

7. Burdin, *Documents historiques,* p. 282.

8. Régistres paroissiaux, 25 February 1737, Municipal Archives of Pont-de-Montvert.

9. *Ibid.,* 4 February 1728.

10. Gagg, *Kirche im Feuer,* p. 120.

11. *Ibid.,* p. 262.

12. Edmond Hughes, ed., *Histoire de la restauration du protestantisme en France au XVIIIe siècle. Antoine Court* (Paris, 1875), p. 32.

13. *Ibid.,* p. 33.

14. Court, *Histoire des troubles des Cévennes,* p. x.

15. *Ibid.,* pp. x–xi.

16. *Ibid.,* p. x.

17. Court, *Mémoires,* ed. Edmond Hughes (Toulouse, 1885), pp. 196–197.

18. *Ibid.,* p. 187.

19. Hughes, *Histoire de la restauration du protestantisme,* p. 204.

20. *Ibid.,* p. 458.

21. *Ibid.,* p. 336.

22. *Ibid.,* p. 445.

23. *Ibid.,* p. 77.

24. *Ibid.,* p. 154.

25. *Ibid.,* p. 155.

26. *Ibid.*

27. See chapter II, page 37.

28. ADH C 231.

29. *Ibid.* There may have been a mistake here. The "judge" would ordinarily have been thought to be Paul Servière, seigneur du Viala and judge for the Knights of Malta. But there was also a sieur Velay, seigneur de Marueilhac. He was not a judge, however. In any case, the point can be made that this lady (whoever she may have been) was an eminently respectable person.

30. *Ibid.*

31. *Ibid.*

32. *Ibid.*

33. 20 June 1739, est ordonné au Sr. Serres et divs. cavaliers de la maréchaussée à residence de la ville de Mende de s'assurer de la Dmlle Servière femme du Sr. Velay habitan de la Paroisse de Fraissinet de Lozère et de la conduire dans le couvent des religieuses ursulines de la ville de Mende ou sa pension sera payée par son mary (ADL H 351).

34. ADH C 240. Roux was eventually released and placed under surveillance at the Pont. His sister was similarly confined at Saint-André-de-Valborgne, where she lived with her "so-called" husband whom she had married *au désert.*

35. The one exception to this rule came in 1793 with the closing down of the Protestant temple. The municipality did not approve of this. When word came

from Mende about the intended closure, it decided "a l'unanimité des suffrages qu'elle entendait conserver son culte public toutes les fois que les lois de la République ne s'y opposeraient pas." The remark is quoted in Louis André's book, *Essai sur la Révolution en Lozère* (Marvejols, 1894), p. 183, and I have not been able to trace it. Perhaps the papers which André used in 1883 were destroyed in the fire of 1887. In any case, it is interesting to speculate about this. In 1702, the lower classes revolted on behalf of Protestantism. During the eighteenth century, they were brought back under the control of the local bourgeoisie through Protestantism, and thus did not revolt in 1793. Since, at this time, this same bourgeoisie momentarily turned its back on organized religion. Protestantism, by binding the poor to the rich, had in this particular instance become the agent of its own undoing. This, however, must remain somewhat hypothetical. In 1793 notables and nonnotables alike may have remained secretly loyal, deciding to bend so as not to break. Nonetheless, the difference between 1702 and 1793 is striking and cannot be explained without making reference to the change in the relations between educated and uneducated, rich and poor, temporizers and rebels.

36. Daniel Robert, *Les Eglises réformées en France (1800–1830)* (Paris, 1961), p. 545.

37. Bonnicel was not the first Protestant pastor to work at the Pont since 1685. In 1756, the pastor Gabriac had been assigned the Pont as one of his parishes by the underground Protestant synod. From that date on, Montipontins always had some spiritual guidance, but of an unofficial sort, of course. See Lise Dupouy, "Les Protestants de Florac," p. 80.

From records of births and deaths, of marriages and notarial documents, M. Albin Pantel has established the following chronology for the *pasteurs du désert:* Teissier, 1744 to 1747; Roux, 1745 to 1746; Molines, 1746 to 1777; Pierredon, 1771 to 1773; Roche, 1773; Gabriac, 1773 to 1778; Desabatière, 1777; Mazauric, 1777; Martin, 1778 to 1780; Bonnicel, 1780 to 1819.

38. *Ibid.,* p. 23. (It is not certain that Jeanbon Saint-André actually said this, but M. Robert thinks it a distinct possibility.)

39. ADL III E 8698, Rouvière notaire, Floréal, Year VII, pp. 16–19.

40. AN F1c III 8.

41. AN D IV 1064–1069.

42. In 1914, a governmental committee was set up to draw up a picture of French agriculture since 1814, and archivists were asked to forward the relevant documents. But Brunel replies that he had nothing to send since everything had been burned in the fire of 1887 (Ministère de l'Instruction Publique et des Beaux Arts, *Notices, inventaires, et documents* [Paris, 1914], p. iii, n.2).

43. In 1797, when Servière had been named "commissaire du pouvoir exécutif pour l'administration du département" he tried to set up some "cercles constitutionnels": they were, he thought, particularly useful and would contribute a good deal "à améliorer l'esprit public et à répandre ses lumières sur la classe ignorante, lui montrer la république telle qu'elle est et ... la perfidie de nos ennemis" (AN F1c Lozère III 8). Surely, Servière would have wanted to set up one of these circles in his own home town, but no records of it survive. We must therefore presume that our knowledge of the Pont during the Revolution is very fragmentary indeed.

44. AN F1c III 8.

45. The Montversois in this instance were the guests of the Villefort battalion. Their hosts were very gracious, and the officers from Villefort did not pull rank on the soldiers from the Pont, who were allowed to stand where they pleased: "A mesure qu(ils) entroient dans le camp, (ils) s'y rengoient sans aucune distinction ni préséances ne devant y avoir dans une assemblée de frères, dont l'égalité fait la principale base [sic]." Then, the Montipontin officer harangued his guests: "Messieurs," he said, "nous venons vous offrir au nom de tous les citoyens du Pont-de-Montvert le vœu qu'ils ont forme de fraternité avec vous. Ils nous ont chargés de vous assurer de leur amitié, de leur secours dans le besoin et de vous demander les vôtres; ils vous prient si leur démarche vous est agréable, de leur permettre de se réunir à vous, par leurs députés, pour pretter le serment civique." Bardy, "Notes et comptes rendus. Sur Le mont Lozère, le 14 Juillet 1790," *Revue du Gévaudan,* (1963), 154–159.

46. One of them, Joseph Tabusse, was more cautious than his colleague and only took the oath conditionally, "sous la réserve expresse du spirituel." Perhaps he was a trimmer. But to no good purpose since he was eventually forced to leave the Pont. Characteristically, however, Tabusse was not hounded out by the locals but by outside agitators from the Gard. The people of the Pont even helped him in his hour of need, and he appears to have been well liked. He returned to the village in 1801 where he served for another twenty-two years. In the end he cannot be said to have suffered grievously at the hands of the Revolution. It is useful to remember this since Tabusse and his colleague Durand, who had been curé at Grizac, were the only Montversois who were driven out or persecuted in any way during these years. For details of the turnover of juring and nonjuring clergy at the Pont, Grizac, and Fraissinet, see vol. 3. pp. 513–515 of the Abbé Pourcher's *Le Clergé de la Lozère* (Saint-Martin-de-Boubaux, 1896–1900) and Foulquier, *Notes historiques sur les paroisses des Cévennes,* p. 385.

47. Both Archives Nationales F1c III Lozère I and F20 349 give 332 active citizens for the canton of Pont-de-Montvert which counted 1,925 habitants. F20 349 also indicates that in the Year II there were at the Pont 225 "votants". But this must refer to potential rather than actual voters. The expression is used in reference to a vote for the Constitution of 1793, but the document antedates January 1, 1794, when the results were published. Moreover, 225 active citizens for the commune of the Pont corresponds to 332 active citizens for the canton of the Pont.

Two hundred twenty-five active citizens represent 20 percent of all Montipontins. This is high but not unreasonable for an area characterized by widespread peasant ownership and the absence of large-scale feudal proprietors. Paul Bois, in his *Les Paysans de l'ouest* (Le Mans, 1960) finds that in the Sarthe the proportion of active citizens to total population varied between 13 and 20 percent.

48. AN B II 237a Pont-de-Montvert.

49. AN B II 754b.

50. Whether this coverage was complete cannot be ascertained with certainty. The numbers involved suggest that everybody was listed, but only two of the sixty-three men involved were artisans. This is obviously an anomaly, and taken at its face value, it suggests that in the Pont the "urban poor" were not as committed as the peasants. But the discrepancy is so large that it may

in fact be a mistake. The clerk who drew up the list of national guardsmen may just have found it easier to write down "cultivateur" and to leave it at that. See ADL L 225.

51. *Délibérations de l'administration départementale de la Lozère,* III, 67 and 106.

52. ADL L 225.

53. ADL IV M1–5. More peculiar still is that all of these men had been given some public significance by the ancien régime itself. Laurent Servière was one of the "consuls" of the Pont, in charge of verifying the apportionment and collection of taxes; and both Jean Servière, and Rouvière were described as "conseillers politiques" in a notarial act of 1788 (ADL III E 8689, Molines notaire, 14 June 1788).

54. ADL L 229.

55. ADL C 377.

56. ADL III E 8694, Molines notaire, 4 April 1793.

57. ADL Q 205. In this he was not unlike another volunteer, Paul Quet, of Finialettes, since another debtor of the same Henri de Pelet was one "Quet of Finialettes."

58. ADL C 377.

59. *Ibid.*

60. Even Revolutionary adultery appears to have been conducted on class lines. In 1795, Louis Boutin went off "aux armées." His attachment to the Republic was probably sincere, since his family had been involved in the purchase of *biens nationaux* the year before (ADL III E 8694), but his wife appears to have been less involved with the new Revolutionary morality. Although of respectable family (all the Boissiers were bourgeois at the Pont or landowners at Grizac and Fraissinet), she soon found herself pregnant "des œuvres de Francois Chaptal de Frutgères" (Etat Civil, 25 Pluviose, Year IV). The curious thing, however, is that like Louis Boutin and Marie Boissier, François Chaptal was also well off. In 1789 he had been the richest man in his hamlet (ADL C 377).

61. ADL Q 24.

62. *Ibid.*

63. ADL C 377.

64. Only one member of the cartel was a bourgeois, Bondurant la Roche, a notary at Genolhac. By local standards, Bondurant was no stranger to the Pont since he was a descendant of the Bondurant La Roche, also a notary at Genolhac, who had in the seventeenth century married Isabelle Velay, the sister of François Velay of Florac and Antoine Velay of Grizac. See Dupouy, "Les Protestants de Florac," p. 155.

65. Benoit bought his for 42,000 francs (Servière, "Commanderie de Gap-Francais," p. 63). Velay sold his for 90,000 francs (ADL III E 8694 1 Floreal, Year III).

66. In 1825, the Albarics of Villeneuve owned more than 150 hectares between them, and in 1914, they were still the largest landowners there by far. Today most of this land has been repurchased by the national forestry service.

67. ADL E 8694 Molines notaire, 26 Fructidor, Year III; and *Bulletin de la Lozère,* 28 May 1953.

68. ADL Q 266.

69. "Livre de raison de Antoine Velay."

70. In theory, peasants chosen for the *milice* were not allowed to buy their way out. Those who tried to evade it were subject to a fine of 500 livres and ten years supplementary duty. See Pierre Rascol, *Les Paysans de l'Albigeois à la fin de l'ancien régime* (Aurillac. 1961). p. 145.

71. This was especially true in the later years of the Napoleonic regime. In 1813, for example, the prefect of the Lozère wrote that everyone had been called up: "Je n'en ai dispensé qu'un seul dans la levée que j'ai faite afin qu'on ne dise pas que la faveur de la dispense était illusoire" (AN F7 3600, 7 June 1813).

72. *Journal de la Lozère,* 14 Brumaire, Year XII, 13 August 1806, 3 January 1807. ADL L 168 (Pont-de-Montvert).

73. ADL III E 8706. Rouvière notaire, 24 August 1812.

74. In December of 1814, the same Jean Servière sold him a field at Rieumal for 1,400 francs (ADL Q 111).

75. Pont-de-Montvert, Etat Civil.

76. Prefect to the mayor of Fraissinet, 20 Nivose, Year 12, Archives de la famille Pantel.

77. Pont-de-Montvert, Etat Civil.

78. The unanimity is all the more admirable for the fact that the events of the Hundred Days were very baffling even to sophisticated political observers. as witnessed perhaps by the shifts and hesitations in the nomenclature used by one of the local notaries. On April 17, 1814, he was as he had been for ten years, a "notaire impérial." On April 24, that was crossed out and replaced by "notaire public," which rubric remained alone on April 28. From June 25, 1814, to March 22, 1815, however, this was altered, as it should have been, to "notaire royal." But on March 1, 1815, Napoleon landed at Antibes, and the notary, broken to the ways of the world, now labeled himself simply as "notaire" with no additions of any sort. This was followed, once again, by "notaire impérial" from April 5, 1815, to June 28 of the same year, the day of Waterloo. From the second to the sixteenth of July, the situation was unsettled and we find mentions of both "notaire" and "notaire public," both of which finally yielded on July 19 of 1815 to "notaire royal," and this for the next thirty-three years.

79. AN B II 904.

80. A good example of this can be found in connection with the old communal rights which the inhabitants of the hamlets had enjoyed on the lands formerly owned by the Order of Malta. When these properties had been sold as *biens nationaux,* the new owners had agreed to maintain these rights— "n'étant en rien dérogé à ceux qui y avaient des anciens droits, qu'ils conserveront en leur entier (ADL III E 8695, Molines notaire, 5 Vendémiaire, Year IV). But very soon afterwards, the new purchasers proved to be more greedy than the old owners. In 1802, they were collectively sued by their poorer neighbors who asserted their right from custom immemorial: "en ont joui en commun et par indivis de la faculté de prendre du bois pour brûler et autrement dans la terre . . . ayant appartenu aux cy-devant commandeurs de gap-français" (ADL II U 99).

81. ADH C 47.

82. *Ibid.*

V. THE BREAKUP OF SOCIAL STRUCTURE

1. Before 1789, population figures were usually based on the capitation count. After 1789, actual counts were made, and the gap between the two sets of figures may have more to do with method than fact. It should be noted however that the numbers of *capités* did decline after 1785, and we can from that infer that an actual decline in population was taking place, linked perhaps with a minor economic crisis.

2. The figure for the 1820s is very high (4.8) and it is due to the fact that so many people had gotten married to avoid the draft before 1815. In the years immediately following, there were therefore more married couples, with more babies, with fewer people getting married. By contrast with the 1820s, the rate of births to marriages fell in the 1840s. Fewer people had married at the Pont in the preceding years. From 1836 to 1841, only forty-eight marriages were celebrated as against ninety-nine in the next six years (in the village, the 1830s had been years of hard times and falling population.) The 1840s however reversed this pattern: many more people were married, but since fewer people had been married before, the result was fewer babies than was usually the case, and more marriages, with a consequent unnatural and eccentric fall in the number of births for marriages (2.6 in 1839–1848).

It should also be said that the rate of births per marriage is biologically meaningless and statistically extremely questionable. It has, however, often been used, notably by Lucien Gachon (in *Géographie d'une commune rurale* [Clermont-Ferrand, 1939], p. 155), since it is extremely simple to establish. The ideal figures would deal with the fertility per marriage, but these are difficult to compute. There are many problems here due to the fact that records are not properly indexed, that many people share the same patronymics, and that many Montipontins' mothers emigrated in the middle of their childbearing career. For the more recent years, calculations are quite hopeless since many if not most children are born in clinics situated in other communes.

The rate of births per marriage, on the other hand, is readily obtainable, but it is not very reliable.

3. L. S. Mercier, *Tableau de la vie parisienne en 1789* (Paris, 1957), pp. 150–151.

4. AN F16 1101, 23 January 1809.

5. *Ibid.*

6. AN F1c III Lozère 6.

7. Robert Tinthouin, "Structure sociale et démographique du Gévaudan au XVIII et XIXme siècle," *Revue du Gévaudan*, 4, (1958), 128.

8. *Statistique générale de la France*, n.s., 1 (1871), 212. Improvement was very swift. In 1811, 2,418 Lozerians caught smallpox (about one in twenty). General vaccination at this point brought a rapid decrease. In 1813, only 129 Lozerians contracted this disease and only 4 died of it as against 227 in 1811.

9. Archives de la famille Chapelle.

10. AN F17 114.

11. ADL Série E, supplément, 19 February 1835.

12. AN F9 209.

13. ADL P 796-P3.

14. ADL Série E, supplément, 31 May 1839.

15. AN F3 II Lozère 5, 23 January 1832.

16. *Appel à la charité des Catholiques par Rouvière curé du Pont-de-Mont-vert* (Mende, 1854).

17. ADL P3 796.

18. G. Géraud, "Notes sur cent ans d'histoire en Lozère au XIXe et XXe siècles," *Revue du Gévaudan*, 13 (1967), 149.

19. Archives de la famille Molines.

20. Archives de la famille Chapelle.

21. ADL C 72.

22. ADL C 377.

23. ADL P 796 P3, Statistique: contrôle de Mende.

24. ADL C 478 (1736).

25. ADL E 12.

26. ADL C 478, Statistics on production 1759–1785.

27. *Bulletin de la Société des Sciences, des Lettres et des Arts de la Lozère* (1828), 210; prix des laines de 1809 à 1828.

28. *Bulletin de la Société des Sciences, des Lettres et des Arts de la Lozère* (1832–1833), p. 16.

29. *Bulletin de la Société des Sciences, des Lettres et des Arts de la Lozère* (1856), p. 294.

30. See pages 56 and 57.

31. The problem here is of the same sort as "which report of the tax inspector do you read?" In 1846 and 1849, a survey lists no carders. Another one, dated 1852, gives 11 carders. It seems most reasonable to assume that these people existed throughout but had been omitted before. On the other hand, it is odd that there should be so many carders and no weavers, when some weavers existed later. Perhaps the ultimate explanation is that there were throughout eleven cloth artisans of all sorts.

32. ADL P 796 P3: contrôle de Mende.

33. ADL Patentes du Pont-de-Montvert, 1890.

34. *Bulletin de la Société des Sciences, des Lettres et des Arts de la Lozère* (1834–1835), 77.

35. ADL 796 P3.

36. AN F1c Lozère 6.

37. There were only 330 sheep at the Pont in 1915, but this low figure may have been due to wartime factors.

38. The exact figures are as follows. For 1891, 151 bulls, 230 oxen, 80 cows, and 316 calves (or 778 in all). For 1903, 65 bulls, 153 oxen, 255 cows, and 184 calves (or 657 in all). For 1925, 30 bulls, 110 oxen, 240 cows, and 130 calves (or 610 in all).

39. ADL M 3036 (1888) (1891); M 3039 (1908); M 3040 (1915); M 5354 (1917–1918).

40. ADL III E 8656, Folcher notaire, 26 February 1728. See also ADL C 1681.

41. In 1789, two Montipontins were described in the capitation rolls as *voituriers*. There may therefore have already been some practicable roads before 1800, but this remains hypothetical. In 1813, the prefect described the road leading northward from the Pont to Le Bleymard and the Causse highway as "un sentier très pierreux dans lequel on ne peut marcher qu'un à un."

42. AN F1c III 5.

43. AN F14 1558.

44. Délibérations du conseil municipal, Municipal Archives of Pont-de-Montvert, 9 May 1863.

45. Even today many of the roads which Montipontins consider essential are unpaved. The village is to the left in a right wing department, and this may have something to do with it as witnessed by the fact that the dirt road which leads to right wing Le Bleymard is only tarred from the border of the two towns to Le Bleymard itself.

46. ADL IV M 8 115 (Pont-de-Montvert).

47. ADL Matrice générale des patentes (Pont-de-Montvert) 1890.

48. ADL P 796 P3: contrôle de Mende.

49. *Bulletin de la Société des Sciences, des Lettres et des Arts de la Lozère* (1850), 73.

50. "Livre de raison" by Antoine Velay, and ADL C 264.

51. If this existed at the Pont, it did so in virtue of a royal declaration of December 13, 1698, which held that "Pour instruire les enfants et nommément ceux dont les pères et mères ont fait profession de la religion prétendue réformée . . . que dans les lieux où il n'y a point d'autres fonds il puisse être imposé sur tous les habitants la somme qu'il manquera pour leur subsistance jusqu'à celle de cent cinquante livres par an pour les maîtres et cent livres pour les maîtresses." See Jourdan et Isambert, *Recueil général des anciennes lois françaises,* xx, 317, cited in Maurice Gontard, *L'Enseignement primaire en France de la Révolution à la loi Guizot (1789–1833),* (Paris, n.d.), pp. 12 and 13.

52. It should also be remembered that literacy was often higher in mountainous areas than in the lowlands. Contemporaries were themselves aware of this, as witnessed by a speech to the Tribunat in 1802 by Pierre-François Duchesne, a Savoyard, who spoke of the "génie actif et entreprenant des habitants des montagnes . . . instruits de bonne heure dans la lecture, l'écriture, et les premiers éléments du calcul parce que la rigueur du climat ne leur permet aucune occupation dans la saison d'hiver." See *Archives parlementaires,* 2e série, vol. 3, p. 529, cited by Maurice Gontard, *L'Enseignement primaire,* p. 21.

At the same time, although overall literacy may have been higher at the Pont than elsewhere, it should be remembered that the rates of literacy varied from class to class. A parallel and confirmation of this can be found in the nature of political participation at the Pont during the French Revolution, which also varied a good deal from one social class to the next. The rich were more involved than the poor, and this was reflected in the high degree of literacy which was evinced by the participants. In May of 1802, for example, on the occasion of the plebiscite for Bonaparte's life consulate, 142 Montipontins came to vote and 108 of them signed the voting lists themselves (ADL VI M2-2). This is a proportion of 70 percent, which is unusually high. Even in the 1820s when education was generally more widespread, only one half or so of the adult Montipontins could sign their name. As late as 1830, 30 of the 62 conscripts for the canton were completely illiterate. Only the more prosperous and more educated villagers voted during the Revolution, and to this one could add also that they did quite well for themselves during those years. Of the twelve people, for example, who had banded together to purchase the most sizable of the Revolutionary *biens nationaux* (see chapter IV) only two could not sign the notarial archive (Servière, "Commanderie de Gap-Français," p. 68).

53. In an essay published some years ago which he had entitled "De La Condition de l'instruction publique dans les hautes Cévennes avant et après 1789," *Mémoires de l'académie de Stanislas* 4th series, vol. 11 (1878), M. Maggiolo claimed that the conditions of education in this region was satisfactory at the turn of the eighteenth century. Most parishes, he thought, had a school and even a schoolteacher who was paid a decent wage. The evidence cited however shows that whatever schools were to be found existed only in the largest towns. There is no reason to suppose that there were any schools at the Pont before 1789, and even if there had been one at the bourg, this would have been of no use to that half of the population which lived in the hamlets. That grievance, in fact, was specifically voiced by the people of the neighboring commune of Saint-Germain-de-Calberte who complained that "on impose sur eux les gages d'un Régent et Régente qui est d'une lieue et demie pour ceux qui sont aux extrémités" (Henri Ausset, "L'enseignement publique dans deux communes rurales des Cévennes à la fin du XVIII*e* siècle," in *Congrès des Sciences Sociales tenus à Nantes* [1901], p. 9). Paying for schooling was bad enough for the people who lived in the bourg, but it was a provocation for those who lived far afield.

54. Delon, *La Révolution dans la Lozère,* p. 720.

55. *Ibid.,* p. 709.

56. AN F1c III Lozère 6, 20 June 1813.

57. ADL IZ, Sous-préfecture de Florac.

58. ADL VI M2-2.

59. ADL IZ, Sous-préfecture de Florac.

60. During the Restoration a great debate raged in France on the methods of education. The left advocated *enseignement mutuel* or mutual teaching, so called because the brighter and older pupils would help the teacher with the younger pupils. For some obscure reason, the right continued to see the hand of the devil in this particular pedagogic technique until the debate died away by common consent in the middle decades of the nineteenth century. At the Pont, however, there was no *enseignement mutuel* although there should have been some, since the village was to the left. In the one school that still existed in 1821, one teacher handled alone thirty-five boys and fifteen girls. It can be added that the inspector who drew up the report for 1821 estimated that the population of school age at that time numbered eighty boys and thirty-five girls. Given the number of children at the Pont, this presupposes that it was thought that schooling should not last for more than three or four years.

61. ADL IZ, Sous-préfecture de Florac.

62. Ferdinand Fabre, *Barnabé* (Paris, 1875), pp. 146–147.

63. AN F17 12508.

64. *Ibid.*

65. ADL IZ, Sous-préfecture de Florac.

66. ADL Série E. supplément, 3 August 1835.

67. *Ibid.,* July 1837.

68. *Ibid.*

69. AN F17 9318.

70. Incapable teachers were not popular at the Pont, and it is perhaps a

measure of parental concern that dissatisfied parents at l'Hospital forced the resignation of one such pedagogue in 1863 by forbidding their children to attend his school.

71. ADL OV 116.

72. *Délibérations du conseil municipal.* 1859 (budget). Municipal Archives of Pont-de-Montvert.

73. *Ibid.*

74. *Délibérations du conseil municipal.* 25 March 1859.

75. *Ibid.,* 13 February 1871.

76. *Moniteur de la Lozère,* 1867. The figures are for the class of 1866.

77. For an acute discussion of this book and of its influence, see Daniel Halévy, *La République des Ducs* (Paris, 1937), pp. 338–339.

78. These figures are reconstituted from the Dénombrement de 1911—Pont-de-Montvert: liste nominative, and the cadastre of 1913, Bureau du Cadastre, Mende.

79. ADL Q 111.

80. Cadastre du Pont-de-Montvert, 1913.

81. Paul Chabanier, *Recueil des usages locaux* (Mende, 1917), p. 25.

82. Emendations to the cadastre of 1825.

VI. POLITICS SINCE 1815

1. AN F7 4067.

2. ADL IV M 5–6.

3. Interview with Emile Servière, 12 July 1963.

4. ADL IV M 4–15.

5. ADL M 4 25.

6. ADL IV M 4 26.

7. AN F9 567.

8. ADL VI M2–2.

9. AN F19 10478.

10. ADL VI M2–2.

11. *Journal de la Lozère,* June 2, 1821.

12. ADL IV M5–6.

13. In a letter dated 22 December 1833. A copy of this letter can be found in the municipal archives of Pont-de-Montvert.

14. AN F1c III Lozère 6.

15. *Ibid.*

16. *Ibid.*

17. For the Plebiscite of 1851, AN B II 1092; 1870, ADL IV M2–5.

18. ADL IV M2–5.

19. For the legislative election of 1857, ADL IV M 4 13; 1863, ADL IV M 4 14; 1869, ADL IV M2 5.

20. ADL IV M2–5.

21. AN F1b II Lozère 10.

22. ADL IV M4–19.

23. AN F1b II Lozère 10.

24. ADL IV M 4 26.

25. ADL IV M 4 27.

26. ADL IV M 4 16. Unfortunately, I have been unable to find the electoral results for the Pont for the elections of February 1871.

27. ADL IV M 4 18.

28. *Ibid.*

29. ADL IV M 4 19.

30. *Ibid.*

31. ADL IV M 4 20.

32. ADL IV M 4 27.

33. ADL M 4 30.

34. ADL IV M 4 32. The fact that Dreyfus gravitated toward the Lozère may not have been a mere accident. According to Robert de Jouvenel, his choice might indeed have been the consequence of a profound sociological law, "A partir de mille mètres d'altitude," wrote the author of *La République des camarades,* "on a le goût de la fortune. Pour les montagnards, généralement pauvres, une élection est une aubaine et le bulletin de vote vaut un effet de commerce. Les Alpes, les Pyrénées, et le Massif Central sont la patrie bénie des millionaires" (R. de Jouvenel, *La République des camarades* (Paris, 1914), p. 20). That is, of course, a very harsh judgment. But, Dreyfus was after all a millionaire, and the Pont, in parts, does lie at an altitude of over 1000 meters.

35. ADL IV M 4 32.

36. ADL IV M 4 31.

37. *Ibid.*

38. ADL IV M 4 26.

39. ADL IV M 4 24.

40. ADL IV M 4 25.

41. ADL IV M 4 27.

42. ADL Série E supplément.

43. ADL IV M 4 13.

44. ADL IV M 4 25.

45. ADL IV M 4 36.

AFTERWORD: VILLAGE STUDIES AND THE HISTORY OF FRANCE

1. Boris Porchneev, *Les Soulèvements populaires en France de 1623 à 1648* (Paris, 1963).

2. Roland Mousnier, "Recherches sur les soulèvements populaires en France avant la Fronde," *Revue d'histoire moderne et contemporaine,* 5 (1958), pp. 81–113.

3. As quoted by Lucien Gachon in *L'Auvergne et le Velay* (Paris, 1948), p. 315.

4. Henri Lefebvre has also drawn up a very interesting history of village histories in an essay entitled "Problèmes de sociologie rurale: La Communauté paysanne et ses problèmes historico-sociologiques," *Cahiers internationaux de sociologie,* no. 6, (1949), pp. 79–100.

5. The importance of land tenure has been particularly emphasized by Henri Lefebvre, notably in his book *La Vallée de Campan* (Paris, 1963). For him, a peasant community is an entity made up of families or "elementary units" which "own both collective and individual property in accordance with

relationships that are always historically determined" (cited in I. Chiva, *Rural Communities: Problems, Methods, and Types of Research,* Unesco Reports and Papers in the Social Sciences, no. 10 [1958], p. 9). See also Henri Lefebvre, *La Vallée de Campan* (Paris, 1963), p. 89. Marc Bloch's attitude was less categorical, but he, too, emphasized the importance of land tenure. For him the determinant of peasant life was the *régime agraire,* a combination of nonintellectual, nonpolitical, social, and technical factors.

6. The creation of schools and the importance of education had been especially emphasized by Roger Thabault in his work entitled *Mon Village, ses hommes—ses routes—son école* (Paris, 1945). This is an important book, and two famous French social historians, Duby and Mandrous, have gone so far as to consider it one of the basic works of modern French historiography. It is nonetheless unusual in its tone. Roger Thabault wrote it during the German occupation of France, and it is hard to escape the conclusion that in its emphasis, and even in its content, *Mon village* is a gesture of democratic defiance. The author is a humane, *républicain,* slightly left-of-center pedagogue, who refuses to accept the verdict of 1940 and the victory of Hitlerite barbarism. For that reason, perhaps, Thabault considers the history of his village largely from the point of view of its schools. Before they had been educated and enlightened, the inhabitants of Mazières-en-Gatine were, he thinks, poor and cut off from the rest of the world. But according to Thabault, the creation through the bounty of the Third Republic of a school system, and to a lesser degree of roads and railways, brought about a complete change in the circumstances of village life.

7. Among the aspects of life at the Pont that are difficult to describe and compare with those of other communities are nearly all of the cultural phenomena which Lawrence Wylie has described so well in his *Village in the Vaucluse* (Cambridge, Mass., 1957). Even if it were possible to reproduce the humane understanding which is evinced in all of its pages, the purpose of that work cannot, unfortunately, be recreated historically. *Village in the Vaucluse* is a study of contemporary social mores. It is especially concerned with the socialization of children and with the origins of those attitudes which we think of as being typically French: fundamental individualism, external conformity to established patterns of behavior, an attachment to the family which is seen as a bastion against the incursions of *les autres,* and a resigned acceptance of both life and death. None of these things can be grasped at the village level for the preceding centuries. We can, it is true, trace the same attitudes in the works of isolated writers. Who could deny, for example, that Montaigne would have understood the cautious and gentle cynicism of the Peyrannais? But the seventeenth-, eighteenth-, and nineteenth-century officials who drew up the documents which form the basis of the history of Pont-de-Montvert did not share the concerns of the author of the *Essays.* They cared instead about taxes, riots, conscripts, elections, and the like. From the archival remains of their handiwork it is possible to reconstruct an economic or social history of the Pont, but it is largely impossible to recreate in detail a cultural history of the village. There are no documents about child rearing in Pont-de-Montvert on the eve of the French Revolution. Never, alas, shall we know if the Montversois parents of the 1760s were more permissive than those of previous generations. Whether the Montipontins of Napoleon's day thought that sex was good or bad, pleasant or unpleasant, we cannot say. This is not

to deny that such questions are of historical importance. It is merely to say that although such questions can be answered for today's villages, as Lawrence Wylie has done, they cannot be answered for Pont-de-Montvert during the period with which I have dealt. A certain history of the Pont can be written, but not as Lawrence Wylie has done for Peyranne.

8. For a description of the organization of rural industries in the villages of the Vendée, see Charles Tilly's *The Vendée* (Cambridge, Mass., 1964), pp. 139–140.

9. See Thabault's *Mon Village,* pp. 106–108, 128.

10. See especially Paul Bois's *Les Paysans de l'ouest,* pp. 50–59 and his descriptions of the *cantons* of Conlie and Vibraye.

11. Edgar Morin, *Commune en France* (Paris, 1967), pp. 190–191.

12. Paul Morin has presented the same problem in the following way: "Dans quelle mesure ai-je pu isoler les traits singuliers, et surtout dégager une individualité, c'est-à-dire les métabolismes particuliers à travers lesquels s'opèrent les processus généraux? Qu'est-ce que l'individualité d'une commune? Qu'ont de commun et, en commun, ses membres? Comment cette individualité renvoie-t-elle à la société générale? Puisqu'il y a quelque lien fondamental entre Plodémet et la société française, que le devenir plodémétien procède du devenir national et s'intègre aujourd'hui dans le courant du devenir national (avec contre-courants, on le verra), peut-on alors élaborer un discours sur Plodémet sans tenir un second discours, latent, filigrané, sur le devenir national et plus largement occidental? Ce second discours ne doit-il pas être lui-même complexe et articulé, au lieu de se borner à quelques schémas unilatéraux sur l'extension de la société industrielle ou de consommation? Comment dialectiser les deux discours, étant donné que la connaissance de Plodémet ne peut induire à la connaissance de la France, mais peut y contribuer, et qu'elle ne peut être déduite de la connaissance du processus français, encore que celui-ci doive nécessairement y contribuer? Comment éviter que la dialectique devienne jonglerie, et se dissolve, soit dans le phénomène singulier et concret, soit dans le discours abstrait et général?" p. 16.

13. Herzen, *My Past and Thoughts,* I, 347.

BIBLIOGRAPHY

MANUSCRIPTS AND DOCUMENTS

Manuscripts and documents in this list are arranged in the following order: depository, general title of series, number of series, description of relevant material, and (in brackets) box numbers in series.

AN—NATIONAL ARCHIVES (PARIS)

National Elections

B II Lozère	Popular Votes (1793, An 3, An 7), Life Consulate, Imperial Heredity, Additional Act, Plebiscite of 1851. [17, 51, 237, 237 bis, 544 a, 544 b, 754 a, 754 b, 904, 1006, 1092]
C	[1327, 1332]

Military Matters

BB	Desertions, 1st Empire, 1842. [30, 470]
BB II	[17, 51, 904, 237 a, 237 b, 414 b, 544 a, 754 a, 754 b]

Legislative Comity

DIII	Revolutionary Communal Correspondence. [138–139]
D IV	Active Citizens. [1064–1069]

General Administrative Affairs

F1a	Communal Administration (1790–1821). [419, 581, 582]
F1b Lozère	Administrative Personnel (1791–Year 5, Year 6–1811, 1812–1820, 1821–1847, 1870–1880). [1, 2, 3, 4, 10]

Bibliography

F1b II   (1791–Year 5, Year 6–1811, 1812–1820, 1821–1847) Pont-
Lozère   de-Montvert: 1870s and 1880s. [1, 2, 3, 4, 6, 10, 11]

Public Opinion and Elections

F1c   Elections (1812–1815) [5, 6]
Lozère
F1c III   Elections (1790–Year 11, 1812, 1812–1815, 1816–1856).
Lozère   Administrative Reports (1791–1809, 1810–1870), National
          Holidays, Oaths, Various, Correspondence (1791–1853),
          1853–1856). [1, 2, 3, 4, 5, 6, 7, 8, 9]

Regional Affairs

F1c V   Conseil Général (Year 1–1817, 1818–1827, 1828–1851).
Lozère   [1]

Communal Administration

F 3 Lozère   [7]
F3 II Lozère Communal Accounts (An 8–1845), Communal Administra-
              tion (1791–1835). [5, 7]

Police Reports

F7   Lozère: Political Prisoners, Military Draft, Lozère General
          Information, Police Reports (1790–1792, 1821–1831, 1842–
          1859—reports for 1848 and 1851 are missing), Various
          (1832–1847, Year 4–Year 11), Papers of the County of Pub-
          lic Safety, Associations, Masons (1816–1830), Administra-
          tive Affairs (1814–1817). [3290, 3600, 3681 13–15, 4065,
          1066, 4067, 4564, 6697, 7136 987, 7165 7144, 7341 8287,
          7435 7629, 7592 961, 7625 1338, 7723 3712, 7738 4937,
          7745 5642, 7760 7228, 8463, 8464, 8110]

Sanitation

F8   Public Hygiene, Vaccination (Year 8–1825). [58, 114]

Military Police

F9   National Guard (1793–1849), Military Conscription (Year
          7–1832), Lozère, Desertions. [567, 568, 209, 310]

Agriculture

F10   Communal lands (1790-Year 8), Agricultural Workers
          (Years 2 and 3), Wolves in the Lozère (Year 14–1812),

196

Cattle (1813), Sheep (1799–1813). [332, 333, 334, 453, 467–468, 531, 534–538]

Food

F11   Foodstuffs (Year 3–1810), Harvests, Lozère (1814–1828). [373, 509]

Commerce and Industry

F12   Lozère (Year 3—Textiles), Maximum, Lozère, Industry (1872–1887). [1346, 1544–15, 4516A]

Roads and Bridges

F14   Accounting, Roads in the Lozère (1792–1820, 1821–1830), Roads in the Lozère (1789–1815), Roads (1814–1840), Lozère: Mines (1746–1876), Lozère: Bridges (1811–1871). [326, 327, 854, 1558, 1559, 8095–98, 11122]

F21   Communal Roads—Lozère (Year 11–1861). [1069]

Poor Relief

F15   Hospitals, Orphans, Charity (1800–1816, 1817–1821, 1822–1824, 1825–1826, 1827–1832), Charity (1811–1819), Indemnities, Charitable Contributions. [867, 868, 869, 870, 871, 2755, 3175]

Jails and Beggars

F16   Mendicity in Mende. [1101]

Public Schools

F17   Primary Education (1833), Primary Education, General Statistics, School Teachers, Schools, Lozère (1884), Schools (1856, 1878–1880, 1850s, 1855–1856, 1847–1893, 1844), Textbooks (1870s and 1880s, 1883, 1884), Protestant Schools (1828–1834). [122, 1041, 2639, 2946–50, 9318, 9267, 9318, 9328, 9627, 11621, 11652, 12508, 2639]

Generalities

F20   Military Draft (Year 7–1832), General Reports (1793–1813), Population, Active Citizens (Year 8–1791). [209, 220, 349]

Bibliography

Religion

F19   Lozère, Religious Affairs (Year 11–1827, 1790–1810), Sta-
               tistics on Protestant Population (1814–1815), Protestant
               Clergy, Lozerian Industry, Wages (1870s and 1880s), Re-
               ligious Affairs, Mende (1804–1830, 1830–1850). [343, 444,
               10478, 10498, 10615, 10873, 5686, 5738]

Government Property

Q   Communal Roads—Lozère (Year 11–1861), Biens Natio-
               naux. [1069, 94, 616 2, 617 3]

ADB-du-R—Departmental Archives of Bouches-du-Rhône
(Marseilles)

Religious Affairs

HOM   Order of Malta. [1920, 1944, 4113]

ADH—Departmental Archives of l'Hérault (Montpellier)

General Administration

C   Administrative Reports, Correspondence between the
               subdélégué of Mende and the Intendant at Montpellier.
               [47, 180, 181, 182, 239, 240, 2925, 2969]

ADL—Departmental Archives of the Lozère (Mende)

General Administration

C   Feudal Rights at Pont-de-Montvert, Noble Property,
               Abandonned Property, Taxes, Population Counts, Capita-
               tions for Frutgères and Grizac, Cloth Trade, Roads and
               Bridges. [19, 20, 26, 55, 62, 72, 264, 376, 377, 478, 486,
               943, 1171, 1681]

E (Supplément) Correspondence between the prefect and the mayor of
               Pont-de-Montvert.

Politics

F   Private Correspondences, Political Agitation in 1815.
               [609, 611, 1177]

Bibliography

Notarial Archives

Folcher 1676–1702 III E 8638–8640
François Pascal 1683–1709 III E 8641–8652
J–P. Folcher 1712–1748 III E 8653–8660
Jean Dubost 1720–1753 III E 8661–8668
Et. Ulpic Dubost 1753 III E 8673–8679
J–B. Filhon 1763–1774 III E 8680–8683
François Boissier 1771–1778 III E 8684–8695
J–A. Molines 1779–1795 III E 8686–8695
Jean Rouvière 1796–1836 III E 8696–8720
J–V. Boissier 1800–1825 III E 8721–8746
J–P. Isidore Boissier 1825–1830 III E 8747–8753
Jean Louis Pantel 1834–1850 III E 8754–8763
Alphonse Rouvière 1836–1850 III E 8770–8783

Religious Affairs

G   Fiefs in the Gévaudan, State of the Clergy, Judicial Affairs,
           Pouillé, Clerical Incomes ca. 1765, Pouillé for the diocese
           of Mende. [63, 459, 990–991, 1005, 1883, 2096, 2097,
           2098, 2101, 2103]
H   Order of Malta. [351, 416, 417]

Commerce

J   Cloth trade in the Gévaudan during the 18th century. [259,
           272]

Agriculture

M   Agricultural statistics, Pont-de-Montvert, Pont-de-Montvert
           1950, Communal Rights at Pont-de-Montvert in 1845.
           [3036, 3039, 3040, 3041, 5992, 6018, 6889, 11853, 11321,
           12264]

Revolutionary Period

L   Elections (1790–An 10), National Guard, Assignats, Vol-
           unteers 1792, Levée en masse, Elections 1792. [112–118,
           119, 125, 141, 156, 163, 165, 167, 168, 229, 934]

Justice

II L   Elections of Justices of the Peace. [3, 114, 253 72]
II U   Justice of the Peace at Pont-de-Montvert. [99–11, 98–100,
           118]

Bibliography

Government Property

Q   *Biens Nationaux* Registers of Sales and Payment, Registry of Sales, List of Émigrés, List of Émigré Properties, Sommier of Confiscated Properties. [24, 26, 28, 35, 111, 72, 73, 75, 84, 44–47, 152, 166, 203, 204, 205, 1937]

National Elections

IV M 4   (1848, 1849, 1852, 1857, 1863, 1869, 1870, 1876, 1877, 1879, 1881, 1885, 1886, 1889, 1893, 1898, 1902, 1905, 1906, 1910, 1914, 1919, 1924, 1928, 1932, 1936, 1945, 1946, 1951, 1956, 1958, 1962.) [9, 10, 12, 13, 14, 15, 16, 18, 19, 20, 22, 23, 24, 25, 26, 27, 28, 29, 30, 31, 32, 33, 34, 35, 36, 38, 39, 40, 42, 43, 44, 45]

VI M2   Subprefecture of Florac. [2]
IV M1   [5]
IV M5   [13, 14, 15]
IV M8   Local Affairs: Pont-de-Montvert. [115 P]

Roads and Bridges

O   [510, 527]
S1   Roads. [35. 71]
S   Electricity at Pont-de-Montvert. [148, 36]

Local Affairs

OV   Communal Administration. [(00160) 116]
P   [355, 480]
P3   Tax Inquests (1845–1880). [796]
IZ   Correspondence between the subprefecture of Florac and the mayor of Pont-de-Montvert.
Z   Subprefecture of Florac, Etat Civil Protestant (1670–1685), Etat Civil (1792–1969), Matrice Générale des Patentes et Professions—Contributions Directs (1890–1969), Cadastres (1825–1969), Listes Nominatives (Census) (1911–1969).

MUNICIPAL ARCHIVES (PONT-DE-MONTVERT)

Compoix de Frutgères 1631
Cadastre 1661
Meetings of the Municipal Council
Other État Civil

Bibliography

PRIVATE PAPERS

Archives of the Chapelle Family (Pont-de-Montvert).
Archives of the Rouvière-Lamarche Family (Fraissinet-de-Lozère).
Archives of M. Albin Pantel (Pont-de-Montvert).

LOCAL SOURCES

Affre, H. *Les Camisards en action: Lettres du prieur Miellet, leur contemporain*. Rodez, 1890.
Alméras, Henri. *La Transmission du patrimoine des parents à leurs enfants dans les familles rurales lozériennes*. Paris, 1934.
André, Ferdinand. *Documents relatifs à l'histoire du Gévaudan: Guerres de religion en Gévaudan*. Vols. 2–4. Mende, 1886–1889.
André, Louis. *Essai sur l'histoire de révolution en Lozère*. Marvejol, 1894.
Anthologie Lozérienne. Ed. mutuelles du Gévaudan. Marvejols, 1948.
Arnal, Paul. *L'Eglise réformée de Florac avant la révolution française*. Vals, 1896.
Atger, Guy. "Les Etats du Gévaudan." Mimeographed. Montpellier, 1957.
Barbot, Jules. "Les Commandeurs du Gap-Français." In *Archives Gévaudannaises, 1909–1914*. Mende: Société d'Agriculture de la Lozère, 1915.
_____ "Les Anciennes Drayes de la Lozère." *Bulletin de la Société des Sciences, des Lettres, et des Arts de la Lozère* (1902).
Bardy, Benjamin. "Notes et comptes rendus: Sur le Mont Lozère le 14 Juillet 1790," *Revue du Gévaudan*, 9 (1963), 154–159.
_____ "Statistiques agricoles et démographiques en Gévaudan à la fin du XVIIe siècle." *Revue du Gévaudan*, 4(1958), 71–90.
Baulig, Henri. *Le Plateau central de la France et sa bordure méditerranéenne*. Paris, 1928.
de Bernis, René. *Précis de ce qui s'est passé en 1815 dans les départements du Gard et de la Lozère*. Paris, 1818.
Berthoud, Gérald. *Changements économiques et sociaux de la Montagne; Mermamière en Valais*. Berne, 1967.
_____ *L'Equilibre agro-sylvo-pastoral dans la région Floracoise*. Montpellier, 1955.
Blanchemain, Antoine. "Possibilités humaines et agricoles sur le Mont Lozère: Essai de monographie du Pont-de-Montvert." Certificat d'aptitude à l'enseignement agricole. Mimeographed. Montpellier, 1955.
Bost, Charles. *La Première Vie de Pierre Corteiz pasteur du désert*. Paris, 1935.
_____ "Les Prophètes du Languedoc en 1701 et 1702," *Revue historique* (1921), no. 136, pp. 1–37, and no. 137, pp. 1–32.
Bouret, J. *Dictionnaire géographique de la Lozère*. Mende, 1852.
Bresoles, Pierre. "Contributions à l'étude des étages de la végétation du Mont-Lozère." *Revue du Gévaudan*, 13 (1967), 72–95.
Brun, Auguste. *Recherches historiques sur l'introduction du Français dans les provinces du Midi*. Paris, 1923.
de Burdin, Gustave. *Documents historiques sur la province de Gévaudan*. 2 vols. Toulouse, 1845–1847.

Bibliography

Cantaloube, Chanoine. "Les Origines de la réforme dans les Cévennes." *Bulletin de la Société de l'Histoire du Protestantisme français (BSHP)* 105 (January–March 1959) 25–26.

Camproux, Charles. *Etude syntaxique des parlers gévaudannais.* Paris, 1959.

_____ *Essai de géographie linguistique du Gévaudan.* 2 vols. Paris: PUF, 1962.

Cavalier, Jean. *Mémoires sur la guerre des Cévennes.* Paris, 1918.

Caziot, Pierre. *La Valeur de la terre en France.* Paris, 1914.

Chabrol, J. P. *Les Fous de Dieu.* Paris, 1961.

de Chambrun, Comte Joseph de Pineton. *Etudes politiques et littéraires.* Paris, 1892.

_____ *Fragments politiques.* Paris, 1871.

_____ *Aux Montagnes d'Auvergne: Nouvelles conclusions sociologiques.* Paris, 1893.

Chaurand, Baron. "Les Billets de confiance en Lozère." *Revue du Gévaudan,* 6(1960), 121–141.

de Chesnel, Adolphe. *Voyage dans les Cévennes et la Lozère.* Paris, 1829.

Coquerel, Charles. *Histoires des églises du désert.* 2 vols. Paris, 1841.

Cord, Ernest. *Etude géologique et agricole des terrains du département de la Lozère.* Paris, 1899.

Cord, Ernest, and Armand Viré. *La Lozère, les Causses, et les Gorges du Tarn.* Paris, 1900.

Corteiz. *Mémoires de Pierre Carrière, dit Corteiz.* Edited by J. G. Baum. Strasbourg, 1871.

Coste, Emile. *Une Famille de nouveaux convertis en Cévennes (1685–1787).* Audincourt, 1899.

Court, Antoine. *Mémoires d'Antoine Court.* Toulouse, 1835.

Cuche, Roger. *Le Conventionnel Servière.* Fédération du Languedoc Méditerranéen et du Rousillon: XXIX congrès. Mende, 1955.

Dainville, François de. *Cartes anciennes du Languedoc XVI–XVIIIe siècle.* Montpellier, 1961.

Délibérations de l'administration départementale de la Lozère et de son directoire de 1790 à 1800. Edited by Ferdinand André. 4 Vols. Mende, 1882–1884.

Delon, J. B. *La Révolution en Lozère.* Mende, 1922.

Devic, Dom, and Dom Vaissete. *Histoire générale du Languedoc.* 15 vols. Toulouse, 1872–2905.

Devos, J. C. "Villars et la pacification des Cévennes (avril 1704–janvier 1705)." In *Actes du 86e Congrès National des Sociétés Savantes.* Montpellier, 1961. Pp. 47–53.

Documents relatifs à l'histoire du Gévaudan: Documents antérieurs à 1790. 5 vols. Mende, 1885–1893.

"Documents. La persécution dans le diocèse de Mende d'octobre 1685 à mars 1688." *Bulletin de la Société de l'Histoire du Protestantisme français.* no. 40, 1906 (July–August) 416–425.

"Documents. Les enfants des nouveaux convertis." *Bulletin de la Société de l'Histoire de Protestantisme français.* no. 31, 1882. 110–117.

Doniol, Henry. "Rapports." In *Travaux et analyses de la Société d'Agriculture.* Mende, 1845.

Bibliography

Douen, Orentin. *Les Premiers Pasteurs du désert (1685–1700).* 2 vols. Paris: Grassart, 1879.

Dubois, Alfred. *Les Prophètes cévenols.* Strasbourg, 1861.

Dumas, G. "Complément aux 'Eléments de recherches lozériennes' de M. Marius Balmelle." *Revue du Gévaudan,* 1 (1955), 43–55.

Durand, Alfred. *La Vie rurale dans les massifs volcaniques des Dores, du Cézallier, du Cantal, et de l'Aubrac.* Aurillac, 1946.

Dupouy, Lise. "Les Protestants de Florac de la révocation de l'édit de Nantes à l'édit de tolérance," *Revue du Gévaudan,* 11 (1965), 46–186.

Fages, E. "L'Industrie de la laine en Gévaudan au XVIIIe siècle." In *Travaux et documents historiques. Année 1903.* Mende: Société des Sciences, des Lettres et des Arts de la Lozère, 1903.

———— "Notes d'histoire Gévaudannaise: Les Anciennes Justices de la Lozère," *Bulletin de la Société des Sciences, des Lettres et des Arts de la Lozère* (1907).

Favié, Mile Pasteur. "Notice sur M. le Pasteur Gabriac." *Archives du christianisme au XIXe siècle,* 2 (1819), 27–35.

Fayet, Albert. *Usages et règlements locaux ayant force de loi dans le département de la Lozère.* Mende, 1885.

Feneyrou, Nicole. "Contribution à l'histoire de la transhumance au XVe siècle." *Revue du Gévaudan,* 9 (1963), 114–136.

Flutre, L. F. *Recherches sur les éléments pre-gaulois dans la toponomie de la Lozère.* Paris, 1957.

———— "Toponymes lozériens d'origine gauloise." *Revue internationale d'Onomastique,* vol. 8, no. 4 (December 1956), pp. 273–282, and vol. 9, no. 1 (March 1957), pp. 31–43.

De Font-Reaulx, J. "L'Exemption fiscale de la seigneurerie de Grizac." *Revue du Gévaudan,* 8 (1962), 137–139.

Foulquier, Achille. *Notes historiques sur les paroisses des Cévennes comprises dans le diocèse de Mende.* Mende, 1906.

Gachon, Lucien. *Une Commune rurale d'Auvergne du XVIIIe au XXe siècle.* Clermont-Ferrand, 1939.

———— *Les Limagnes du sud et leurs bordures montagneuses.* Tours, 1939.

———— "Récentes Reprises et reprises humaines sur les massifs anciens du centre de la France," *Revue de Géographie Alpine,* 40 (1952), 265–290.

Gachon, Lucien, and J. A. Senèze. *Notre Commune: Petite Etude de géographie locale,* Paris, 1945.

Gallon, G. *Mouvement de la population dans le département de la Lozère au cours de la période 1821–1920 et depuis la fin de cette période.* Mende, 1932.

Geisendorf, Paul. "Recherches sur l'émigration huguenote du Gévaudan vers Genève avant et après la révocation de l'édit de Nantes." *Revue du Gévaudan,* 6 (1960), 110–120.

Géraud, G. "Notes sur Cent Ans d'Histoire en Lozère," *Revue du Gévaudan,* 13 (1967), 121–173.

Grimaud, Albert, and Marius Balmelle. *Précis d'histoire du Gévaudan.* Mende: Planchon, 1925.

Hughes, Edmond. *Histoire de la restauration du Protestantisme au XVIIIe siècle. Antoine Court.* 2 vols. Paris, 1875.

Bibliography

Jerphanion, Préfet. *Statistique du département de la Lozère.* Mende, 1802.
Journal de la Lozére
La Gorce, A. de, *Camisards et dragons du Roi.* Paris, 1950.
Lapadu-Hargues, Pièrre. *Les Massifs de la Margeride et du Mont-Lozère et leurs bordures.* Paris, 1948.
de la Roque, Louis. *Armorial de la noblesse de Languedoc, généralité de Montpellier.* 2 vols. Montpellier, 1860.
De Las Cases, Emmanuel. *Ce n'est rien, rien qu'une vie.* Mende, 1961.
Lelièvre, Mathieu. *Portraits et récits huguenots.* Toulouse, 1903.
Leroy-Ladurie, Emmanuel. *Les Paysans du Languedoc.* 2 vols. Paris: SEVPEN, 1966.
Lescure, Vicomte de. *Armorial du Gévaudan.* Lyon, 1929.
Louvreleuil, Le Révérend Père. *Le Fanatisme renouvellé.* 3d ed. 2 vols. Avignon, 1868.
_____ *Mémoires historiques sur le pays de Gévaudan et sur la ville de Mende, qui en est la capitale.* Mende, 1825.
Lorblanchet, Michel. "Géographie préhistorique, protohistorique et gallo-Romaine des Cévennes méridionales et de leurs abords. Mimeographed. Montpellier, 1967.
Lordat, Marquis de. *Les Pereyenc de Moras 1685–1798: Une Famille cévenole au service de la France.* Toulouse: Privat, 1959.
Maggiolo, M. "De La Condition de l'instruction publique dans les Hautes Cévennes avant et après 1789," *Mémoires de l'Académie de Stanislas,* 4th ser., 11 (1878), 46–87.
Magne, P., and Clave, A. "Les Drailles de transhumances dans le Gard et la Lozère." *Fédération Française d'Economie Alpestre,* no. 6 (1956).
Marres, Paul. *Les Grandes Causses: Études de géographie physique et humaine.* Tours, 1936.
_____ "Modernisation de la vie rurale cévenole." In *Mélanges offerts au Doyen Bénévent.* Edited by M. J. Blache. Ophrys: Gap, 1954. Pp. 255–269.
Martel, E. A. *Les Cévennes et les régions des Causses.* Paris, 1890.
Masseguin, Monique. "Les Parlementaires Royalistes Lozériens de 1815 à 1893." *Revue du Gévaudan,* 4 (1958), 146–166.
Mazel, Abraham. *Mémoires inédites d'Abraham Mazel et d'Elie Marion sur la guerre des Cévennes 1701–1708.* Edited by Charles Bost. Paris, 1931.
Mazoyer, Louis. "La Jeunesse villageoise du Bas Languedoc et des Cévennes en 1830." *Annales d'histoire économique et sociale* (November–December 1938), 500–507.
_____ "Les Origines du prophétisme cévenol 1700–1702." *Revue historique,* 197 (January–March 1947), 23–55.
Merle, A., ed. *Carte topographique.* 2d ed. 1923.
Mitard, E. A. "Ardèche et Lozère," *Revue de Géographie Alpine,* 20, fasc. 3 (1932), pp. 591–600.
_____ "Pluviosité de la bordure sud-orientale du Massif Central." *Revue de Géographie Alpine,* 15, fasc. 1 (1927), pp. 5–70.
Moniteur de la Lozère
Morel, Charles. "Fouilles et recherches inédites: Sépultures tumulaires." *Revue du Gévaudan,* 7 (1961), 103–159.

Bibliography

Mortillet, A. de. *Les Monuments mégalithiques de la Lozère*. Paris, 1905.

Nissolle, Jean. "Récit manuscript de Jean Nissolle, marchand de la ville de Ganges réfugié en Suisse. 1685." *Bulletin de la Société de l'Histoire du Protestantisme français*, 10 (1861), 442–457.

Nauton, Pierre. *Atlas linguistique et ethnographique du Massif Central*. 4 vols. Paris: CNRS, 1957–1963.

Nègre, Maurice. "L'Aménagement du Mont-Lozère." *Revue des eaux et forêts* 70, nos. 3 and 4 (March–April 1932).

———— "Les Forêts de la Lozère." *Le Chêne*, no. 11 (1934).

Pantel, Albin, and Emile Servière. "Seigneureries cévenoles." *Revue du Gévaudan* (1966), 13–55.

Pauc, Camille. *La Lozère: Géographie et histoire à l'usage des élèves*. Mende 1941.

Peyrat, Napoleon. *Histoire des pasteurs du désert 1685–1789*. Paris. 1842.

Peytavin, Abbé. "Notice sur St. Julien du Tournel par l'abbé Peytavin, curé. 1763." In *Bulletin de la Société des Sciences, des Lettres, et des Arts de la Lozère: Chroniques et Mélanges*. Mende, 1940.

Pin, Marcel. *Un Chef Camisard, Nicolas Jouanny*. Montpellier, 1930.

Pons, Pierre, "Extraits des mémoires de Pierre Pons, natif du Pont-de-Montvert, réfugié à Génève où il est mort." *Bulletin de la Société de l'Histoire du Protestantisme français*, 32 (1883), 218–230.

Porée, Charles, "Notes et documents sur les anciennes mesures de grains du Gévaudan." In *Etudes d'Histoire et d'Archéologie sur le Gévaudan*. Mende, 1919.

Pourcher, l'Abbé. *L'épiscopat français et constitutionnel et le clergé de Lozère durant la Révolution de 1789*. 3 vols. Saint-Martin-de-Boubaux, 1896–1900.

Prieur, J. "Le Mont Lozère: Evolution économique et humaine." *Revue du Gévaudan*, 4 (1958), 188–212.

Prouzet, Abbé. *Annales pour servir à l'histoire du Gévaudan*. 2 vols. St. Flour, 1843–1844.

Puaux, Franck. "Origines, causes, et conséquences de la guerre des Camisards," *Revue Historique*, 129, nos. 1 and 2 (September and October 1918), 1–22, and 209–243.

Rabaut, P. *Paul Rabaut, ses lettres à Antoine Court*. Edited by Charles Dardier. Paris, 1884.

Ramel, François de. *Les Vallées du pape d'Avignon: Essai sur vie de quelques familles en Languedoc Cévenol au XIVe siècle*. Dijon, 1954.

Rascol, Pierre, *Les paysans de l'Albigeois à la fin de l'ancien régime*. Aurillac, 1961.

Remize, l'Abbé. *Biographies lozériennes*. Toulouse, 1948.

Robert, Albert. *Les Débuts de l'insurrection des Camisards: L'Affaire du Pont-de-Montvert*. Nîmes, 1910.

Robert Labarthe, Urbain de. *Histoire du protestantisme dans le Haut-Languedoc, le Bas Quercy, et le Comté de Foix*, 2 vols. (Paris: Grassart, 1892–1896.)

Roqueplo, Paul. *La Dépopulation dans les arrondissements de Mende et de Marvejols (Lozère)*. Rodez, 1914.

Bibliography

Roucaute, Jean. *Un Pays de la France centrale au temps de la Ligue: Essai historique sur le Gévaudan*. Paris, 1900.

Rouquette, Pierre. *La Transhumance des troupeaux en Provence et en bas Languedoc*. Montpellier, 1913.

Servière, Emile. "Commanderie de Gap-Français, Ordre des Hospitalliers de Saint-Jean de Jérusalem." *Revue du Gévaudan*, 10 (1964), 41–72.

Siegfried, André. "Le Groupe protestant cévenol." In *Protestantisme français*. Paris, 1945. Pp 22–32.

Sinègre, Henri. *Essai sur le département de la Lozère*. Mende, 1937.

Stevenson, Robert Louis. *Travels Through the Cévennes on a Donkey*. Collected Works, vol. 12. New York, 1903.

Tinthoin, Robert. "Commerçants des hautes Cévennes au XIXe siècle." In *Compte rendu du Congrès des Sociétés Historiques du Languedoc*. Rodez, 1958.

———— "Le Pont-de-Montvert." *Lou Pais* nos. 57, 58, 59 (1959).

———— "Structure sociale et démographique du Gévaudan aux XVIIIe et XIXe siècle." *Revue du Gévaudan*, 4 (1958), 116–145.

———— "Vie économique et sociale urbaine en Gévaudan au XVIIIe siècle." *Revue du Gévaudan*, 2 (1956).

Trapenard, Camille. *Le Pâturage communal en Haute-Auvergne (XVIIe– XVIIIe siècle)*. Paris, 1904.

Velay, Jean. "Petit Livre de mémoires des affaires domestiques de Jean Velay, viguier de Florac." Edited by Auguste Boyer. Documents relatifs à l'histoire du Gévaudan, 1889. Vol. 2. pt. 3.

Vincens, P. P. *Dictionnaire des lieux habités du département de la Lozère*. Mende, 1879.

Waksman, Pierre. "La surveillance des religionnaires du Languedoc et de la vallée du Rhône de 1685 à 1705: Leurs communications." In *Actes du 86e Congrès Nationale des Sociétés Savantes*. Montpellier, 1961. Pp 29–45.

Weiss, N. "Précisions documentaires sur l'histoire des Camisards." *Bulletin de la Société de l'Histoire du Protestantisme français*, 58 (May–June 1909), 243–253.

Wemyss, Alice. *Les Protestants du Mas d'Azil: Histoire d'une résistance (1680–1830)*. Toulouse: Privat, 1961.

Weyd, Paul Marie. *Les Forêts de la Lozère*. Paris-Lille, 1911.

GENERAL SOURCES

Agulhon, Maurice. *La Sociabilité méridionale*. 2 vols. Aix-en-Provence: La Pensée universitaire, 1966.

Appolis, Emile. *Un Pays languedocien au milieu du XVIIIe siècle: Le Diocèse civil de Lodève*. Lodève, 1953.

Arbos, Philippe. *L'Auvergne*. Paris, 1952.

Archives statistiques du ministère des travaux publics, de l'agriculture et du commerce. Paris, 1835.

Ariès, Philippe. *Histoire des populations françaises et leurs attitudes devant la vie depuis le XVIIIe siècle*. Paris, Self, 1948.

Babeau, Albert, *Le Village sous l'ancien règime*. Paris, 1882.

Bibliography

Baehrel, René. *Une Croissance: La Basse-Provence rurale (fin XVIe siècle– 1789)*. Paris, 1961.

Barruel, J. *Du Désert au réveil*. Dieulefit, 1938.

Bernardy, André. *Euzet, mon pays*. Uzès, 1958.

Bernot, Lucien, and René Blancard. *Nouville: Un Village français*. Paris, 1953.

Bloch, Marc. *Les Caractères originaux de l'histoire rurale française*. Paris, 1952.

Bois, Paul. *Les Paysans de l'ouest*. Le Mans, 1960.

Bouillet, J. B. *Nobiliaire d'Auvergne*. 7 vols. Clermont-Ferrand, 1846–1853.

Bourderon, H. "La Lutte contre la vie chère dans la généralité du Languedoc au XVIIIe siècle. *Annales du Midi,* vol. 66, no. 26 (April 1954), pp. 155–170.

Bourgeois, Jean. "Le Mariage, coutume saisonnière: Contribution à l'étude sociologique de la nuptialité en France." *Population,* vol. 1, no. 4 (October–December 1946), pp. 623–643.

Bozon, Pierre. *La Vie rurale en Vivarais: Etude géographique*. Valence, 1961.

Braudel, Fernand. *La Méditerranée et le monde méditerranéen à l'époque de Philippe II*. 2nd ed. 2 vols. Paris: Presses Universitaires de France (PUF), 1966.

Brunhes, Jean. *La Géographie humaine*. 4th ed. 3 vols. Paris, 1934.

Caillet, Armand. *Puiselet-le-Marais, village de France*. Largentière, 1951.

Carrère, Paul, and Raymond Dugrand. *La Région méditerranéenne*. Paris, 1960.

Chaptal, Jean-Antoine. *De l'Industrie française*. 2 vols. Paris, 1819.

Chiva, I. *Les Communautés rurales: Problèmes, méthodes, et exemples de recherches*. Paris, 1958.

Clément, Pierre. *Le Salavès: Étude monographique du canton de Sauve (Gard)*. Montpellier, 1952.

Cobb, Richard. *Les Armées révolutionnaires des départements du Midi*. Toulouse, 1955.

Commission centrale d'études relatives au coût de la vie. *Compte rendu des travaux*. Paris, 1920.

Daudet, Ernest. *Histoire des conspirations royalistes du Midi sous la Révolution*. Paris, 1881.

Dauzat, Albert. *Le Village et le paysan de France*. Paris, 1941.

Dedieu, Joseph. *Le Rôle politique des protestants français. 1715–1734*. Paris: J. Gabalda, 1925.

Demangeon, Albert, "Enquête sur l'habitation rurale en France." *Annales de Géographie,* 257 (15 Sept. 1936).

Ducros, Louis. *La Société française au XVIIIe siècle*. Paris, 1922.

Durand, Charles. *Histoire du protestantisme français pendant la Révolution et l'empire*. Geneva, 1909.

Dutil, Léon. *L'Etat économique du Languedoc à la fin de l'ancien régime*. Paris, 1911.

Enquêtes parlementaires sur les actes du gouvernement de la défense nationale. Paris: Imprimerie Nationale, 1875.

Faucher, D. *La Vie rurale vue par un géographe*. Toulouse, 1962.

Fel, André. *Les Hautes Terres du Massif Central: Tradition paysanne et économie agricole*. Paris: PUF, 1962.

Bibliography

Fleury, Michel, and Louis Henry. *Des Régistres paroissiaux à l'histoire de la population: Manuel de dépouillement et d'exploitation de l'état-civil ancien.* Paris, 1956.

Friedman, G. "Communauté rurale et milieu natural." *Annales,* 9 (1954), 191–207.

Gachon, Lucien. *L'Auvergne et le Velay.* Paris, 1948.

Gagg, Robert. *Kirche im Feueur: Das Leben der sudfranzösischen Huguenotten Kirche nach dem Todesurteil durch Ludwig XIV.* Stuttgart: Zwingli Verlag, 1961.

Garaud, Marcel. *La Révolution et la propriété foncière.* Paris, 1958.

Gobin, Leon, *Essai sur la géographie de l'Auvergne.* Clermont-Ferrand, 1896.

Godechot, Jacques. "Démographie et subsistances en Languedoc du XVIIIe siècle au début du XIXe siècle." *Bulletin d'histoire économique et sociale de la révolution française* (1964), pp. 23–63.

Halévy, Daniel. *Visites aux paysans du centre.* Paris, 1921.

D'Hombres, Maximum, and Gratien Charvet. *Dictionnaire languedocien-français.* Alais, 1884.

Hyslop, Beatrice. *Répertoire critique des cahiers de doléances pour les états-généraux de 1789.* Paris, 1933.

Joanne, Adolphe. *Itinéraire général de la France.* Paris, 1933.

Joanne, Paul. *Dictionnaire géographique et administratif de la France.* 7 vols. Paris: Hachette, 1892–1905.

Joly, Robert, and Pièrre Estienne. *La Région du centre.* Paris, 1951.

Lapraz, Y., R. Burdet, and A. Bitou. "Connaître une population rurale." *Economie et humanisme,* 108 (1957), 1–91.

Latreille. André, and André Siegfried. "Les Forces religieuses et la vie politique: Le Catholicisme et le protestantisme," *Cahiers de la Fondation des Sciences Politiques,* no. 23 (Paris, 1951).

Le Bras, Gabriel, *Introduction à l'histoire de la pratique religieuse en France.* 2 vols. Paris: PUF, 1942–1945.

Lefebvre, Georges. *Les Paysans du nord pendant la révolution française.* Paris, 1924.

Lefebvre, Henri. "Perspectives de la sociologie rurale." *Cahiers internationaux de sociologie,* no. 14 (1953), pp. 122–140.

_____ "Problèmes de sociologie rurale: La communauté paysanne et ses problèmes historico-sociologiques." *Cahiers internationaux de sociologie,* no. 6 (1949), pp. 79–100.

Leonard, E. G. *Histoire ecclésiastique des réformes français au XVIIIe siècle.* Paris, 1940.

Leonard, E. G. *Le Protestant français.* Paris: PUF, 1953.

_____ "Les Protestants français du XVIIIe siècle," Annales d'histoire sociale, 2 (1940), 5–20.

Livet, Roger. *Habitat rural et structures agraires en basse Provence.* Gap, 1962.

Marion, Marcel. *La Dîme ecclésiastique en France au XVIIIe siècle.* Paris, 1912.

_____ *L'Impôt sur le revenu au XVIIIe siècle, principalement en Guyenne.* Toulouse, 1901.

Maury, Léon. *Le Réveil religieux dans l'église réformée à Genève et en France (1810–1850).* 2 vols. Paris, 1892.

Mazoyer, Louis. "Essai critique sur l'histoire du Protestantisme à la fin du XVIIIe siècle." *Bulletin de la Société de l'Histoire du Protestantisme Français,* 79 (January 1931), 33–57.

Mélanges géographiques offerts à Philippe Arbos. 2 vols. Paris: Les Belles Lettres, 1953.

Mendras, Henri. *Sociologie rurale.* Paris: Les Cours de droit, 1957.

_____ *French Bibliographical Digest: Rural Sociology.* New York. 1964.

_____ *Sociologie de la campagne française.* Paris: PUF, 1959.

Meynier, André. *Géographie du Massif Central.* Paris, 1938.

_____ *Ségalas, Lévezou, Châtaigneraie: Etude géographique.* Aurillac, 1931.

Ministère de l'Instruction publique et des Beaux-Arts. *La Statistique agricole depuis 1814.* Comités des travaux historiques. Section d'histoire moderne depuis 1715 et d'histoire contemporaine. Paris, 1914.

Mours, Samuel. *Les Eglises réformées en France.* Paris, 1958.

Morin, Edgar. *Commune en France.* Paris, 1967.

Neufbourg, Comte de. *Paysans: Chronique d'un village du Xe au XXe siècle.* Paris, 1945.

Orcibal, Jean. *Etat présent des recherches sur la répartition des "nouveaux catholiques" à la fin du XVIIe siècle.* Paris: J. Vrin, 1948.

Peake, Harold. "Village Community." In *The Encyclopedia of the Social Sciences.* New York, 1954. Vol. 15, pp. 253–259.

Perrot, C. *Report on the Persecutions of French Protestants.* London, 1816.

Pigeire, Jean. *La Vie et l'œuvre de Chaptal.* Paris, 1932.

Poitrineau, Abel. *La Vie rurale en Basse Auvergne au XVIIIe siècle.* 2 vols. Paris: PUF, 1965.

Pomaret, Charles. *L'Abandon des campagnes.* Paris, 1928.

_____ *Le Dernier Témoin.* Paris, 1969.

Rivers, P. H. "Social Class in a French Village." *Anthropology Quarterly* 32 (January 1960).

Robert, Daniel. *Les Églises réformées en France (1800–1830).* Paris, 1961.

Rostaing, Charles. *Les Noms de lieux.* Paris: PUF, 1948.

Roupnel, Georges. *Histoire de la campagne française.* Paris, 1932.

Schmidt, Charles. *Les Sources de l'histoire de France depuis 1789 aux Archives Nationales.* Paris, 1902.

Sée, Henri. *La Vie économique et les classes sociales en France au XVIIIe siècle.* Paris, 1924.

Segondy, Jean. *Cernon-sur-Orb.* Montpellier, 1949.

Sentou, J. "Impôts et citoyens actifs à Toulouse au début de la Révolution." *Annales du Midi,* vol. 61 n.s., nos. 3 and 4 (1948), pp. 159–179.

Shaw, William, ed. *Naturalization of French Protestants in England.* Publications of the Huguenot Society of London, 27. Manchester, 1923.

Siegfried, André. *Tableau politique de la France de l'ouest sous la IIIe république.* Paris, 1913.

Soboul, Albert. "La Communauté rurale française XVIIIe–XIXe siècle." *La Pensée,* 73 (1957), 65–81.

Soreau, Edmond. *L'Agriculture du XVIIIe siècle à la fin du XVIIIe siècle.* Paris, 1952.

Statistique Générale de la France. Ministère de l'Agriculture et du Commerce. 2 vols. 1835.

Statistique de la France publiée par le ministre de l'agriculture, du commerce et des travaux publics. Prix et salaires à diverses époques. Vol. 12. Strasbourg, 1863.

Statistique de la France, publiée par le ministre des travaux publics, de l'agriculture et du commerce. Agriculture 1840–1841. Paris, 1840 and 1841.

Statistique Générale de la France. Salaires et coûts de l'existence à diverses époques jusqu'en 1910. Paris, 1911.

Stéphan, Raoul. *Histoire du protestantisme français.* Paris: Fayard, 1961.

Valarché, Jean. *L'Économie rurale.* Paris, 1959.

Varagnac, André. *Civilisation traditionnelle et genres de vie.* Paris, 1948.

INDEX

Index

212

Index

213

Index

Harvard Historical Studies

OUT OF PRINT TITLES ARE OMITTED

33. *Lewis George Vander Velde*. The Presbyterian Churches and the Federal Union, 1861–1869. 1932.

35. *Donald C. McKay*. The National Workshops: A Study in the French Revolution of 1848. 1933.

38. *Dwight Erwin Lee*. Great Britain and the Cyprus Convention Policy of 1878. 1934.

48. *Jack H. Hexter*. The Reign of King Pym. 1941.

58. *Charles C. Gillispie*. Genesis and Geology: A Study in the Relations of Scientific Thought, Natural Theology, and Social Opinion in Great Britain, 1790–1850. 1951.

62, 63. *John King Fairbank*. Trade and Diplomacy on the China Coast: The Opening of the Treaty Ports, 1842–1854. One-volume edition. 1953.

64. *Franklin L. Ford*. Robe and Sword: The Regrouping of the French Aristocracy after Louis XIV. 1953.

66. *Wallace Evan Davies*. Patriotism on Parade: The Story of Veterans' and Hereditary Organizations in America, 1783–1900. 1955.

67. *Harold Schwartz*. Samuel Gridley Howe: Social Reformer, 1801–1876. 1956.

69. *Stanley J. Stein*. Vassouras: A Brazilian Coffee County, 1850–1900. 1957.

71. *Ernest R. May*. The World War and American Isolation, 1914–1917. 1959.

72. *John B. Blake*. Public Health in the Town of Boston, 1630–1822. 1959.

73. *Benjamin W. Labaree*. Patriots and Partisans: The Merchants of Newburyport, 1764–1815. 1962.

74. *Alexander Sedgwick*. The Ralliement in French Politics, 1890–1898. 1965.

75. *E. Ann Pottinger*. Napoleon III and the German Crisis, 1865–1866. 1966.

76. *Walter Goffart*. The Le Mans Forgeries: A Chapter from the History of Church Property in the Ninth Century. 1966.

77. *Daniel P. Resnick*. The White Teror and the Political Reaction after Waterloo. 1966.

78. *Giles Constable*. The Letters of Peter the Venerable. 1967.

79. *Lloyd E. Eastman*. Throne and Mandarins: China's Search for a Policy during the Sino-French Controversy, 1880–1885. 1967.

80. *Allen J. Matusow*. Farm Policies and Politics in the Truman Years. 1967.

81. *Philip Charles Farwell Bankwitz*. Maxime Weygand and Civil-Military Relations in Modern France. 1967.

82. *Donald J. Wilcox.* The Development of Florentine Humanist Historiography in the Fifteenth Century. 1969.

83. *John W. Padberg, S.J.* Colleges in Controversy: The Jesuit Schools in France from Revival to Suppression, 1813–1880. 1969.

84. *Marvin Arthur Breslow.* A Mirror of England: English Puritan Views of Foreign Nations, 1618–1640. 1970.

85. *Patrice L.-R. Higonnet.* Pont-de-Montvert: Social Structure and Politics in a French Village, 1700–1914, 1970.